Human Resource Management

Human Resource Management

By

Dr. Naga Raju Battu

MHRM, M.A., B.L., B.Ed., M.Phil., Ph.D.,
Faculty in Human Resource Management
Department of Sociology, Social Work and IRPM
Acharya Nagarjuna University
Nagarjuna Nagar–522510
Andhra Pradesh

DISCOVERY PUBLISHING HOUSE
NEW DELHI

First Published – 2006

Reprinted – 2025

ISBN: 978-81-8356-089-4

Human Resource Management

Published by:

DISCOVERY PUBLISHING HOUSE

4383/4B, Ansari Road, Darya Ganj
New Delhi-110 002 (India)
Phone: +91-11-23279245; 23253475; 43596065
Mobile: +91 9811179893 / +91 9871656464
E-mail: discoverybooksindia@gmail.com
orderdphbooks@gmail.com
namitwasan9@gmail.com
web: www.discoverypublishinggroup.com

Printed at:
Infinity Imaging Systems
Delhi

Dedicated
to

My Beloved Wife
Naga Malliswari Battu

and

Daughter
Satya Pushyami

Son
Jeswin Battu

Preface

Human resources are important and invaluable assets of an organization. Its performance and survival depend to a large extent on the effective and optimum utilization of human resources. The notion that the prosperity of a business enterprise revolves round the technological progress and innovations, has been widely shared.

Human resource management refers to the people dimension in management. It is now realized that efficient management of human resources is a crucial factor in determining the growth and prosperity of a business enterprise. This is particularly true in the case of dairy units where people (at village level societies, district level milk unions and state level federation) are expected to plays a crucial role. Unless the district milk unions which control the milk processing/product units, develop close rapport with employees at all levels and develop co-operative relationships, it would be impossible for them to meet production targets, quality standards and cope with the intense competition from their counterparts. Improper handling of human resources through haphazard personnel policies and practices may have deleterious effects upon the efficient functioning of the organization in the long run. In dairy industry which is agro based and traditional in nature, it is necessary to have the support and strength of HRM interventions, particularly when it is about to take a big leap. The human factor thus acts as a limiting factor to organizational survival, growth and effectiveness. Without positive contributions from human beings, it would be an arduous task to assess the growing mortality rate in dairy industry. It is time for the milk units to think about good HRM practices aimed at improving the quality of work life in dairy industry.

The growth of employment in dairy industry and the growing dependence on skilled personnel necessitate the adoption of scientific techniques for managing people. Effective management of human resources spells the difference between success and failure even in the case of dairy units and hence, is the biggest challenge now. Dairy industry needs enlightened, hardworking and positively motivated people who are capable of applying their minds in a wise and judicious fashion in the use of critical resources. There have been many impressive writings eulogizing the virtues of veterinary aspects, dairy technology, marketing, financial and quality management in dairy industry but, quite surprisingly the human resource management dimension hardly received any attention. Studies or writings in this area are conspicuous by their absence. There is, thus an imperative need to understand practices followed in dairy industry. In this context the present study assumes importance and represents a modest attempt to fill the knowledge gap in this area.

Dr. Naga Raju Battu

Acknowledgements

I wish to record my deep sense of gratitude to my research director Prof. B.S. Murty, former head of the department and Chairman, Board of Studies, Department of Industrial Relations and Personnel Management (HRM), Colleges of Arts and Commerce, Andhra University, Visakhapatnam, for his inspiration, unfailing help, constant guidance, academic encouragement and cooperation he has given me in getting this work done. Words cannot express my indebtedness to him.

I am personally thankful to Dr. DBRNK Benerjee, Head of Department of IRPM, and I am also thankful to Prof. (Mrs). P. Devakidevi, Chairperson, Board of Studies, Department of IRPM, Andhra University, Visakhapatnam, for their constant support and valuable suggestions which I received during the period of my research work.

I take this opportunity to express my sincere thanks to Prof. K. Ramesh, former head of the department and Dean CDC, Andhra University, Visakhapatnam, Dr. D. Prabhakara Rao, executive council member, Andhra University, Prof. G. Muralidarsan, Dr. P.D. Raju, Dr. T. Subbarayudu, for their co-operation and encouragement in various respects.

I am profoundly indebted to Prof. M. Laxmipathi Raju, Head of the department of sociology, social work and IRPM, Dr. M.V. Rama Kumar Ratnam, Associate professor, CMBS, Prof. S. Vijaya Raju, department of commerce and management, executive council member of Nagarjuna university for their kind cooperation and timely help.

I owe my gratitude to Prof. D.K. Lal Das, principal, R.M. College of social work, Hyderabad, Prof. A.V. Dattatreya Rao, department of statistics, Nagarjuna university for their valuable suggestions and the keen interest they have evinced in the pursuance of my research work.

I wish to express my thanks to the Managers and staff, Sangam dairy and Vijaya dairy for providing information in pursuance of my research work. I am also thankful to the library staff of Dr. B.R. Ambedkar memorial library, Nagarjuna University, Dr. V.S. Krishna memorial library, Andhra University, central libraries of, Osmania, O.U., Main library, university of Hyderabad, for their co-operation.

I take it an opportunity to express my gratitude to my colleagues Dr. GBVLN Rao senior faculty member, Sri. M.V. Nageswara Rao, Asst. Commissioner of Labour, Sri. M. Trimurthi Rao for their affectionate encouragement, constant support, and cheerful company during the completion of work.

It is my pleasant duty to thank my wife Mrs. B.N. Malleswari who has shown patience and perseverance in going through my drafts and enabled me to complete the work by providing me moral support at all times during the course of this work. The work would not have been possible without her constant encouragement and continuous support, words can't express my heart felt feelings to her—my wife.

I will be failing in my duty if I do not express my sincere gratitude to my beloved parents, sisters and brothers-in-law, uncle and aunty for their encouragement and constant support during the completion of this work.

I wish to express my affectionate thanks to my students Phani Vardhan Radhika, Sumabala, Shakeela, Satish and Madhu, students of human resource management, Nagarjuna University, for their assistance in collection of data.

Last but not least, I thank Mr. K.L. Koteswara Rao, Director for U.S. Data Systems, G. Satyanarayana, office in charge and Chand Basha, Nagarjuna University, for their secretarial work.

Abbreviations

AITUC	All India Trade Union Congress
AMC	Any time milk counter
APDDCF	Andhra Pradesh Dairy Development Co-operative Federation
ATM	Any time milk
BMS	Bharathiya Mazdoor Sangh
CITU	Centre for Indian Trade Unions
EEC	European Economic Community
FAO	Food and Agricultural Organization
GDCC Bank	Guntur district co-operative central bank
GDMPMA Co.U.LTD	Guntur district milk producers mutually aided co-operative union limited
IDC	Indian Dairy Corporation
ILO	International Labour Organisation
INTUC	Indian National Trade Union Congress
JAC	Joint Action Committee
KDMPCO.U.LTD	Krishna District Milk Producers Co-operative Union Ltd.
MT	Metric Tonnes
MTD/MTPD	Metric Tonnes per day
NCL	National Commission on Labour
NDDB	National diary development board
NMR	Nomial Mustar Roles

SMT	Square Metre
SNF	Solids Not Fat
TCB	Transporter Com Distributor systems
TLPD	Thousand Litres Per Day
TLts	Thousand liters
TNTUC	Telugu Nadu Trade Union Congress
UHT	Ultra high temperature
UNICEF	United Nations Children's Emergency Fund
VRS	Voluntary Retirement Scheme

Contents

1

Problem and Methodology

INTRODUCTION

India with a vast population has a great problem in providing each citizen with adequate food, both in terms of quality and quantity. Most of the regions in the country are undernourished and suffer from malnutrition. A large number of people depend on milk and its products as the most important source of nourishment. Thus dairying promises to be a vitally significant occupation of the farmers. Besides, organised dairying also creates substantial employment opportunities. Dairy industry not only provides additional employment but reduces the burden of population on agricultural sector. Keeping this in view, it is necessary to develop the dairy industry very fast for overcoming the problems of income, employment and nutrition in the country. Not only the Union Government, but also the State Government has undertaken different programmes "Operation Flood" is an important programme in this regard. Dairying in India is not only dominated by the Government but by the co-operative sector as well.

GROWTH OF THE DAIRY INDUSTRY

Before the Independence of India in the first half of the 20th century, dairying in the country was largely unorganised. Fluid milk and its products were generally, not easily marketable commodities and there was no transport of these products to far distances. Organised dairying, as was understood in the west, located in a small way when military dairy farms and creameries were established towards the end of the 19th century to meet the demands of the armed forces and their hospitals. Some private dairies, such as 'Kaventers' and 'Polson's', with more or less modern processing facilities were encouraged to make pasteurised butter, primarily for the use of the British army. As a result, the Imperial Institute of Animal Husbandry and Dairying was established in 1923 at Bangalore. There has been another major effort in the early 1940's where milk produced in rural areas of Kaira District was collected in bulk, pasteured 'and transported by rail for distributing in Bombay by "The Bombay Milk Scheme" operated by the Bombay Municipality.

When India became independent in 1947, one of the major milk schemes launched in the country was "The Greater Bombay Milk Scheme (GBMS)". This consisted of a market for Milk in Bombay supplied by the Kaira District Co-operative Milk Producer's Union, although Dairy existed in this country since 1913 for mostly collecting and selling fresh milk to the local consumers. The first large scale and systematic breakthrough in Dairy in India was made in 1948 by the Kaira District Co-operative Milk Producers Union at Anand. Ultimately, this union came to be known as the Anand Milk Union Limited, abbreviated as "AMUL" which in the vernacular language means "highly valuable" or "Priceless".

Dairy Development Under the Five Year Plans

Dairy Development in India received an impetus after the independence when industrialisation and public awakening necessitated the establishments or organised collection, processing and distribution of Milk to cater to the needs of the expanding urban areas.

The planned development of dairying was actually taken up in the First National Five Year Plan (1951-1956) and the inadequacy of suitable marketing structure was noticed as one of the inhibiting factors for milk production.

This expressed itself in an accentuated form in remote rural areas, where, for want of quick transport and marketing facilities, Milk was marketed in the converted form of Ghee, which did not provide sufficient income to the farmers.

To solve this problem the Indian Dairy Corporation (IDC) was established in 1970 as a specialised institution to promote and finance dairy development in India. Its function includes financing Co-operative Dairy Development in India and promoting expansion of Milk Processing and marketing facilities.

Growth of Dairying in Andhra Pradesh

Andhra Pradesh has made rapid strides in the past three decades and has emerged as a major milk producing state. Dairying has proved to be the main stay of rural development. The Operation Flood Programme and Dairy Co-operatives have become instruments for change and growth in villages.

Tremendous efforts were made for creation of infrastructure for dairy development. Dairy as an organisation passed through different phases... beginning as a Pilot Milk Supply Scheme (1960) then as an Integrated Milk Project with UNICEF assistance leading on to a Dairy Development Department (1971) which in turn became a Dairy Corporation (1974) and finally, a Co-operative Federation (1981).

The Mission statement reads that professionalisation and decentralisation should help Management of Dairy Co-operatives to function with profitability and with thrust on industrialisation of rural dairying.[1]

The Government of Andhra Pradesh set the following objectives for the dairies. (i) To provide assured year—round market for the surplus milk produced in the rural areas; (ii) Supply wholesome milk and milk products to the urban consumers; and (iii) to stimulate milk production and to develop the required infrastructure.[2]

Achievement

Today nearly 9 lakh farmers are supplying milk through 9144 collection centres, covering about 15,595 villages in the state. The milk procurement has grown to touch 3112.25 lakh litres and sale of milk has touched 2262.18 lakh litres during 1997-98.

Operation Flood Programme

A.P. Dairy Development Co-operative Federation Limited was started in 1981 to implement Operation Flood Programme in the State, with financial assistance from N.D.D.B with the objective of replicating "Anand pattern"[3] dairy co-operative structure in other parts of the country. The project aims at getting back to the rural milk producers a larger share of the urban consumers rupees spend on milk and milk products.

Operation Flood-I was in June 1970. The Guntur District Milk Producers Co-operative Union was organised and the Sangam Dairy was established.

Operation Flood-II was in October, 1979. 16 Districts have been covered under Operation Flood-II. Several schemes have been implemented for establishment, expansion and strengthening of the dairy units. One of those scheme is expansion of milk plant at Vijayawada and Sangam at Vadlamudi.

Operation Flood-III was started in March, 1987 In addition to 16 districts, Nellore district is also covered under Operation Flood-III. During this flood period major schemes have been taken up for the dairy development in the 17 districts.

Dairy Programmes for Rural Women

Organisation of All-Women Dairy Co-operatives has been taken up to enhance the status of women by inducting them in dairying, with financial assistance from the Ford Foundation, Netherlands Government and Indo-Swiss

Project. All these societies are being managed by the Women themselves.

Andhra Pradesh Dairy Development Co-Operative Federation

It was felt right from the beginning that only a strong organisation could mobilize and channelise the interest of the people and help them to adopt modern practices to improve their productivity.

Andhra Pradesh Dairy Development Cooperative Federation was constituted in October, 1981, to implement operation Flood programme through active involvement of producers in organising milk production, procurement, processing and marketing on 'three-tier' cooperative structure as per the National Policy of Government of India. The three-tier system consists of milk producers cooperative society at the village level and cooperative milk producers union at the district level and Federation as an apex body at the state level. Mr. V. Kurien is the father of the three-tier system and Operation Flood.

The National Dairy Development Board (NDDB) identified this three-tier system project which is meant for the implementation of Operation Flood programme in 17 districts out of 23 districts.

Regardless of their industry, size, or location, companies today face five critical business challenges. Collectively, these challenges require organisations to build new capabilities. Who is currently responsible for developing those capabilities? Every-one and no one. That vacuum has given human resources an opportunity to play a leadership role in enabling organisations to meet the following competitive challenges.

GLOBALISATION

Gone are the days when companies created products at home and shipped them abroad "as is". With the rapid expansion of global markets, managers are struggling to balance the paradoxical demand to think globally and act locally. That imperative requires them to move people, ideas, products, and information around the world to meet local needs. They must add new and important ingredients to the mix when making strategy volatile political situations, contentious global trade issues, fluctuating exchange rates, and unfamiliar cultures. They must be more literate in the ways of international customers, commerce, and competition than ever before. In short, globalisation requires that organisations increase their ability to learn and collaborate and to manage diversity, complexity, and ambiguity.[4]

Profitability through Growth

During the past decade, most western companies have been clearing debris, using downsizing, reengineering, delayering, and consolidation to increase efficiency and cut costs. The gains of such yard work, however, have largely been realised, and executives will now have to pay attention to the other part of the profitability equation: revenue growth.

The drive for revenue growth, needless to say, puts unique demands on an organisation. Companies seeking to acquire new customers and develop new products must be creative and innovative, and must encourage the free flow of information and shared learning among employees. They must also become more market focused—more in touch with the fast changing and disperate needs of their customers. And companies seeking growth through mergers, acquisitions, or joint ventures require other capabilities, such as the finely honed skills needed to integrate different organisations' work processes and cultures.

Technology

From videoconferencing to the Internet, technology has made our world smaller and faster. Ideas and massive amounts of information are in constant movement. The challenge for managers is to make sense and good use of what technology offers. Not all technology adds value. But technology adds value since it can have its affect on the mode and the place of work. In the coming years, managers will need to figure out how to make technology a viable, productive part of the work setting. They will need to stay ahead of the information curve and learn to leverage information for business results. Otherwise, the risk being swallowed by a tidal wave of data-not ideas.

Intellectual Capital

Knowledge has become a direct competitive advantage for companies selling ideas and relationships (think of professional service, software, and technology-driven companies) and an indirect competitive advantage for all companies attempting to differentiate themselves in the manner they serve their customers. From now on, successful companies will be the ones that are the most adept at attracting, developing, and retaining individuals who can drive a global organisation that is responsive to both its customers and the burgeoning opportunities of technology. Thus the challenge for organisations is to make that sure they have the capability to find, assimilate, develop, compensate, and retain such talented individuals.

Change, Change, and More Change

Perhaps the greatest competitive challenge companies face is adjusting to-indeed, embracing-nonstop change. They must be able to learn rapidly and continuously, innovate ceaselessly, and take on new strategic imperatives faster and more comfortably. Constant change means organisations must create a healthy discomfort with the status quo, an ability to detect emerging trends quicker than the competition, an ability to make rapid decisions, and the agility to seek new ways of doing business. To thrive, in other words, companies will need to be in a neverending state of transformation, perpetually creating fundamental and enduring change.

Human Resource's New Role

The five challenges described above have one overarching implication for business; the only competitive weapon left is organisation. Sooner or later, traditional forms of competitiveness-cost, technology, distribution, manufacturing, and product features can be copied. They have become table stakes. You must have them to be a player, but they do not guarantee your win.

In the new economy, winning will spring from organisational capabilities such as speed, responsiveness, agility, learning capacity, and employee competence. Successful organisations will be those that are able to quickly turn strategy into action; to manage processes intelligently and efficiently; to maximize employee contribution and commitment; and to create the conditions for seamless change. The need to develop those capabilities brings us back to the mandate for human resources. Let's take a closer look at each human resource imperative in turn.

First, human resources (HR) should be held responsible for defining an organisational architecture. In other words, it should identify the underlying model of the company's way of doing business. Several well-established frameworks can be used in this process. Jay Galbraith's star model, for example, identifies five essential organisational components Strategy, structure, rewards, processes, and people. The well-known 7-S framework created by McKinsey & Company distinguishes seven components in a company's architecture strategy, structure, systems, staff, style, skills, and shared values.

It is relatively unimportant which framework the HR staff uses to define the company's architecture, as long as it is robust. What matters more is that architecture be articulated explicitly. Without such clarity, managers can become myopic about how the company runs and thus about what drives strategy implementation and what stands in its way. They might think only of structure as the driving force behind actions and decisions, and neglect systems or skills. Or they might understand the company primarily in terms of its values and pay inadequate attention to the influence of systems on how work—that is, strategy execution—actually gets accomplished.

Senior management should ask HR to play the role of an architect called into an already constructed building do draw up its plans.[5] The architect makes measurements; calculates dimensions; notes windows, doors, and staircases; and examines the plumbing and heating infrastructures. The result is a comprehensive set of blueprints that contains all the building's parts and shows how they work together.

Next, HR must be accountable for conducting an organisational audit. Blueprints can illuminate the places in a house that require immediate improvement; organisational architecture plans can be similarly useful. They are critical in helping managers identify which components of the company must change in order to facilitate strategy execution. Again, HR's role is to shepherd the dialogue about the company's blueprints.

In a company in which HR has defined the organisation's architecture in terms of its culture, competencies, rewards, governance, work processes, and leadership, the HR staff can make use of that as a model to guide the management through a rigorous discussion on the fitness of the organisations architecture in aspects like culture competencies etc.

The liberalisation of the economy has presented the Indian Industry with numerous opportunities and challenges. One of the major challenges has been to upgrade ourselves to global standards, whether or not the operations extend to countries outside India.[6] With the transformation of world's economies from a production based to a skill and knowledge based proposition, our industry has realised that technology, IT infrastructure, economies of scale and capital merely provide a foothold, but not the necessary competitive edge for doing so. Organisations can gain a competitive edge through a culture of innovation, effective use of the entrepreneurial abilities of its people, and acquiring, creating and using knowledge for increasingly higher value additions for all.

In the new millennium[7], one slogan that would stay painted across many corporate doors would be 'We are people driven" according to Mclagan (1997), this is because their market value depends increasingly on intangibles. Knowledge, loyal customers and other expressions of human capital. Most organisations had focused on how they acquired monetary capital and how their hard assets were deployed. Now the wealth of business and nations, depend on the knowledge and skills of their people. There has been a revival of interest in the resource based view of the firm, however, the difference being that people are being viewed as the key strategic resource management sources like C.K. Prahlad, Gary Hamal, David Ulrich who have given wider currency to this by suggesting that inimitable firm heterogeneity or the possession of unique 'competencies' or 'capabilities' may be an important source of enduring competitive advantage (Prahlad & Hamal, 1990; Ulrich, 1997). This perspective talks about building a competitive advantage—how organisations can outperform competition—through focusing on better management and development of their people.

Review of Literature

Numerous research studies have been conducted on various HR aspects all over the globe. An attempt is made in the following paragraphs to review the literature and research on various aspects of HRM. First some of the international studies are presented followed by Indian studies.

Robert and Margo have presented the report of a world-wide human resource survey on seventeen (17) Multinational companies in 1974. The study found that in many developing countries a proper approach to human resource management is lacking. The study which covered 17 companies with employees ranging up to 6,000, operating in both developed and developing countries, took four months through personal visitation. Staff directors and human resources expert were involved in the study. In the local companies managing director and the local personnel manager were interviewed.[8]

Recent researches worldwide have shown that good HR practices and policies can go a long way in influencing business growth and development.[9] The researches indicate that the companies gain competitive advantage through people. Yeung and Berman (1997) point out that HR practices can play three major roles. These are building critical organisational capabilities, enhancing employee satisfaction and improving customer and shareholder satisfaction

Macduffie and Krafcik (1992) studied 70 automotive assembly plants representing 24 companies and 17 countries worldwide. This study indicated that manufacturing facilities with 'lean production systems' are much higher in terms of both quality and productivity than those with 'mass production systems'.

Ostroff (1995) developed an overall HR Quality Index based on the aggregate ratings of all HR activities of a firm. On the basis of this index, firms were grouped into four categories. The firms that scored higher on the HR quality index consistently outperformed than those with a lower index on four financial measures market/book value ratio, productivity ratio (i.e., sale/employees), market value and sales.

Macduffie (1995, cited by Pfeffer, 1998, 32) observed from his studies that innovative HR practices are likely to contribute to improve economic performance only when employees possess knowledge and skills managers lack, employees are motivated to apply this skill and knowledge through discretionary effort and when employees contribute to such an effort.

Huselid (1995) found that in a sample of 3,452 firms representing all kinds of industries, one standard deviation increase in management practices was associated with increase in sales, market value and profits. A subsequent study by Huselid and Becker (1997) found that one standard deviation improvement in HR system index was associated with an increase in shareholder wealth of $41,000 per employee.

Similar results were found in Germany by Bilmes et al. (1997). This study found a strong link between investing in employees and the stock market performance of the corporation. Companies that laced workers at the core of their strategies produced higher long-term returns than those who did not.

In a 1989 study by Macduffie (1995) on 70 automobile plants representing 24 companies from 17 different countries, the results revealed the quality and productivity were much higher in the flexible rather than in the mass production system and the two systems differed substantially on how they managed their people-in terms of emphasis on training, use of teams, reduction of status differences, and the use of contingent performance-related compensation.

Arthur (1994) studied the impact of two different management approaches on the productivity of steel mills. His study of the 30 of the 44 existing steel mills in the US at that time differentiated the 'control' approach to human resource management (HRM) from that of the 'commitment' approach. After statistically controlling age, size, union status and business strategy of the mills, the results showed that using a commitment strategy was significantly related to improved performance in terms of labour hours and scrap rate. Mini-mills using the commitment approach required 34 per cent fewer labour hours to produce a tone of steel and showed a 63 per cent better scrap rate.

'A number of studies spanning different organisations operating in various service industries provide evidence for a positive relationship between employee attitudes, customer service and satisfaction and profits' (Pfeffer, 1998, 55).

Schneider and Bowen (1985) reported in a study of bank branches that when the branches had sufficient numbers and quality of people to perform its tasks (called the service imperative) customers reported receiving higher levels of service. In another study Schneider (1991) found that customer perceptions and attitudes were affected by what employees experienced. Organisational practices that are both service related and human resources related seem to provide cues to customers to evaluate bank's service.

A study by Johnso, Ryan and Schmit (1994) at the Ford Motor Credit revealed that attitudes concerning workload, teamwork, training and development, satisfaction with the job, and satisfaction with the company were all related to customer satisfaction. Schmit and Allscheid (1995) found that customer satisfaction and perceptions of service quality were significantly related to measures of employee attitudes about the fairness of pay, whether management was concerned about employee welfare and treated people fairly, and whether supervisors encouraged an open and participative work environment. Employee attitudes are in turn related to profits. For example, in a study of an eye care company a significant relationship was found between employee attitudes and profits (Moeller and Schneider, 1986).

Delery and Doty (1996) in a study of nearly 200 banks found that differences in HR practices accounted for large differences in financial performance. Huselid concluded that 'prior empirical work has consistently found that use of effective human resource management practices enhances firm performance' (Huselid, 1995, 640).

A study of the bibliographical research work in the field of personnel management in India reveals that bulk of literature relates to the papers published by personnel executives written on the basis of their experience. Their observations are mostly impressionistic in nature.

Another category of work belongs to the text book type without much of empirical basis. Some scholars have attempted to study the personnel management theories in the context of live cases. Some of them include T.N. Kapoor (1965); Ram S. Tarneja (1968); R.C. Goyal (1970); and Monappa and Saiyadain (1979). Empirical research on academic venture has been taken up by some researchers. Their works mostly remained unpublished and they have neither reached the professionals nor academics. Very few research works were published. Some of them include Sivayya[10] (1968); Rudrabasavaraj (1969);[11] Lallan Prasad (1973);[12] Jacob (1973);[13] Gopalji (1983); G.C. Patro (1989);[14] CH Ram Prasad Rao (1990);[15] and VSP Rao (1991).[16]

Myeiars (1958)[17] discussed the labour problems caused by the industrialising process and links the labour problems to the changing social, economic and political institutions of India.

Takkar (1962)[18] has made a study of the 15 mills in Bombay covering many aspects such as their scope, industrial relations, and union management relations. Nicholson's (1976)[33] research study does not reveal any logical connection between job-satisfaction, pay, promotion, supervision, co-workers and absenteeism. Baldev Sarma (1983)[34] noted that many of the problems confronting industrial relations in India can be traced back to the weak trade union movement.

Sexena (1970)[19] gave socio-economic background of workers in the five selected units in Meerut district and discussed promotion policies, training; transfer, welfare measures, bonus, remuneration and the functioning of trade unions.

Gangadhara Rao (1970)[20] has studied some aspects of personnel administration and union management relations in the Indian railways in the post-independence period. Singh and Sudha (1973)[21] revealed the potential effect of need for achievement on the relationship between employees' performance and job-satisfaction.

Bhushan (1973)[22] pointed out some effective steps for the proper management of personnel in the cooperative institutions. (1) need to retain experienced employees both in small and large scale cooperative units; (2) need for development of professional management in cooperation; (3) growth and expansion of business in large cooperative organisations; (4) need for adopting modern technology calling for the newer skills; (5) need to ensure viability of cooperative institution by keeping the manpower cost to minimum; and (6) need to fill up positions in the cooperative institutions calling for business and administrative expertise.

According to Jurgen Von Muralt (1973),[23] the peculiarities of the management of cooperative societies results from the distinct features of a cooperative society as a combination of two organisational entities a business enterprise, on the one hand; and a social institution or association of persons who unite to use the services provided by the business enterprises, on the other. Manpower planning has not received due attention in the cooperative sector in spite of the expansion of business and diversification of economic activities. Goyal (1974)[24] reviews the industrial relations policy through the five year plan. Sharma (1974)[25] made an analysis of the problems of industrial workers in India.

E.A. Ramaswamy (1977)[26] observed that 'humble-down to earth empiricism' is the need of the hour in Indian labour studies. An empirical study of the practices relating to the application of tools and techniques will be of great importance. Studies in this regard are very few.

Kamat (1978)[27] emphasised the need for adoption of modern personnel administration and management practices in cooperatives. He felt that careful situation of managerial personnel will give much better results. Kutumba Rao (1978)[28] considered cooperatives as a third rate organisation in the market. Employees are not enthusiastic because of poor prospects and poor working and other facilities.

Dinesh (1978)[29] expressed that there are certain serious drawbacks in the employer-employee relationship, viz., the entire process of recruitment, coordination, control, personnel and manpower planning, induction and training, performance appraisal and promotion policies, etc., in the cooperative and small industry sectors in general and cooperative industries in particular.

Venkata Ratnam (1978)[30] studied some aspects of human factor in Visakapatnam Port. The study discussed the growth and characteristics of human resources, work organisation and employment practices, employee earnings, productive efficiency, employee welfare, unionism and union involvement, and union management relations.

Manju Gupta (1978)[31] conducted studies on personnel and union management relations in the Hindustan Shipyard Limited. Murthy (1983)[32] in his study discussed the trade unionism in Orissa.

There is great need to take up more research studies in the vital area of human resource management. Particularly case studies making an indepth study of human resource management practices in individual enterprises are conspicuous by their absence. Hence there is a need for comprehensive and objective study of human resource management practices. As for dairy industry in A.P. no study has so far been taken up. The present work is an humble attempt to fill the knowledge gap and seeks to contribute to an understanding of the HRM practices in this vital and growing Dairy sector of A.P.

Conceptual Framework

Some managers misunderstand that human resources management is a dignified term of personnel management, while some are of the opinion that both the terms represent the same concept or identical functions. In this context, one should understand that human resources management is not personnel management, though the latter is included in the former. The very outlook of philosophy of human resources management is different from that of personnel management.

According to Flippo, "Personnel management is the planning, organizing, directing and controlling of the procurement, development, compensation, integration, maintenance and separation of Human Resource to the end that individual, organisational, Societal objectives are accomplished".[33] This highlights that various managerial functions relating to procurement and maintenance of people in an organisation come under personnel management.

In the words of Jucius "Personnel management may be defined as that field of management which has to do with planning, organising and controlling the functions of procuring, developing, maintaining and utilising a labour force, such that (a) the objectives for which the company is established are attained economically and effectively; (b) objectives of all levels of personnel are served to the highest possible degree; and (c) objectives of society are duly considered and served".[34]

According to Leon C. Megginson, the term human resources can be thought of as, "the total knowledge, skills, creative abilities, talents and aptitudes of an organisation's workforce, as well as the value, attitudes and beliefs on the individuals involved."[35] The term human resource implies that the management can get and use the skill, knowledge, ability etc., through the development of skills, tapping and utilising them again and again. Human resources are also regarded as human factor, human asset, human capital and the like.

The term the researcher has chosen for the title of the thesis and which appears use through out the work, is human resource. It has gained widespread acceptance over the last decade because it expresses the belief that workers are a valuable and some times irreplaceable resource. Effective human resource management (HRM) is a major component of any manager's job.[36]

Human Resources Management (HRM) is concerned with the human beings in an organisation. It reflects a new philosophy, a new outlook, approach, and strategy, which views an organisation's manpower as its resources and assets, and not as liabilities or mere hands. It is essentially 'developmental in nature. If the approach under personnel management could be described as direction and control, the approach under human resource management could be termed as supportive and facilitative. It seeks to realize the optimum potential of human beings and utilised the same for organisational ends as well as for individual development through a proactive approach.

The Present Study

The present study is undertaken in the dairy industry of Andhra Pradesh. Two dairy units viz., Krishna district Milk Producers Cooperative Union Ltd (Vijaya Dairy), Guntur District Milk Producers Mutually Aided Co-operative Union Limited (Sangam Dairy) situated in Krishna district and Guntur district respectively, have been selected. Their contribution to the 'white revolution' in the state is substantial. Both the units have registered incremental growth year after year. They are in the process of taking a big leap and have embarked upon ambitious expansion programme. The co-operatives which have roots in the villages engage over two thousand employees. If these units have to cope up with the competitive environment and make rapid strides, they have to manage their human resources effectively besides taking care of capital and other physical resources. Needless to mention that the growth and viability of the organisation depend upon the quality of its human resources. In this context the policies and practices of HRM play a vital role. The present study is an attempt to examine closely the policies and practices adopted in this regard in the two units. Recruitment and selection is the first vital function in HRM. One of the concerns of the study is to examine this aspect. Besides, the management has to adopt appropriate methods and strategies to develop the potential of human beings so inducted in organisations. The study seeks to examine the developmental strategies and approaches of human potential.

Payment of just and appropriate compensation and promotion of employee welfare is another major aspect of HRM. The study seeks to probe the compensation package offered in the units vis-a-vis other organisations of the industry.

The tone and tenor of industrial relations is another important aspect covered under study. The different mechanisms which aim at preventing industrial conflict and promoting harmony between management and labour are sought to be examined in detail. In this regard collective bargaining practices, participative management and joint consultation, grievance redressal mechanism, discipline maintenance and the approach of the parties in resolving conflict are important aspects in this regard. The status and role of the trade unions in industrial relations is also sought to be examined.

Job satisfaction and employee commitment are also examined in detail. In the present study an attempt is also made to study the profile of the respondents in terms of age, educational background, marital status, urban/rural background, salary, dependents, and indebtedness and to study the relationship between these personal variables and the major functions of human resource management in each unit in terms of managerial and non-managerial background.

The study, in a nutshell seeks to review the personnel policies and practices as perceived by the employees and to provide necessary inputs to improve the practices for effective and sound human resource management.

Importance and Scope

The review of literature presented earlier reveals that the bulk of literature in the field of HRM has no empirical basis. The articles written by executives, are based mostly on their experiences and stray thoughts. And the textbooks written by Indian authors are without field investigation.

Studies based on field study are very much limited. As for the dairy industry in Andhra Pradesh it remains 'untrodden' and no study has been undertaken in this vital industry so far. It is in this context the present study assumes importance and seeks to contribute for a clear understanding of the HRM approaches, procedures, policies and practices.

As for its scope, the study is confined to two major dairy units located in Krishna and Guntur districts of Andhra Pradesh. They are selected in view of their growth potential, contribution to the rural economy, the technology and the size of workforce employed in two units. Of the seventeen dairy units in Andhra Pradesh of various sizes and description, the units selected for the study are major ones and with a standing of nearly two decades. All important human resource functions viz. recruitment and selection, HRD, wages and employee welfare, industrial relations, job satisfaction and employee commitment are sought to be covered. The human resource policies and the practices which are meant for translating these policies into action are also covered under the scope of the present study.

Objective of the Study

The major objective of the study is to assess the human resources management practices in the two dairies. The following are the sub-objectives of the study,

(*a*) To study the employment policies and procedures of the organisation and to evaluate the same.

(*b*) To assess the HRD practices in the organisation and to find out the employee perceptions about them.

(*c*) To examine the employee compensation system in the organisations and to know the views of employees in this regard.

(*d*) To evaluate the industrial relation climate prevailing in the organisation and to study the employees' feelings in this respect.

(e) To analyse employee welfare and social security measures available in the organisations.

(f) To assess the extent of commitment and job satisfaction among the employees of the dairy industry; and finally.

(g) To study the causal factors that effected commitment and job satisfaction among the employees.

HYPOTHESES

1. Recruitment and selection is likely to be associated with personal variables (age, sex, caste, salary, education, indebtedness, dependents, rural/urban background etc) and organisational variables (organisation, category).

2. Employee welfare is likely to be associated with personal variables (age, sex, caste, salary, education, indebtedness, dependents, rural/urban background, etc) and organisational variables (organisation, category).

3. Commitment is likely to be associated with personal variables (age, sex, caste, salary, education, indebtedness, dependents, rural/urban background... etc) and organisational variables (Organisation, category).

4. Job satisfaction is likely to be associated with personal variable (age, sex, caste, salary, education, indebtedness, dependents, rural/urban background. etc.) and organisational variables (organisation, category).

METHODOLOGY

(a) Method of Study

Application of appropriate methods and adoption of scientific procedure is a sine-qua-non of systematic enquiry. This has an important bearing on the collection of reliable and accurate information as well as on the outcome of the study. The present study uses a combination of case study and survey method.

Case study method is adopted to make an indepth analysis of human resource policies and practices. Opinion survey of the respondents constitutes the survey method in the study.

(b) Universe and Sample

The Krishna District Milk Producers Co-operative Union Limited, Vijayawada and the Guntur District Mutually Aided Milk Producers Cooperative Union Limited, Vadlamudi and the employees constitute the universe. The total population of the two units at the end of June 2002 was 1901 (1040+861). It includes both managerial and non-managerial employees. The managerial employees are classified into managers, deputy managers and assistant managers; whereas the non-managerial group into supervisors, technical staff, clerks, drivers and workers. Thus the sample is selected by giving representation to the various strata following the principles of stratified random samples. The details are furnished in Table 1.1.

Table 1.1: Sample Design

	Vijaya Dairy		*Sangam Dairy*		*Total*
	Managerial	*Non-Managerial*	*Managerial*	*Non-Managerial*	
Total strength of the organisation	63	977	55	806	1901
Sample taken	30	150	25	100	305
Percentage	47.61	15.35	45.45	12.40	16.04

Data Collection

Data has been collected both from primary and secondary sources. Two elaborate schedules are designed for collection of information. One is management schedule, covering various aspects such as organisational background on policies, procedures and practices of human resource management. With the help of this schedule the organisational data has been collected through informal discussions with the officers. The second schedule has been designed to find out the employees background and their opinions on various aspects of human resources management practices in the organisation. This schedule has been administered among the sample managerial and non-managerial employees. Some of the non-managerial employees have adequate knowledge of English. In cases where the employees have no proficiency in the language the questions have been asked in mother tongue (telugu) and opinions are elicited. The personal presence of the researcher throughout data collection has highly facilitated in getting relevant information. Collection of data from the field is not an easy task. The respondents have not been spontaneous in extending co-operation in the initial stages. They even suspected the researcher to be either the representative of the management or person from a government agency. He had to establish rapport with the respondents by establishing his identity and explaining the objectives of the study. The help of some managers and trade union officials has come handy in this regard. When they were convinced that the study was academic in nature, they were uninhibited in their approach and began extending their co-operation. Personal interviews have been held with the respondents by arranging prior appointment according to the convenience of the respondents. Some interviews involved single session of an hour or so whereas in some cases the interviews staggered over more than one session. In addition to the primary method of data collection, secondary sources of the data have also been in the study which include annual reports, files, vouchers and records of the two dairies.

Data Processing and Techniques of Analysis

The information collected from the organisation has been analysed qualitatively by using the method of content analysis. The information collected from the employees has been processed, tabulated, and analysed quantitatively by using a number of statistical measures such as chy-square test, Pearson's coefficient of correlation, partial correlation and regression analysis.

Presentation of the Study

The entire work is presented in ten chapters. Chapter one focuses on the nature of the problem and the methodology adopted in the study. It is followed by a brief profile of the sample dairy units and the profile of the respondents in chapter two. The recruitment and selection practices are reviewed in chapter three. Chapter four makes an attempt to analyse the human resource development practices. Chapter five discusses the aspects of wage and employee welfare. Chapter six deals with the pattern of industrial relations in the dairy units. Chapter seven studies the aspects of employee commitment. In chapter eight, an attempt is made to find the level of job satisfaction of the employees. Chapter nine examines the causal factors affecting commitment. Chapter ten summarises the main findings and conclusions of the study besides offering some important suggestions.

Limitations

The study has the following limitations.

(i) Since the principal method of study is the case study method, it has all the limitations associated with the method. The generalisations of the study cannot be expected to have Universal application. Even when we try to apply to the units of similar nature these must be applied with caution.

(ii) The records and files have not been maintained systematically and the researcher had to labour very hard to collect necessary information by running from 'pillar to post'.

(iii) Employees were hard pressed for time in view of the job demands and rigorous work schedule. The researcher had to persuade them for sparing time for conducting interviews. When he found that the respondents were not

in a position to spare adequate time for the purpose, he had to request them to spare time after the shift timings.

(iv) There are quiet a few standardised instruments to measure job satisfaction and commitment. However this study pertains to a new sector i.e., Dairy industry which is significantly different from conventional industries. To be very specific dairy units are more or less co-operative societies which follow most of the human resource practices. Generally the instruments to measure job satisfaction etc. have been developed keeping in view conventional industries. Hence it is felt that it would not be appropriate to use already existing instruments. As such self anchored instruments have been developed for this study. Therefore these instruments have their own limitations.

REFERENCES

1. Government of Andhra Pradesh, (1990). *Andhra Pradesh Dairy Development Cooperative Federation Limited.* Hyderabad: Department of Publications, 3.

2. *Ibid.,* 3.

3. The most Successful Dairy Experiment Carried out in India by the Government of Gujarat State.

4. Dave, Ulrich. (1997). A New Mandate for Human Resources, in *Harvard Business Review* Harvard Business School Press, 126-128.

5. *Ibid.,* 128.

6. Ramesh, Galley. (2000). *Going Global Leveraging Human Potential,* National HRD Network, Hyderabad Chapter. New Delhi: Tata McGraw Hill Publishing Company Limited, iii.

7. Archana, Arcot. (2000). *Competency Rooted Human Resource Management,* New Delhi: National HRD Network, 254.

8. Michael, V.P. (1996). *Human Resource Management and Human Relations.* Mumbai: Himalaya Publishing House, 32.

9. Rao, T.V., (1999). *HRD Audit, Evaluating the Human Resource Function for Business Improvement.* New Delhi: Sage Publications, 20.

10. Sivayya, K.V. (1968). *Industrial Relations in Visakhapatnam Port.* Waltair: Andhra University Press.

11. Rudrabasvaraj, M.N. (1969). *Personnel Administration in India.* Poona: Vaikunth Mehta National Institute of Co-operative Management.

12. Prasad, Lallan (1973). *Personnel Management and Industrial Relations in Public Sector.* Mumbai: Progressive Publisher.

13. Jacob, K.K. (1973). *Personnel Management in India,* A study of Training and Functions of Personnel Officers. Udayapur: SJC Publications, i.

14. Patro, G.C. (1989). *Human Resources Management.* New Delhi: Discovery Publishing House.

15. Ram Prasad Rao, Ch. (1990). *Human Resource Management in Municipalities.* New Delhi: Discovery Publishing House.

16. Rao, V.S.P. (1991). *Human Resource Management in Small Industries.* New Delhi. Discovery Publishing House.

17. Myers, C.A. (1958). *Labour Problems in the Industrialisation of India,* Cambridge Harvard University Press.

18. Thakkar, G.V. (1962). *"Labour Problems of Textile Industry",* A Case Study of the Labour Problems of the Cotton Mill Industry in Bombay. Bombay: Vora & cc.

19. Saxena, R.C. (1970). *"Industrial Relations in Selected Units".* New Delhi: R.P.C Planning Commission of India.

20. Gangadhara Rao, M. (1970). *"Industrial Relations in Indian Railways"* An unpublished thesis. Waltair: Andhra University.

21. Singh, A.P. and Sudha, Srivasthava. (1983, Jan). *"Effect of Need for Achievement on the Job Performance, Job Satisfaction Relationship",* Industrial Relations, V. 18, 436-447.

22. Bhushan, Y.K. (1973 February-April). Personnel Development in the Cooperative Sector. *Cooperative Perspective,* 15-17.

23. Jurgen, Von Muralt. (1973 January-March). Cooperative Law and Management, *Cooperative Perspective.* Pune : Vaikunth Mehta National Institute of Cooperative Management, 111.

24. Goyal, R.C. (1974 July-September). "Industrial Relations Policy through the Five Year Plans". *Indian Journal of Public Administration,* 20(3), 638-652.

25. Sharma, B.R. (1974). *"The Indian Industrial Worker".* Delhi: Vikas Publishing House Pvt. Ltd.

26. Ramaswamy, E.A. (1977). *The Worker and his Union—A Study in South India.* Bombay: Allied Publishers Pvt. Ltd., 8.

27. Kamat, G.S. (1978). *New Dimensions of Co-operative Management.* New Delhi, Himalaya Publishing House, 177-78.

28. Kutumba Rao, M. (1978 September). Management of Co-operative Enterprise, *the Indian Management,* 29-33.

29. Dinesh, C. (1978). *Introducing Personnel Management in Co-operatives,* Pune Harshad Prakashan, 52.

30. Venkata Ratnam, C.S. (1978). *"A Study of Some Aspects of Human Factor in Visakapatnam Port",* an unpublished thesis. Waltair: Andhra University.

31. Manju, Gupta. (1978). *"Industrial Relations in Indian Ship-building Industry".* Visakapatnam: An unpublished thesis, Andhra University.

32. Murthy, B.S. (1983, January). "Trade Unionism in Orissa". *Indian Journal of Industrial Relations,* Vol. 18(3), 397

33. Flippo, Edwin B. (1976). *Personnel Management.* New York: McGraw Hill Book Company, Seventh Edition, 5.

34. Michael, J. Jucious. (1976). *Personnel Management,* Home Wood, Lichard D. Irwin, 25.

35. Megginson, Leon, C. (1977). *Personnel and Human Resources Administration,* Homewood: Richard D. Irwin Inc., Illinois, 4.

36. Gomez-Mejia, Luis R., Balkin, David B., and Cardry, Robert L. (2003). *Managing Human Resources,* Third Edition, Delhi: Pearson Education (Singapore) Pte. Ltd. 2.

2

Profile of the Organisations Under Study

The preceding chapter provided the introduction, literature review followed by the methodology of the study. This chapter describes the profile of the two organisations and their employees, so as to form a backdrop of the entire study. In this connection, importance, progress and problems of the dairy units and the salient aspects of the histories of the two units have been narrated. Further, the socio-economic background of the employees employed in these units has also been presented.

THE KRISHNA DISTRICT MILK PRODUCERS CO-OPERATIVE UNION LIMITED (HEREAFTER CALLED VIJAYA DAIRY) VIJAYAWADA

Origin and Growth

The three and half decade old Vijayawada Milk Project managed by "The Krishna District Milk Producers Union", was commissioned in 1965 with Rs. 1.50 crore as an aid given by the UNICEF (United Nations Children's Emergency Fund), to cater to the needs of the coastal district.

Vision

Dairying in the district is the major instrument of strengthening rural economy and making available safe and milk products.

Mission

Farmers' prosperity can be achieved through technical innovations and customer orientation with specific focus on quality and cost.

Quality Policy

The aim of Vijaya Dairy is to be a technologically advanced unit with global outlook providing products and services of higher quality delighting the customer.

Objectives

Major objectives would be to accelerate the pace of increasing rural income and employment through dairy development; adopting modern Technology to improve productivity, reduce operational costs and ensure greater availability of Milk and Milk Products.

1. Evolving long term policies to encourage and develop milk production and productivity in the district.
2. Achieving Co-ordination among various programmes in the district to optimise resource utilisation.
3. Providing remunerative and assured market for the milk produced by the farmers round the year.
4. Improving efficiency in milk collection, transport, processing and marketing with the emphasis on reducing the cost of operations at every stage from rural farmer to urban consumer.
5. Increasing the availability of milk and developing the market for milk and milk products.
6. Developing the manpower of the organisation to reach excellence in their working life and create a pro-active organisational culture for achieving competitive edge.
7. Consolidation and expansion of co-operative structure with special attention to small farmers and weaker sections of milk producing community.

Genesis

The aspects like seasonal surplus, surplus milk after household consumption, have drawn the attention of UNICEF, FAO and Government of India. A survey was conducted in the coastal delta of Andhra Pradesh, and viewed that there could be bright future for dairy in the areas.

As a result of the survey, a scheme "The Integrated Milk Project, Hyderabad, Vijayawada", costing Rs. 4.35 crores was set up to make full utilisation of the surplus milk of the area and to link it up with the milk deficit areas of twin cities of Hyderabad and Secunderabad. The project comprised the Milk Processing Plant at Hyderabad, with a capacity of 50,000 liters per day, and milk conservation and production factory at Vijayawada, with a capacity of 1.25 lakh liters per day. Both were in the first phase.

By the time, the products factory at Vijayawada was pressed into operation, a Milk supply scheme had been started in February, 1965 by commissioning one milk chilling centre at Pamarru, which is a feeder unit to the milk products factory, Vijayawada

The centre which had a humble start of 600 litres has gone upto handle beyond 20,000 liter per day subsequently. Later the scheme was extended to cover greater area in the district by opening other milk chilling centres and also increasing the area of operations.

Originally, the milk products factory, Vijayawada was commissioned on 11-4-1969. This factory has the handling capacity of 1.28 lakh litres per day in the first stage with the provision for expansion to 2.50 lakh litre per day in the second stage. This products factory at Vijayawada has the distinction of being the first products factory in South India. Further, it has the distinction of handling milk to its capacity in the second year of the operations. Apart from handling milk from Krishna district, it also handles surplus milk received from the districts of Vizag, East and West Godavari, Prakasam and Nellore.

The factory had peak handling during 1982-83, with a view to handling the increased surplus milk from Nellore, Prakasam and Godavari districts. A second spray drying plant with latest design to produce about 14.19 tonnes of milk powder has been established and commissioned during December, 1982.

The factory has a provision to make S.M.T of cleulter, 6 M.T. of ghee and 22.0 M.T. of milk powder per day. Vijaya Ghee in consumer sachets is being done only from Milk Products factory, Vijayawada in the state. And it also bags the distinction, as the first public sector organisation in the country to produce infant milk food in consumer packs.

And at last in 1983, the Milk Products factory was emerged as "The Krishna District Milk Producers Cooperative Union Limited", with the change in the policy of unions in 1978, and took over the management of the ongoing activities of Krishna District in February, 1985.

This is the first milk union in the state to be formed with the Financial Assistance of UNICEF. The Krishna District has the distinction of starting organised dairying activities by commissioning a Milk chilling center at Pamarru, in 1965, February, the first one of its kind in Andhra Pradesh.[2]

Infrastructural Facilities

- Total Villages covered - 918
- Dairy Co-operative Societies functional - 521
- Dairy Co-operative Societies defunct - 46
- All Women Dairy Cooperative Societies - 81
- Total Number Producers - 1,02,610
- Milk Producers Association Centres - 342
- Centres with Buildings - 538
- Veterinary First Aid Centres - 530
- Artificial Insemination Centres - 55

- Breeding Bulls in Operation - 206
- Electronic Milk Testers Functional - 352
- No. of Milk Routes - 35
- Total Distance covered per day (kms) - 66520

The type of products manufactured are Milk in Sachets, Ghee, Butter, Skim milk powder, UHT Products. The UHT Products include Milk 100 ml; Milk 200 ml, Merre Milk 200 ml, Ghee and Lassi each 200 ml, Cream 100 ml, Cream 200 ml, and D. Magic 200 ml

Products and Byproducts

Basically, the Vijaya Dairy is a product oriented organisation and also a service-oriented cooperative society, since its motto is to "Help the Milk Producers".

The main product is pure, refined and pasteurised milk and byproducts are of different forms of milk and other variety of sweets.

The list of various byproducts are pasteurised milk is 500 ml polypacks, pasteurised milk in 200 ml polypacks, Vijaya Gold (fat 7%, SNF 9%), Vijaya Special (fat 6%, and 8.5 SNF), Vijaya Premium (Fat 4.5% and 8.5% SNF) fortified with Vitamin 'A', Vijaya Low Fat Milk (Fat 1.5%, 9% SNF) fortified with Vitamin 'A'. Vijaya Diet Milk (Fat 0.1%, SNF 9%) fortified with Vitamin 'A', UMT Milk aseptic pack of 100 ml, UMT Milk aseptic pack of 200 ml, sterilised cream of 100 ml sterilised cream of 200 ml, Vijaya Ghee, in packs of ½, 1, 2, 25 kgs, Flavoured Milk 200 ml pack, Lassi 200 ml polypack, Cooking Butter in 500 gm and 20 kgs pack, Skim Milk Powder in 1 kg/25 kg Pack, Curd (125 ml, 100 ml cups) Sweet Yoghurt 100 ml cups, Butter Milk 200 ml polypack, Paneer 100 and 200 gms polypack, Doodh Peda (25 gms, 250 gms) pack, Basundi 500 gms cup, Khova (unsweetened), Vijaya Cattle Feed- 50 kgs/25 kgs pack, Mineral Mixture in 1 kilo and 25 kgs pack.

Marketing

The marketing of milk is one of the important areas in the Dairy Industry, as this will fetch immediate revenue realisation, and at the same time meet the requirements of the consumers. It can be taken that the milk which 'is distributed should reach the consumer in time and with full assurance of quality.

The Krishna Milk Union area of operation covers three urban towns (Machilipatnam, Gudiwada and Jaggaiahpet) and one major city Vijayawada. The union has achieved a sales growth rate of 12 per cent during the current year. It is proposed to start ATMs and open milk depots at strategic locations to cater to the requirements of agents, parlours, consumer hostels and institutions. The agents will be appointed by studying the zonewise population and identifying new areas.

The survey of existing suppliers will be made for hotels and institutions. Moreover transporter-cum-distributor (TCD) system will be employed for servicing hotels and institutions along with distribution. It is also proposed to start any time milk counters over a period of time. The Cijaya milk will also be made available through opening of day counters which would run from 7 AM to 11 PM. The entire range of Vijaya milk and fresh products will be distributed to the day counters.

The details of the AMC counters which have been proposed to be established in a phased manner are given in Table 2.1.

Table 2.1: Anytime Milk Counters

Sl.No.	*Name of the counter*	*Existing*	*Proposed*
1.	Vijayawada	126	150
2.	Machilipatnam	18	20
3.	Gudivada	8	15
4.	Jaggaiahpeta	8	15
5.	Others	10	12

The Table 2.1 reveals centrewise existing and proposed any time milk counters. 126 existing milk counters are proposed to 150 AMCs at Vijayawada. In Machilipatnam the existing AMCs are 18 and it is proposed to increase them to 20. In Gudiwada and Jaggaiahpeta the existing AMCs are 8 each and it is proposed to increase them to 15 each. Presently the existing AMCs in various places are 10 and it is proposed to increase them to 12.

Finance Profile

In February 1985 the Krishna Milk Union was started with initial capital of 51 million and 27 acres of land as area. Besides the initial capital it has got the authorised capital of Rs.5 crores and paid up capital of Rs. 1.5 crores. Calculated at 1987 prices, the cost of the project for the period 1987-94 is estimated at approximately Rs. 9150 million, in which the participation of the following agencies is shown below.

World Bank	-	Rs. 4,860 million
EEC	-	Rs. 2,227 million
NDDB	-	Rs. 2,063 million.

Including the investments already made during 1985-87, the toal project cost for the period 1985-94 was approximately Rs. 11,960 million.

The financial performance right from the year 1984-85 upto 2000-2001 is presented below from which the profit or loss and depreciation can be estimated.

The following table 2.2 depicts yearwise financial performance of the Vijaya dairy.

The table 2.2 shows yearwise financial performance in terms of total turnover of income, profit/loss, with depreciation, the accumulative profit and loss and profit/loss in terms of cash from 1984-85 to 2000-2001. The total turnover of income increased from Rs. 667.58 lakhs (1984-85) to

Table 2.2: Financial Performance

Year	Total income (Turnover) Rs. Lakhs	Profit/Loss Rs. in lakhs	Depreciation	Cash Profit/Loss (Rs. Lakhs)	Cummulative	
					Profit/Loss	Cash Profit/Loss (Rs. Lakhs)
1984-85	667.58	-13.95	9.76	-4.19	-	-
1985-86	1964.36	-114.49	17.00	-97.49	128.44	-101.68
1986-87	2220.22	6.67	24.57	31.24	-121.77	-70.44
1987-88	1755.88	6.35	24.57	30.92	-115.42	-39.52
1988-89	2455.92	-22.24	37.92	15.68	-137.66	-23.84
1989-90	2612.66	5.85	41.70	47.55	-131.81	23.71
1990-91	2740.61	-19.81	38.09	18.28	-151.62	41.99
1991-92	3371.06	-8.82	57.00	48.18	-160.44	90.17
1992-93	4230.22	-162.66	47.17	-115.49	-323.10	-25.32
1993-94	4785.35	-20.32	42.28	21.26	-343.42	-3.36
1994-95	4847.33	25.59	77.33	102.92	-317.83	99.56
1995-96	4730.77	-53.41	67.09	13.68	-371.24	113.24
1996-97	5611.30	-18.71	56.1	37.39	-389.95	150.66
1997-98	5933.99	5.94	41.8	47.74	-384.01	198.40
1998-99	7606.65	34.86	45.01	79.87	-349.15	278.27
1999-00	9246.18	9.06	50.09	59.15	-340.09	337.42
2000-01	10188.40	32.80	61.66	94.46	-307.29	431.88

Source: Annual audit report of Vijaya dairy.

Rs. 10,188.40 lakhs (2000-01). The yearwise profit/loss, account shows ultimately profit of Rs. 32.80 lakhs in the year 2000-01. After deducting the depreciation cost the profit/loss in terms of cash showed ultimately Rs. 94.46 lakhs in the year 2000-01. While the cumulative profit/loss account showed loss of 307.29 lakhs in the year 2000-01, the profit/loss account in terms of cash was Rs. 431.88 lakhs in the said year.

The table 2.3 presents yearwise Manpower cost profile and its proportion in the total income.

Table 2.3 reveals the yearwise annual income and year wise percentage increase. The yearwise income has increased from Rs. 667.58 lakhs (1984-85) to Rs. 10188.40 lakhs (2000-01). During the year 1985-86 the percentage of increase was 66.01. Thereafter there was no consistent increase or decrease. During the years 1991-92 and 1992-93 there was substantial percentage increase of 18.70 and 20.31 respectively. The maximum percentage increase of 28.50 was noticed in the year 1988-89 during the year 1987-88 it has come down to -26.44. There was consistent increase of manpower cost from Rs. 117.60 lakhs (1984-85) to Rs. 1624.20 lakhs (2000-01). There was maximum percentage increase of 59.33 of manpower cost in the year 1985-86 and it was reduced to -17.69 in the year 1987-88. The proportion of employee cost in income was maximum of 21.83 in the year 1995-96. The proportion of employee cost was reduced to 15.94 during 2000-01. Since the Vijaya Dairy introduced voluntary retirement scheme (VRS) the proportion of employee cost started declining from 21.83 (1995-96) to 15.94 (2000-01).

The table 2.4 presents fixed cost profile of the Vijaya Dairy.

As revealed from the table 2.4 the annual fixed cost of staff wages and welfare expenses, administrative expenses, maintenance of buildings, lease rentals, interest on working capital, interest on capital and depreciation is Rs. 1622.04 lakhs. The cost per liter for the above items at

Table 2.3: Manpower Cost Profile

Year	*Total income Rs. Lakhs*	*Percentage increase*	*Manpower Cost Rs. Lakhs*	*Percentage Increase*	*Proportion of Employee cost in Income*
1984-85	667.58	0	117.60	0	17.62
1985-86	1964.36	66.01	289.19	59.33	14.72
1986-87	2220.22	11.52	372.69	22.40	16.79
1987-88	1755.88	-26.44	316.67	-17.69	18.03
1988-89	2455.92	28.50	457.15	30.73	18.61
1989-90	2612.66	5.99	511.01	10.54	19.56
1990-91	2740.61	4.66	564.42	9.46	20.59
1991-92	3371.06	18.70	670.45	15.81	19.89
1992-93	4230.22	20.31	735.17	8.80	17.38
1993-94	4785.35	11.60	858.65	14.38	17.94
1994-95	4847.33	1.27	996.64	13.85	20.56
1995-96	4730.77	-2.46	1032.92	3.51	21.83
1996-97	5611.30	15.69	1192.38	13.37	21.25
1997-98	5933.99	5.43	1226.49	2.78	20.67
1998-99	7606.65	21.98	1364.93	10.14	17.94
1999-00	9246.18	17.73	1557.96	12.39	16.85
2000-01	10188.40	9.24	1624.20	4.08	15.94

Table 2.4: Fixed Cost Profile 2001-2002

Source of Cost	*Annual Cost Rs. In lakhs*	*Cost per Lt @100% cap. Rs.*	*Cost per Lt@ 37% cap. Rs.*	*Proportion of Total%*
Staff wages and welfare expenses	1318.46	1.44	3.90	81.3
Administrative expenses	53.52	0.06	0.16	3.3
Maintenance of Buildings	38.50	0.04	0.11	2.4
Lease rentals	12.00	0.01	0.04	0.7
Interest on working capital	60.00	0.07	0.18	3.7
Interest on capital	67.06	0.07	0.20	4.1
Depreciation	72.50	0.08	0.21	4.5
Total	1622.04	1.77	4.80	100.00

Source: Office information of Management Information Systems (MIS) department of Vijaya dairy.

the rate of 100 per cent capital value is Rs. 1.77; the cost per liter at the rate of 37 per cent capital value is Rs. 4.80. The staff wages and welfare expenses constitute higher proportion (81.3%) in the total fixed cost. The proportions of other items vary from 0.7 to 4.5 per cent.

Technology Management

The milk union has milk processing and conservation plant at Vijayawada with initial capacity of 1.25 lakh ltrs per day and subsequently expanded to 2.5 lakh ltr. per day, drying capacity of 22 M.Ts (two plants) and Ghee manufacturing capacity of 18 M.Ts. Vijaya Ghee in consumer tin packs is being made only at Vijayawada. It also has advanced milk processing and packaging technology (UHT and Aseptic Packaging in Tetra Brik Packages) with a capacity of 0.35 lakh packs of 1000 ml/day and 0.50 lakh packs of 200 ml/day. This station has the distinction of putting out quality product besides being the highest milk packaging station in the country. This station has successfully developed sterilised cream in aseptic packs with shelf life of 4 months at ambient environment.

Mastering, manufacturing and making use of technology for the organisation, is crucial for the survival of the organisation. This will be integrated with the base of the organisation, its people and systems.

Human Resources Position

Human Resources at work are the essential ingredients in every organisation. The way in which people are recruited, developed and utilised by management largely determines whether the organisation will achieve its objectives.

The table 2.5 gives manpower status of the Vijaya Dairy as on June, 2002.

As shown in table 2.5 the total manpower is 1040. Among them the majority of the employees are time scaled dairy attendants/cleaners etc. (584) followed by junior drivers/junior assistants/L.D.As' etc. (281), supervisors, senior assistants etc (68), plant mechanics, Boilor operators etc. (43), Managers grade II cadre (37), Manager grade I cadre (15), Deputy director cadre (6) and General manager 1.

Table 2.5: The Manpower Status as on June, 2002

Sl. No.	*Category*	*No. of Persons Working*
1.	General Manager	1
2.	Deputy Director Grade	6
3.	Manager Grade I Cadre	15
4.	Manager Grade II Cadre	37
5.	J.Ms./Marketing Supervisors	4
6.	Supervisors /Sr. Assts /U.D. Accountants	68
7.	Plant Mechs/ B.Os/D.Os /Sr.Drs	43
8.	Jr. Drivers/Jr. Assts/L.D.A.s/ Typists/Marktg.Assts/F.As. etc	281
9.	O.Cs/T.S.D.As/Cleaners/F.Hs.	584
10.	Contingent Workers	1
	Total	1040

Organisation Structure

The organisation structure which is entirely based on functional type is shown in exhibit 2.1. The management and control of the organisation is vested in the hands of General Manager. He reports to the chairman, Vijaya dairy (The Krishna District Milk Producers Cooperative Union Limited) a district level cooperative union created by the state government of Andhra Pradesh. The functional heads of the dairy unit viz. Deputy director (Procurement and inputs), Special Officer (Aseptic packaging section), Dairy manager, personnel officer, senior accounts officer, deputy material manager, marketing manager, quality control officer, MIS—manager, Grade-II and assistant engineer civil have to report the General manager about the performance

Exhibit 2.1
Organisation Chart of Vijaya Dairy

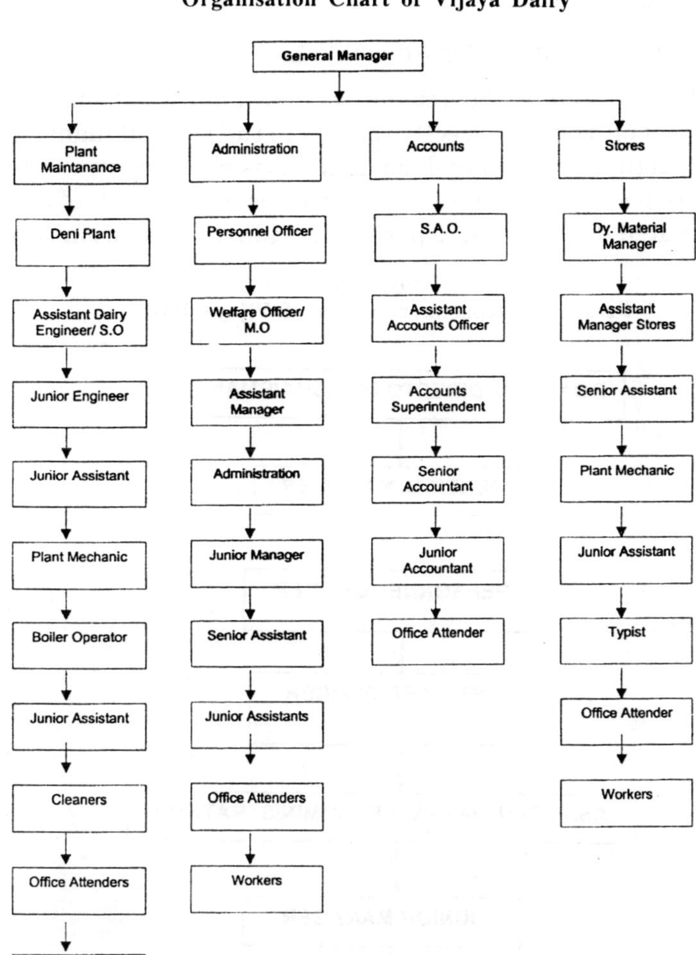

and progress of the operations under their jurisdiction. The exhibit 2.1 also shows the major functions that fall under the purview of each executive. For instance deputy director (P&I) has to look after all the matters relating to procurement of milk from all routes, veterinary, Fodder department and inputs. Similarly other functional heads have to look after all the matters relating to their jurisdiction.

Structure of Personnel Department

The personnel department in Vijaya dairy is headed by personnel officer. He directly reports to the general manager. The structure of personnel department is provided in exhibit 2.2. The personnel department serves as an example of staff coordinated department. Apart from industrial relations and

Exhibit 2.2
Personnel Department Chart of Vijaya Dairy

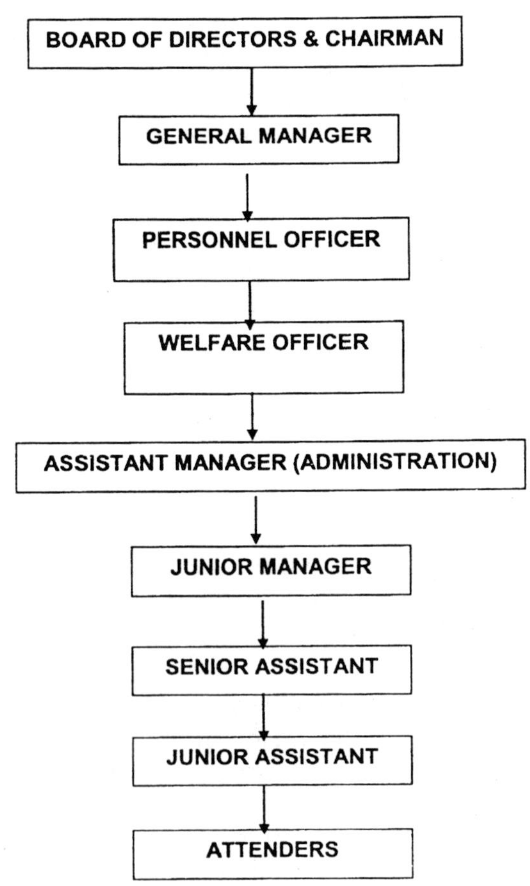

personnel management, a number of other staff functions such as quarter's administrative medical, security, etc. have been clustered together in this department. Broadly, the staff functions of industrial relations, personnel department, labour welfare, legal, executive personnel department, general administration, human resource development, medical, security have been included under the purview of human resource department. The personnel officer is assisted by one welfare officer who coordinates the functions such as intra-mural and extral-mural employee welfare, sports, cultural activities, quarters, and counseling. While personnel administration functions including time office, security, staff attendance, leave administration, legal etc. are coordinated by assistant manager (Administration). The junior manager will assist Assistant Manager (Administration).

Corporate Strategy[3]

The salient aspects of the corporate strategy are as follows.

- Milk procurement activities would be intensified for securing increased share in existing marketable surplus.
- Concentration of milk production enhancement programmes with special emphasis on Animal Breeding, Fodder Development and Animal Health.
- Marketing in the district will be intensified for better remuneration; privatising beyond department level.
- Major strength of union being aseptic technology; emphasis on value-added aseptic milk and milk products.
- To survive and grow in the emerging competitive environment, there would be more and more delegation of work across the organisation calling for accountability through well defined parameters.
- Productivity improvement by Corporate restructuring with change in managerial system to make people more system dependent rather than individual dependent.

- Intensive training for all levels of staff which can really help to improve functioning of organisation.
- Introduction of "Reward and Punishment" system.
- Financial re-structuring of the organisation with the help of Government of India, Government of Andhra Pradesh and NDDB.

The Guntur District Milk Producers Mutually Aided Co-operative Union Limited (hereafter called Sangam dairy) Vadlamudi

Origin and Growth of the Organisation

Under the operation flood programme Guntur district has been selected to develop dairy activities on "Amul" pattern to keep in view the 3 tier system of Village Dairy Co-operative Societies at village level which is managed by elected representatives of milk producers. A Co-operative Union at District Level is managed by representatives of Village Dairy Cooperative Societies. A co-operative federation at state level is an apex body. Milk producers of Guntur, Krishna and West-Godavari districts have generally donated for purchase of 34.46 acres of land at the rate of 1.5 lakhs per acre before initiation of this project during 1973-74. Further 53 acres of land was purchased for location of technical inputs and for staff quarters.

National Dairy Development Board was started in the year 1971. In 1976, they started this Guntur District Milk Producers Co-operative Union. Rs. 104 crores was used for the 18 district level dairies and for infrastructure development.

The management of the dairy was handed over to Guntur District Milk Producers Co-operative Union Limited by the Andhra Pradesh Dairy Development Co-operative Federation Limited on 1-8-1978.

The Guntur District Milk Producers Co-operative Union Limited was registered under the Andhra Pradesh

Co-operative Societies Act, 1964, with registration number 836 DD dated 23-02-77 with 81 affiliated milk producing co-operative centres. Presently there are 640 milk producing co-operative societies and 320 milk collection centers functioning in the area of Guntur District Milk Producers Co-operative Union Limited.

The Guntur District Milk Producers Co-operative Union Limited was converted and got registered on 1-2-1997 under Andhra Pradesh Mutually Aided Co-operative Societies Act, 1995 and attained full autonomy and freedom from the Government Control. Thus the union is named as the Guntur District Milk Producers Mutually Aided Co-operative Union Limited. This is the first milk union in India itself to come under the new Cooperative Societies Act. This union is popularly called "Sangam Dairy", it is purely under the Co-operative sector.

In this Guntur District Milk Producers Mutually Aided Co-operative Union there are 12 Elected Board of Directors. They are elected from the Village Dairy Co-operative Societies with 5 ex-officio members. The Board directly comprises the representatives each from Andhra Pradesh Dairy Development Co-operative federation, Director of Animal Husbandry, Registrar of Co-operative Societies, representative of finance agent and chief-executive of the Union.

So far 130 milk producing societies are brought under the purview of the new Act. The union has planned to convert the remaining in the phased manner.

At present the union is collecting around 2 lakh litres milk per day from 955 villages in 43 milk routes. There are 598 functional dairy cooperatives and 135 procurement milk centres. The Sangam Dairy is called "Feeder Balancing Dairy" for Madras and the Calcutta Dairy.[4]

Nature of Products

In this organisation the main product is milk. The byproducts of the Sangam Dairy are as follows:

Ghee, Mango Mix, Table Butter, White Butter, Dudpeda, Milk Milk, Mineral Water, Skim Milk Powder, Whole Milk Powder, Sweetened Lassie. The types of milk produced by the Sangam dairy are tonned milk, double tonned milk, Standardised milk, whole milk or full cream milk, skim milk, Sterilised favoured milk, Soft milk, UHT large life in tetrapack

Nature of Activities

The activities include procuring milk from various societies, skimming milk, preparation of milk products and marketing of products.

Items of Milk Products and Existing Production Capacities

The various items of milk products and the existing productive capacity of the machinery include milk handling capacity (2.5 lakhs), table butter (8 metric tones per day), ghee (10 metric tones per day), storage capacity of butter (700 metric tones per day), boiler sections (2 oil fired boilers) and 2 coal fired boilers), refrigerators (350 metric tones), milk chilling centre Narasaraopet (50,000 liter per day), Milk chilling centre Gurazala (30,000 liters per day), cattle feed plant (100 metric tones) and aseptic packaging section (50,000 liters per day).

It is observed from table 2.6 that the production of skim milk powder increased from 1170 metric tones during 1990-91 to 2,548 metric tones in 2001-02 whereas the production of whole milk powder has decreased from 130 metric tones (1991-92) to 10 metric tones (1992-93) and increased in the year 1996-97 to 98 metric tones. There was no production of the said item from the years 1997 to 2002. The production of table butter increased from 1024 metric tones (1990-91) to 1802 metric tones (1994-95) and in subsequent years decreased to 477 (2001-02). There is no consistent increase or decrease in production during the years under study. The production of white butter increased gradually from 1265 metric tones (1990-91) to the maximum of 3,684 during 2001-02 except in the years 1994-95 (1728 metric tones)

Table 2.6: Yearwise Production Particulars for various items in Sangam Dairy from 1990 to 2002

	Production Particulars of Sangam Dairy											
Description	*1990-91*	*1991-92*	*1992-93*	*1993-94*	*1994-95*	*1995-96*	*1996-97*	*1997-98*	*1998-99*	*1999-00*	*2000-01*	*2001-02*
Skim milk powder	1.170mts	1.098	1.552	2.507	1751	1050	1137	1450	1032	1168	1828	2548
Whole milk powder	130	168	10	-	43	20	98	0	0	-	-	-
Table Butter	1.024	1.562	708	910	1802	1197	727	692	841	842	906	477
White Butter	1.265	1.042	2.782	3.326	1728	1195	2070	2493	2308	2789	3154	3684
Ghee	870	417	1.871	2.268	1040	970	1111	1063	718	679	827	871
Dudpeda	9	12	9	9.6	10	12	15	15	16	18	20.6	38.2
S.F. Milk [1000 bottles]	63.9	158.3	214.6	185.1	185.1	201	463	251	200	133	278.6	390.7
Lassie	665.5	714.3	933.4	797.4	798	1534	1622	2050	2165	1299	1736.5	2118.3

Source: Consolidate statement prepared by the production department of Sangam dairy.

and 1995-96 (1195 metric tones). The ghee production increased from 870 metric tones (1990-91) to the maximum of 2268 (1993-94) and it was again reduced to 871 in the year 2001-02. The production of dudpeda increased from 9 metric tones (1990-91) to 38.2 metric tones during 2002-02 except in the years 1992-93 (9 metric tones) 1993-94 (9.6 metric tones). The S.F. milk production is measured in terms of units, each unit consisting of 1000 bottles. The production of this item increased from 63.9 units (1990-91) to 390.7 units (2001-02). The production of lassie increased from 665.5 metric tones (1990-91) to 2118.3 metric tones (2001-02). It can be noted here that there is no consistent increase or decrease in the production of the above items during the years under study.

Financial Profile

The financial profile of the organisation includes initial capital, long term finance, loan repayment, working capital loan, borrowing from primary milk societies/centres, turnover, profit and loss.

The initial capital was Rs. 81 lakhs and it was revised to Rs. 2 crores. The initial authorised share capital was Rs. 500 lakhs which was enhanced to Rs. 1000 lakhs from 1-2-1997. The milk unions' paid-up share capital as on 31-3-1998 was Rs. 200 lakhs and share suspense was Rs. 346 lakhs.

Long-term Finance

The National Dairy Development Board has been providing financial assistance for capital projects in the union. Totally an amount of Rs. 1422.55 lakhs has been released by National Dairy Development Board towards loans and grant. Out of this, loan portion is Rs. 995.49 lakhs.

Loan Repayment

National Dairy Development Board installments are being paid and no dues are outstanding. The entire loan drawn amounting to Rs. 279.16 lakhs has been repaid to National Dairy Development Board.

Working Capital Loan

The National Dairy Development Board had providec working capital loan upto 31-3-1992. From 1-4-1992 th(National Dairy Development Board has withdrawn thi: facility to the union. From 1992-93 onwards the union ha: been availing working capital limit with Andhra Pradesl State Co-operative Bank through G.D.C.C. Bank. Th(present limit with Co-operative Central Bank is Rs. 50(lakhs at the rate of 19.5 per cent interest per annum. Ther(is no outstanding balance as on 1-5-1997.

Borrowing from Primary Milk Societies/Centres

The union is also accepting deposits from milk societie: at the save of 12.5 per cent per annum. Till now it is tc the extent of Rs. 192 lakhs.

Turnover Profit and Loss

The turnover of the union was Rs. 4.09 crores in 1978-79 and it has gone up to Rs. 67 crores in 1994-95 and it was Rs. 91.94 crores in 1997-98. The union has earned profits for all the years since inception except in 1985 86 and 1993-94. In 1985-86 the loss was Rs. 46.85 lakhs after proving Rs. 52 lakhs depreciation. The loss during the year was due to higher milk purchase price fixed by the Government of Andhra Pradesh. The loss in 1993-94 was Rs. 64.35 lakhs after providing Rs. 84 lakhs depreciation. The loss was incurred due to heavy milk procurement and low market for the milk products. The loss incurred during these two years was recovered in the succeeding years. The turnover of Rs. 86 crores in the year 1998-99 was estimated Rs. 100 crores in the year 1999-2000.

The table 2.7 depicts the financial position of the organisation from 1994-95 to 2000-2001.

Table 2.7: Financial Position from 1994 to 2001

Years	*Gross Turnover (Rs.)*	*Amount paid to Producers (Rs.)*	*Interest paid as Working Capital (Rs.)*
1994-95	611796420.92	379098580.37	3036817.90
1995-96	566757917.01	395286789.47	1478577.95
1996-97	653112010.75	46069967.79	558040
1997-98	805475591.41	543808750.37	404959
1998-99	1007050769.23	605042688.20	276000
1999-00	1214665684.99	722935960.81	12840277.40
2000-01	1316045384.15	769784093.20	10911376.01

Source: Annual audit reports of Sangam dairy.

The table 2.7 reveals the increase in gross turnover from Rs. 61,17,96,420.92 (1994-95) to Rs. 131,60,45,384.15. So also the amount paid to producers also increased from 37,90,98,580.37 (1994-95) to Rs. 76,97,84,093.20 (2000-01). There is also an increase in the interest paid as working capital from Rs. 30,36,817.90 (1994-95) to Rs. 1,09,11,376.01 (2000-01). There has been consistent increase in the gross turnover and the amount paid to producers from 1997-98 to 2000-01.

The table 2.8 shows yearwise Interest repayment to N.D.D.B. from 1994-2001.

Table 2.8: Interest Repayment to NDDB (term loan)

Year	*Interest repayment NDDB term loan (Rs.)*	*Depreciation Fund (Rs.)*	*Net Profit (Rs.)*
1994-95	8648625.18	7364097.17	108936.51
1995-96	8560611.01	6466535.37	408571.18
1996-97	9509015.26	574668.93	246619.52
1997-98	9631254.61	5174170.66	2521167.77
1998-99	8863614.94	5766922.88	9205993.51
1999-00	15788578.00	1998698.03	1125369.25
2000-01	16913207.98	10320993.06	547401.57

As depicted from table 2.8 there was increase of interest repayment from Rs. 8648625.18 (1994-95) to Rs. 16913207.98 (2000-01). The depreciation fund also increased from Rs. 7364097.17 (1994-95) to Rs. 10320993.06 (2000-01). The net profit was the minimum of Rs. 2,46,619.52 during the year 1996-97. The maximum net profit was Rs. 92,05,993.51 during the year 1998-99. The net profit declined in the succeeding years 1999-2000 and 2000-2001.

Table 2.9: Dividend Paid to Government Last 8 Years

Sl. No.	*Year*	*Amount in Rs.*
I	1990-91	7290
II	1991-92	25920
III	1992-93	12960
IV	1993-94	0
V	1994-95	16470
VI	1995-96	16474
VII	1996-97	36061
VIII	1997-98	1202046

The Table 2.9 gives the yearwise particulars of dividend paid to Government from 1990-91 to 1997-98. The dividend paid to government varied from year to year during the period under study. There was no payment of dividend in the year 1993-94. The dividend payment increased from the minimum of Rs. 7290 (1990-91) to the maximum of Rs. 1202046 during 1997-98.

Technology Profile

The table 2.10 presents technological profile in Sangam Dairy.

The machinery installed in the processing section is mostly Indian made except homogenize machinery which is imported from Germany. The machinery with their respective production capacities are shown in table 2.10.

Table 2.10: Technological Profile of Processing Section

Machine Name	*India Made (or) Imported*	*Capacity (per day)*
Alfa Level Milk Chiller	Alfa Level Company from Pune	20000 liters
Alfa Level Milk	Alfa level company from Pune	10000 liters
Alfa Level Cream	Alfa level company from Pune	5000 liters
Alfa Level Cream	Alfa level company from Pune	10000 liters
Homogenize Machinary	Germany	10000 liters

The table 2.11 shows the profile of the machinery in butter section.

Table 2.11: Butter Section

Machine Name	*India Made (or) Imported*	*Capacity (per day)*
Top Butter cherak	Denmark	10 tones
Continuous butter machine (CBM)	HMT Aurangabd	10 tones
500 butter packing machine	Through, National Dairy Development Board (NDDB)	20 tones
Sig Pack Machine	Italy	5 tones
10 grams chip laced packing machine		1 tones

The table 2.11 shows that two of the machines namely top butter cherak and sig pack machine have been imported from Denmark and Italy respectively. The rest of the machines are Indian made. The machines with their capacities are shown in table 2.11.

The profile of the machinery in the ghee section is given in the table 2.12.

Table 2.12: Ghee Section

Machine Name	*India Made (or) Imported*	*Capacity (per day)*
Ghee Sawset	Nicro	5 tones
Ghee clamber	Alfa Level Company from Pune	10 tones
12 Ghee Packing	Faltabad	10 tones

The machinery in the ghee section are Indian made. The capacities of machines vary from 5 to 10 tones per day.

The table 2.13 shows the particulars of the machinery installed in tetra pack milk and mango drink section.

Table 2.13: Tetra Pack Milk and Mango Drink Section

Machine Name	*India Made (or) Imported*	*Capacity (per day)*
Tetra pack machine	Sweden	½ liter 23000 packets
A-B-10 Machine	Sweden	1 Liter -2400 packets

The two machines installed in the section are imported from Sweden. The production capacity of machines is shown in table 2.13.

Table 2.14: Powder Section

Machine Name	*India Made (or) Imported*	*Capacity (per day)*
Make Larsen & Turbo	Denmark week collaboration (1977)	12 tones
Stinco	India (1980)	10 tones

The table 2.14 shows the machinery installed in powder section. Out of two machines one is Indian made and the other is made with Denmark collaboration. The production capacities of the machines vary from 10 to 12 tones per day.

Manpower Particulars

Departmentwise and cadrewise current manpower position has been discussed in table 2.15.

As revealed from the table 2.15 there are 12 departments each department having different cadres of employees from managers to workers. The table shows that there are 55 managerial personnel including managers, deputy managers and Assistant managers, 77 supervisors, 216 technical staff, 83 clerks, 20 drivers and 410 workers working in the organisation. In all the total strength is 861.

Table 2.15: Sangam Dairy Current Manpower Particulars as on End of June 2002, Vadlamudi

Sl. No.	*Department*	*Mgr*	*Dy. Mgr*	*Asst. Mgr*	*Supervisors*	*Tech. Staff*	*Clerks*	*Drivers*	*Workers*	*Total*
1.	Procurement and Inputs Chilling Centres	1	3	4	18	9	5	-	25	65
2.	Production	1	2	6	6	30	2	-	166	213
3.	Engineering	-	2	7	2	85	3	20	37	156
4.	Quality Control	1	-	1	7	10	-	-	23	42
5.	Purchase and Stores	-	1	-	2	3	16	-	18	40
6.	MIS and PR	1	-	-	-	-	2	-	1	4
7	Marketing	-	-	3	11	4	7	-	29	54
8.	Finance and Accounts	-	-	3	2	3	27	-	4	39
9.	Administration	1	1	2	-	10	10	-	6	30
10.	Chilling Centres	-	-	12	29	52	9	-	82	184
11.	APS	1	-	2	-	9	-	-	17	29
12.	Labour Welfare	-	-	-	-	1	2	-	2	5
	Total	6	9	40	77	216	83	20	410	861

The table 2.16 shows various cadres of employees and their strength.

Table 2.16: Various Cadres of Employees

Sl.No.	*Employees*	*Strength*
1.	Regular employees	861
2.	NMRS	50
3.	Security Guards	46
4.	Contract Labour	152

From table 2.16, it can be understood that the regular employees are 861. Besides the regular employees NMRS (50), security guards (46) and contract labour (152) are working.

Table 2.17: Contract Labour Particulars as on End of June 2002

Sl.No.	*Position*	*Strength*
1.	Drivers	7
2.	Milk Tester	5
3.	Pump holes maintainer	1
4.	Doctors	1
5.	Compounders	5
6.	Can Cleaners	30
7.	Coal Feeders	20
8.	Chairman Car Drivers	2
9.	Tetra Packing	1
10.	Powder Packing	15
11.	White Butter Packing	6
12.	Coal Crushing	9
13.	Tubes Leading	50
	Total	152

The Table 2.17 shows that 152 contract labour are engaged in Sangam Dairy. They are drivers (7), milk testers

(5), pump holes maintainer (1), doctor (1), compounders (5), can cleaners (30), coal feeders (20), chairman car drivers (2), tetra packing (1), powder packing (15), white butter packing (6), coal crushing (9) and tubes leading (50).

Organisation Structure

The organisation structure which is entirely based on functional type is shown in exhibit 2.3. The management and control of the organisation is vested in the hands of managing director. He reports to the chairman, Sangam Dairy a mutually aided cooperative union registered under AP Mutually Aided Cooperative Societies Act, 1995 (attained full autonomy and freedom from the government control), to manage the district level milk union and 640 registered MPCSs and 320 milk collection centres and 955 villages in 43 milk routes. The functional heads of the organisation are production (manager), procurement and inputs (senior manager), dairy engineer, senior accounts officer, quality control (manager), personnel manager, labour welfare officer, MIS office (assistant manager), APS (manager), marketing (manager) and material (manager) have to report to the managing director about the performance and progress of the operations under their jurisdiction. The chart also shows the major functions that fall under the purview of each manager. For instance, manager (production) has to look after all the matters relating to production shops, RMRD and pre-pack processing, butter and ghee, powder and by-products and office management. Similarly senior accounts officer has to look after all the matters relating to accounts, finance, internal audit etc.

Personnel Department Structure

The personnel department in Sangam Dairy is headed by personnel manager. He directly reports to the managing director. The internal organisation of personnel department is provided in exhibit 2.4. The personnel department serves as an example of staff coordinated department. Apart from

Exhibit 2.3
The Guntur District Milk Producers Mutually Aided Co-op Union Ltd. Sangam Dairy

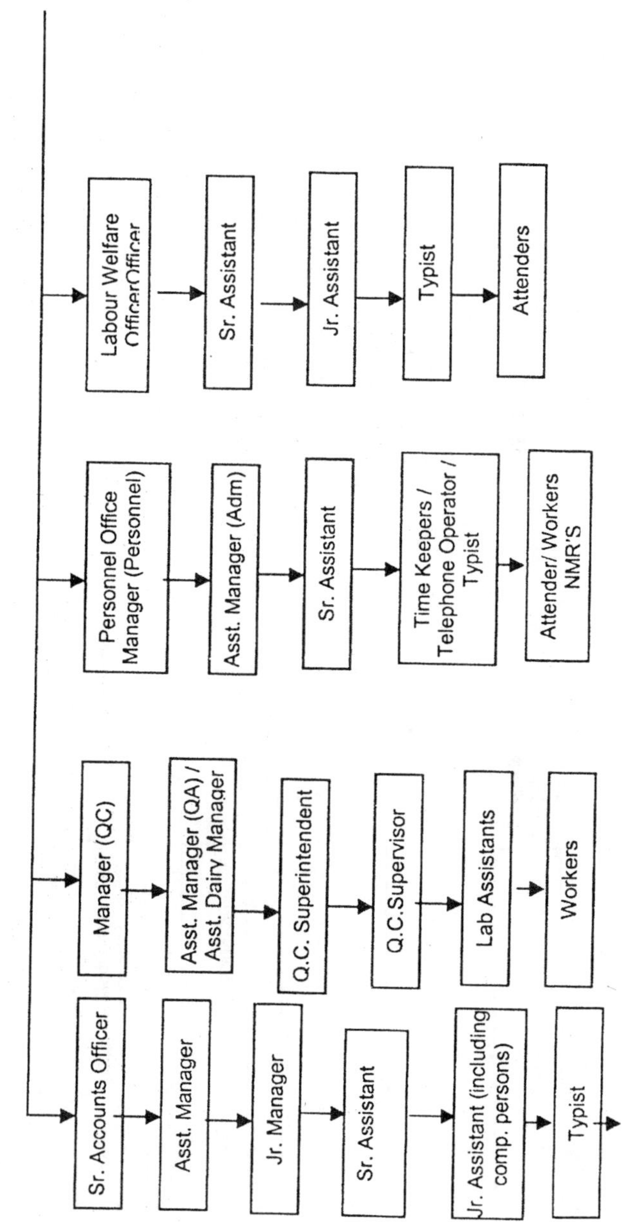

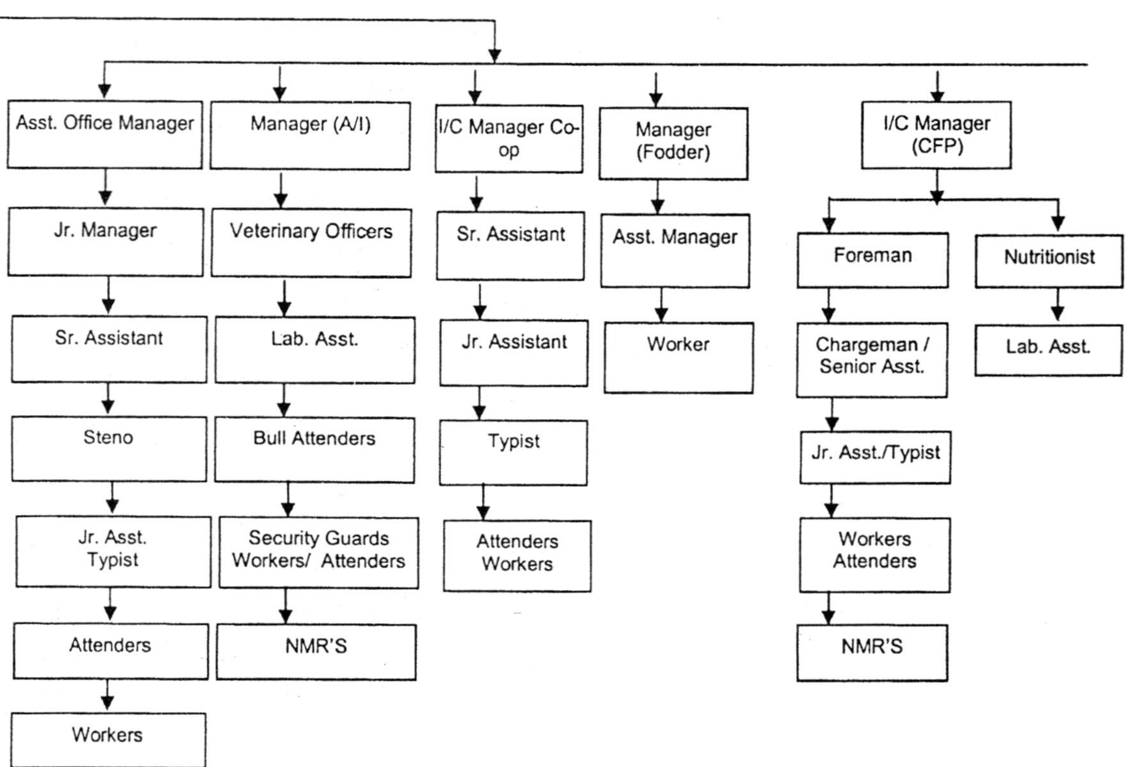
Asst. Office Manager
Jr. Manager
Sr. Assistant
Steno
Jr. Asst. Typist
Attenders
Workers
Manager (A/I)
Veterinary Officers
Lab. Asst.
Bull Attenders
Security Guards Workers/ Attenders
NMR'S
I/C Manager Co-op
Sr. Assistant
Jr. Assistant
Typist
Attenders Workers
Manager (Fodder)
Asst. Manager
Worker
I/C Manager (CFP)
Foreman
Chargeman / Senior Asst.
Jr. Asst./Typist
Workers Attenders
NMR'S
Nutritionist
Lab. Asst.

Exhibit 2.4
Personnel Department Chart of Sangam Dairy

BOARD OF DIRECTORS
↓
CHAIRMAN
↓
MANAGING DIRECTOR
↓
PERSONNEL MANAGER
↓
ASSISTANT MANAGER (ADMINISTRATION)
↓
JUNIOR MANAGER
↓
SENIOR ASSISTANTS
↓
JUNIOR ASSISTANTS
↓
ATTENDERS

industrial relations and personnel management a number of other staff functions such as office administration, medical, security etc., have been clustered together in this department. The assistant manager (administration) assists the personnel manager who coordinates the functions of leave administration, legal matters, time office and quarters.

Future Development Plans of the Sangam Dairy

I. To increase procurement upto 3,00,000 litres per day.

II. To increase sales upto 50,000 litres per day

III. To Increase turnover upto 200 crores

IV. To get ISO 9000 certificate

V. To supply electronic milk testers to each and every Co-operative Societies.

The Sangam Dairy and the Vizag Union have planned to form "The matha milk market federation" to market to dairy's product on its own through a joint venture. The entire marketing process will be run through the above joint venture.

Awards

- The Sangam Dairy got distinctions in record level milk production on 8th march 1994.
- The Sangam Dairy was awarded excellence and the Chairman of the organisation was awarded "Udyoga Ratna" on 24-2-97 by the Institute of Economic Survey of India, New Delhi.
- The Council for Business Entrepreneurs Organisation (New Delhi) awarded gold star and gold medal on August 24th, 1998.
- "Mulakanuru Viswanatha Reddy"was given to Sangam Dairy for the year 1998 by the Cooperative Development Foundation, Hyderabad on 16-11-1998.
- For 1999-2000, 2000-01 and 2001-02 the dairy was graded 'A' in auditing which is highest in audit ratings.

Profile of the Respondents under Study

Human resources play a significant role in influencing the effective functioning of an organisation. The quality of goods and services provided by the organisation and the goodwill created in the eyes of public at large depend upon the efficiency with which the personnel perform the tasks.

In view of the significant role of personnel in the effective functioning of organisation, it would be fruitful to examine and understand their socio-economic characteristics which influence in a large measure, their behaviour and performance. Therefore, an attempt is made in the following pages to present the socio-economic profile of the employees under study.

Table 2.18: Distribution of Respondents by Organisation

Organisation	*Frequency*	*Per cent*	*Cumulative Per cent*
Vijaya Dairy	180	59.0	59.0
Sangam Dairy	125	41.0	100.0
Total	305	100.00	

The Table 2.18 shows that majority of the respondents are from Krishna District Milk Producers Co-operative Union Limited, also known as Vijaya Dairy. The remaining of the respondents are from Guntur District Milk Producers Mutually Aided Co-operative Union Limited also known as Sangam Dairy.

Table 2.19: Categorywise Respondents

Category	*Vijaya Dairy*	*Per cent*	*Sangam Dairy*	*Per cent*	*Total*	*Per cent*
Managerial	30	54.54	25	45.46	55	18.03
Non-managerial	150	60.00	100	40.00	250	81.97
Total	180		125		305	100

Table 2.19 reveals that a large majority (81.97%) of the respondents are non-managerial category and the remaining 18.03 per cent of the respondents are managerial category from both sample units.

Table 2.20 explains departmentwise distribution of respondents; it covers sixteen departments and others, 12.5 per cent of the respondents from finance and accounts, 8.9 per cent of the respondents from Marketing, 7.9 per cent of the respondents from Sales, 6.9 per cent of the respondents from Quality Control, 5.2 per cent of the

Table 2.20: Respondents by Department

Sl. No.	Department	Frequency	Per cent	Cumulative Per cent
1.	Procurement	15	4.9	4.9
2.	Production/plant	13	4.3	9.2
3.	Engineering	14	4.6	13.8
4.	Quality control	21	6.9	20.7
5.	Purchase and stores	13	4.3	24.9
6.	MIS and PR	16	5.2	30.2
7.	Marketing	27	8.9	39.0
8.	Finance and accounts	38	12.5	51.5
9.	Admn and personnel	16	5.2	56.7
10.	APS	16	5.2	62.0
11.	Labour welfare	2	.7	62.6
12.	Transport	16	5.2	67.9
13.	Sales	24	7.9	75.7
14.	Direct routes	9	3.0	78.7
15.	Processing and pre-packed	9	3.0	81.6
16.	Electrical dept	1	.3	82.0
17.	Others	5	18.0	100.0
	Total	305	100.0	

respondents from the departments of MIS & PR, Administration and Personnel, APS and Transport respectively. Another 4.9 per cent of the respondents from Procurement, 4.6 per cent of the respondents from Engineering and each 4.3 per cent of the respondents from Production/Plan, Purchase and Stores. The other respondents from Direct routes (3%), Processing and Pre-packed (3%), Labour Welfare (.7%) and Electrical Department (3%) responded. The respondents who have not mentioned their departments are treated as others. As per table 2.20 others constitute 18 per cent of the respondents.

Table 2.21: Age

Age	*Frequency*	*Per cent*	*Cumulative Per cent*
27-43	77	25.25	25.25
44-51	156	51.15	76.40
52-57	72	23.60	100.00
Total	305	100.00	

The exposure, maturity and individuality depend upon the age of the individual. Table 2.21 narrates that a little more than one-fourth of respondents' age is in between 27 and 43 years. More than half of the respondents' age is in between 44 and 51 years. The remaining respondents' age is below 57 years. It is clear that large number of employees belong to middle age category. The average age of the respondents is 46 years.

Table 2.22: Sex

Sex	*Frequency*	*Per cent*	*Cumulative Per cent*
Male	268	87.9	87.9
Female	37	12.1	100.0
Total	305	100.0	

In the olden days, women used to attend to domestic activities only. But now a days they also seek employment on par with men. The table 2.22 reveals that the male group constitutes the highest percentage of respondents (87.9%) followed by female group (12.1%).

Marriage is an important event in one's life. It influences the style of living and also the attitude, disposition and commitment towards work. Table 2.23 indicates that an overwhelming per cent of the respondents are Married. From the remaining nearly five per cent of the respondents are unmarried, one per cent of respondents are divorced and the rest of them are widowed.

Table 2.23: Marital Status

Marital Status	*Frequency*	*Per cent*	*Cumulative Per cent*
Married	286	93.8	93.8
Unmarried	14	4.6	98.4
Widowed	2	.7	99.0
Divorced	3	1.0	100.0
Total	305	100.0	

Table 2.24: State of Domicile

Domicile	*Frequency*	*Per cent*	*Cumulative Per cent*
A.P.	289	94.8	94.8
Other than A.P.	16	5.2	100.0
Total	305	100.0	

The table 2.24 narrates that 94.8 per cent of the respondent's state of domicile is Andhra Pradesh whereas the rest of them represent other states.

Table 2.25: Respondents by Migration

Migrant	*Frequency*	*Per cent*	*Cumulative Per cent*
Yes	36	11.8	11.8
No	269	88.2	100.0
Total	305	100.0	

The composition of the employees is likely to consist of a mix of natives and immigrants. The table 2.25 describes that 97.4 per cent of the respondents are not migrated whereas the remaining respondents are migrated from neighbouring districts.

welfare. This is followed by low (76) level of satisfaction. To test whether there is any significant association between the two variables, chi-square test was used. The results show that the association is statistically not significant. That is the respondents' indebtedness does not tell us about their level of satisfaction.

As revealed from the above analysis the indebtedness of the employee has no effect on their satisfaction about employee welfare. If employee welfare is taken care of by the management the indebtedness will not effect the level of satisfaction of the employees. The employees whether indebted or not are happy with the welfare amenities.

Is employee welfare associated with the number of dependents of the respondents? To find out the answer, data relating to the number of dependents of the respondents and their employee welfare have been cross tabulated. The results of the analysis are presented in Table 5.35.

Table 5.35: Employee Welfare by Number of Dependents

Number Dependents	*Employee welfare regrouped*			*Total*
	Low	*Moderate*	*High*	
0.00	1	2	1	4
1.00	10	8		18
2.00	26	23	14	63
3.00	45	28	7	80
4.00	36	42	13	91
5.00	12	22	8	42
6.00	1	6		7
Total	131	131	43	305

$X^2 = 22.982$ df = 12 p = .028 Conti. Coeff = .265

It is understood from the table that in a majority of the respondents, number of dependents and their level of satisfaction on employee welfare is moderate. This is followed by low level of satisfaction. Whereas 43 respondents are highly satisfied on employee welfare. To test whether there is any significant association between the two variables, chi-square test was used. The results show that the association is statistically significant. From this it may be inferred that there is significant association between employee welfare and number of dependents of the respondents.

The above analysis tells that the number of dependents will influence the level of satisfaction about employee welfare. Employees with less number of dependents may have higher level of satisfaction about welfare amenities.

Is employee welfare associated with the Rural/Urban background of the respondents? To find out the answer, data relating to the Rural/Urban background of the respondents and their Employee Welfare have been cross tabulated. The results of the analysis are presented in Table 5.36.

Table 5.36: Employee Welfare by Rural/Urban Background

Rural/Urban	*Employee welfare regrouped*			*Total*
	Low	*Moderate*	*High*	
Rural	118	108	36	262
Urban	13	23	7	43
Total	131	131	43	305

X^2 = 3.348 df = 2 p = .187 Conti. Coeff = .104

It is evident from table 5.36 that the level of satisfaction and employee welfare in the case of 131 of the respondents from both the Rural and Urban background is moderate. This is followed by low level of satisfaction. 36 respondents from the rural and 7 respondents from urban scored high level of satisfaction. To test whether there is any significant association between the two variables, chi-square test was used. The results show that the association is statistically not significant. Hence the employees'

It is evident from Table 5.32 that 131 respondents from both sexes and their level of satisfaction on employee welfare is moderate. However further analysis reveals that comparatively larger proportion of male respondents' employee welfare is moderate. This is followed by equally scored to low level of satisfaction. 32 male respondents and 11 female respondents are highly satisfied about employee welfare facilities. To test whether there is any significant association between the two variables, chi-square test was used. The results show that the association is statistically significant. Hence the sex of the respondents indicates some significance with employee welfare.

From Table 5.32 more than one-third respondents scored to low level of satisfaction it may alert the management of the sample units to design and provide wider range of employee welfare facilities. As studies emphasised, for every six months, management is to feel the pulse of the employees, and provide facilities according to their requirements. Every employer should realise that investment on employee is a productive investment.

Is employee welfare associated with the educational background of the respondents? To find out the answer, data relating to the educational background of the respondents and their Employee Welfare have been cross tabulated. The results of the analysis are presented in Table 5.33.

It is evident from the table 5.33 that 131 respondents' educational background, and their level of satisfaction on employee welfare is moderate. Another 131 respondents scored 'low' level of satisfaction. Other 43 respondents are 'highly' satisfied. To test whether there is any significant association between the two variables, chi-square test was used. The results show that the association is statistically significant. Hence, the employees' educational background tells us about their level of satisfaction about employee welfare.

In general where the educational background is high, their level of satisfaction is low on benefits and services offered by the management. In the dairy units also the same trend has been noticed.

Table 5.33: Employee Welfare by Educational Background

Education Background	*Employee welfare regrouped*			*Total*
	Low	*Moderate*	*High*	
Elementary level	8	7		15
High school level	53	58	2	113
Intermediate	24	23	15	62
Graduation	24	33	16	73
Post-graduation/ professional	22	9	10	41
Technical		1		1
Total	131	131	43	305

X^2 = 36.905 df = 10 p = .000 Conti. Coeff = .329

Is employee welfare associated with the indebtedness of the respondents? To find out the answer, data relating to the indebtedness of the respondents and their employee welfare have been cross tabulated. The results of the analysis are presented in Table 5.34.

Table 5.34: Employee Welfare by Indebtedness

Indebtedness	*Employee welfare regrouped*			*Total*
	Low	*Moderate*	*High*	
Yes	76	67	23	166
No	55	64	20	139
Total	131	131	43	305

X = 1.264 df = 2 p = .531 Conti. Coeff = .064

It is indicated that from Table 5.34 that more than half of the respondents (166) have indebtedness among whom 23 respondents expressed high satisfaction and 67 respondents expressed moderate satisfaction about employee caste of the respondents and their employee welfare have been cross tabulated. The results of the analysis are presented in Table 5.39.

Table 5.39: Employee Welfare by Caste

Caste	*Employee welfare regrouped*			*Total*
	Low	*Moderate*	*High*	
OC	83	105	35	223
BC	40	19	3	62
SC	8	7	5	20
Total	131	131	43	305

$X^2 = 17.687$ df = 4 p = .001 Conti. Coeff = .223

It is evident from table 5.39 that in the case of 131 of the total respondents from all the castes and the level of satisfaction on employee welfare is moderate. However further analysis reveals that again in the case of 131 respondents from all castes satisfaction is low. To test whether there is any significant association between the two variables, chi-square test was used. The results show that the association is statistically significant.

It can be inferred from the above analysis that caste has influence on the level of satisfaction about employee welfare. That means the higher castes that is OCs may have better satisfaction about welfare amenities than BCs and SCs.

Is employee welfare associated with the Age of the respondents? To find out the answer, data relating to the age of the respondents and their employee welfare have been cross tabulated. The results of the analysis are presented in Table 5.40.

It is evident from table 5.40 that in the case of a majority of the respondents from all the ages the level of satisfaction on employee welfare is moderate. It is followed by 131 respondents from all the age group having low level of satisfaction. To test whether there is any significant association between the two variables, chi-square test was used. The results show that the association is statistically not significant. That is the employees' age does not have any relation to employee welfare.

Table 5.40: Employee Welfare by Age

Age	*Employee welfare regrouped*			*Total*
	Low	*Moderate*	*High*	
27-43	31	33	13	77
44-51	57	76	13	146
52-57	43	22	17	82
Total	131	131	43	305

$X^2 = 15.924$ df = 4 p = .003 Conti. Coeff = .223

The above analysis reveals that there is no relationship between age and satisfaction about the welfare amenities. Irrespective of the age group the employees have expressed satisfaction about welfare amenities.

Is employee welfare associated with the gross salary of the respondents? To find out the answer, data relating to the gross salary of the respondents and their employee welfare have been cross tabulated. The results of the analysis are presented in Table 5.41.

Table 5.41: Employee Welfare by Gross Salary

Gross Salary (in Rs.)	*Employee welfare regrouped*			*Total*
	Low	*Moderate*	*High*	
3900-7400	44	35		79
7401-11000	55	53	33	141
11001-70000	32	43	10	85
Total	131	131	43	305

$X^2 = 26.314$ df = 4 p = .000 Conti. Coeff = .282

background either rural or urban does not tell us about their level of satisfaction on employee welfare.

From the above analysis it may be understood that the rural or urban background has no differential impact on employee welfare. In other words the welfare amenities that are provided do not have their impact on the level of satisfaction between the Rural and Urban employees.

Is employee welfare associated with the organisation of the respondents? To find out the answer, data relating to the organisation of the respondents and their Employee Welfare have been cross tabulated. The results of the analysis are presented in Table 5.37.

Table 5.37: Employee Welfare by the Organisation

Organisation	*Employee welfare regrouped*			*Total*
	Low	*Moderate*	*High*	
Vijaya Dairy	78	81	21	180
Sangam Dairy	53	50	22	125
Total	131	131	43	305

$X^2 = 2.286$ df = 2 p = .319 Conti. Coeff = .086

It is evident from Table 5.37 that in the case of 131 of the respondents from both the organisations, the level of satisfaction on employee welfare is moderate. This is followed by low level of satisfaction by 131 respondents of both the organisations. 21 respondents from Vijaya Dairy and 22 respondents from Sangam Dairy scored high level satisfaction. To test whether there is any significant association between the two variables, chi-square test was used. The results show that the association is statistically not significant. That is whether the employees of Sangam Dairy or Vijaya Dairy does not tell us about their level of satisfaction on employee welfare.

From the above analysis one can understand that the employees of both the organisations are equally happy about the welfare amenities. That is to say irrespective of the organisations respondents expressed satisfaction about employee welfare.

Is employee welfare associated with the category of the respondents? To find out the answer, data relating to the category of the respondents and their Employee Welfare have been cross tabulated. The results of the analysis are presented in Table 5.38.

Table 5.38: Employee Welfare by Category

Category	*Employee welfare regrouped*			*Total*
	Low	*Moderate*	*High*	
Managerial	25	27	3	55
Non-Managerial	106	104	40	250
Total	131	131	43	305

$X^2 = 4.243$ df = 2 p = .120 Conti. Coeff = .117

It is evident from the table that the level of satisfaction of 131 respondents from both the categories on employee welfare is moderate. This is followed by low level of satisfaction by 131 respondents. 40 non-managerial and 3 managerial respondents are highly satisfied with employee welfare. To test whether there is any significant association between the two variables, chi-square test was used. The results show that the association is statistically not significant. That is whether the employees are of managerial or non-managerial category the category does not have its influence on the level of satisfaction on employee welfare.

It is obvious from the above analysis that both managerial and non-managerial employees are happy with the welfare amenities. That means irrespective of the category and cadre the employees have satisfaction about welfare amenities.

Is employee welfare associated with the caste of the respondents? To find out the answer, data relating to the

2. Biswas, R.K. (1982, March). Concept of Wages Under Different Labour Laws. *Labour Gazette,* 761-772.

3. Suri, G.K. and Chellappa, H.V.V. (1973, July). 'Wage-cost-productivity Nexus and Incomes Policy'. *Indian Journal of Industrial Relations,* Vol. 9, No. 1, 69.

4. Papola, T.S. (1981). *Urban Informal Sector in a Developing Economy.* New Delhi: Vikas Publishing House Pvt. Ltd. Kashyap, S.P. and Himal Singh (1987, July) 'Urban Informal Sector. Issues Arising Out of Gujarat's Experience'. *Indian Journal of Industrial Relations,* Vol. 23, No. 1, 49.

5. Munshi, N.M. (1983). *'Personnel Management in Small Industry of Saurashtra'.* Unpublished Doctoral Thesis Submitted to Saurashtra University.

6. Government of India (1966). *Report of the National Commission on Labour,* 230.

7. In a Series of Adjudication Cases in Respect of Wage Disputes, the Courts have Laid down this Principle in Unequivocal Terms.

8. Government of India, (1969). *Report of the Committee on Fair Wages,* 9.

9. *Ibid.,* 11.

10. *Report of the National Commission on Labour* (1966). New Delhi: Government of India Publications, 236.

11. The Hindustan Times Vs. Their Workmen, AIR, 1963, S.C. 1322.

12. Express Newspapers Pvt. Ltd. Vs Union of India, 1958, S.C. 578.

13. *The Management of People at Work,* 643-644 and 652.

14. Belchar, David W and Heneman, Jr., Herbert G, "How to Make a Wage Survey", Technical Report Series No. 2, Industrial Relations Centre, University of Minnesota (1948, July). Quoted in David W. Belchar, *Wage and Salary Administration,* 45.

15. Ross, Arthur M. *"The Dynamics of Wage Determination under Collective Bargaining".* 800.

16. Government of India (1973). *Report of the 3rd Central Pay Commission,* New Delhi: Minister of Finance.

17. International Labour Organisation, (1956). *Problems of Wage Policy in Asian Countries,* Geniva, 39.

18. Government of India, *Report of the National Commission on Labour,* op.cit, 220.

19. In the aftermath of the Industrial Unrest Immediately Prior to and after Independence, a Tripartite Conference was Convened by the Government in 1947, to Suggest Remedial Measures for Industrial Unrest. At this Conference an Industrial Truce Resolution was Adopted.

20. Moorthy, M.V. (1958). *Principles of Labour Welfare,* Visakhapatnam: Gupta Brothers, 1.

21. Sarma, A.M. (1998). *Personnel and Human Resource Management,* Mumbai: Himalaya Publishing House, 240.

22. International Labour Organisation (1942). *Approach to Social Security—An International Survey,* Geneva: the Auditor, 83.

23. William, Beveridge (1942). *Social Insurance and Allied Services,* Report Presented to Parliament by Command of His Majesty, London: H.M.S.O. 120.

24. Vaid, K.N. (1970). *Labour Welfare in India,* New Delhi: Sri Ram Centre for Industrial Relations, 251.

25. Government of Andhra Pradesh (1980). Andhra Pradesh Dairy Development Co-operative Federaion. Hyderabad : Department Publication, 6.

26. *The Report of the Committee on Labour Welfare,* Government of India, (1969) Delhi: 252.

27. *International Labour Organisation* (1947). Planning for Labour, 107.

28. *Report of the Labour Investigation Committee,* (1946). Government of India, New Delhi: 343.

29. Suman Swarup., (2001, September) *Employers Guide,* New Delhi. Employees' State Insurance Corporation, Director General.

30. *Report of Royal Commission on Labour in India,* (1929). Government of India, Delhi, 270.

31. *Report of the Labour Investigation Committee,* op.cit., 362.

32. Giri, V.V. (1962). *Labour Problems in India Industry,* (2nd edition), Bombay: Asia Publishing House, 299.

It is evident from table 5.41 that in the case of 131 respondents from all the employees the level of satisfaction on employee welfare is moderate. This is followed by low level of satisfaction whereas the other respondents are highly satisfied. To test whether there is any significant association between the two variables, chi-square test was used. The results show that the association is statistically significant. Hence the employee's gross salary has association with employee welfare.

From the above analysis it may be noted that the gross salary will influence the level of satisfaction of the employees about welfare amenities. The more the gross salary the more may be the satisfaction.

Is employee welfare associated with the Net Salary of the respondents? To find out the answer, data relating to the Net Salary of the respondents and their employee welfare have been cross tabulated. The results of the analysis are presented in Table 5.42.

Table 5.42: Employee Welfare by Net Salary

Net Salary (in Rs.)	*Employee welfare regrouped*			*Total*
	Low	*Moderate*	*High*	
1800-3800	31	33	9	73
3801-6700	73	56	29	158
6701-16000	27	42	5	74
Total	131	131	43	305

$X^2 = 18.807$ df = 4 p =.000 Conti. Coeff = .508

It is evident from table 5.42 that in the case of 131 of the respondents from all the employees' the level of satisfaction on employee welfare is moderate. This is followed by low level of satisfaction scored by 131 respondents. The remaining respondents scored high satisfaction. To test whether there is any significant association between the two variables, chi-square test was used. The results show that the association is statistically not significant.

The above analysis denotes that the net salary has no impact on the level of satisfaction of the employees about welfare amenities. The net salary may not influence the satisfaction of the employees about welfare amenities.

It is found that the level of satisfaction of male respondents is higher than the female. It may be because of the fact that both dairies do not provide any special welfare facilities to the female respondents other than the statutory benefits. In respect of educational background, the study found that the higher the levels of the education the lower the level of satisfaction on employee welfare. It may be because education brings more awareness and increases the level of aspiration. When the aspirations are not met, the dissatisfaction increases. It is further found that the higher the number of dependents of the respondents the lower the level of satisfaction with employee welfare. The rationale behind this might be the increased number of dependents of the employee may increase the expectations of the respondents as he has to meet the requirements of his dependents. With regard to association between caste background of the respondents on satisfaction with employee welfare, it is found that the level of satisfaction of open category (upper caste) is higher than that of others. It might be because of the status on the benefits they enjoy in the society, upper caste people may not expect more from the organisation.

Based on the above analysis presented in this chapter it can be concluded that the employee welfare has association with sex, educational background, number of dependents, caste and gross salary.

REFERENCES

1. Seal, K.C. (1965, July). 'A Critical Review of Research and Literature on Wages in India'. *Indian Journal of Industrial Relations,* Vol. 1, No. 1, 41-59.

for the stability and progress of industry. When good understanding prevails between them, each party tries to serve the other to the best of its ability. Workmen try to give their best and improve productive efficiency, and the management acknowledges its satisfaction and attractive working conditions. In such a state of relations marked by amity, there is little scope for grievances and disputes. But the maintenance of good labour management relations is very often a difficult job.

In a realistic sense, complete harmony, peace or co-operation can be elusive. The objectives of the parties are so different that only 'antagonistic co-operation' is possible in labour management relations.[3] "Despite the heavy accent in recent times on common good and virtue of industrial peace and harmony, the pursuit of opposite aims continues to cause strife."[4] Wage earners form trade unions to safeguard their interests and to register protest in an organised way. Unions assume the form of defense or combative mechanism aimed at meeting the exploitative tactics of employer. This evokes a reaction in employer who wants to serve his interests well by taking recourse to counter-defensive measures such as employers' association, economic pressures, hiring strike-breakers or invoking the help of police and in the interest' of law and order. Thus, the whole gamut of human relations arising from the sale of services by working for price and their working on the premises of the employers under their control forms the subject matter of industrial relations. These relations exist and grow out of employment and involve relationship between the employers and employees as well as their organisations.[5]

Role of State

Employment conditions in industry are not regulated merely by employees and employers, though both have a major role in it. State intervention in the regulation of labour management relations has been on the increase and, therefore, the role played by the state and its interaction with employers and employees legitimately forms part of industrial relations. What is intended in the present chapter is the study of the pattern of labour management relations that arise and the institutions and forums created by the parties to resolve these problems and to regulate the relations between them.

Industrial Relations Strategy in Dairy Industry

An attempt is made below to describe the industrial relations strategy in dairy industry based on the information collected from the managers of both dairies through interviews. The discussions revealed that the dairy units aim at improving productivity and profitability and also a fair deal to workers. Management of dairy units and employees' unions believe that industrial peace and harmony are the hallmark of optimum production. Both of them have agreed to maintain industrial peace and are committed to make efforts to ensure high level of performance with safety, health inputs and sustained efforts. The parties, recognised that future prosperity and efficiency of the undertaking rest heavily on the ability of the parties to work in co-operation to achieve higher productivity trends. The management gives importance to personnel and industrial relations matters. The personnel and industrial relations matters are entrusted to the personnel department. The company's personnel and industrial relations policy is to provide benefits to employees through negotiations. The parties would discuss their mutual issues through negotiations before they think of other methods to resolve their conflicts. The management has been favourably disposed in revising wage scales periodically taking into account the principles of equity and fairness and the capacity of the industry to pay. The management seeks to streamline and change the system of working of the organisation to make it sound and buoyant. Through discussion with the union, shop floor discipline has been tightened. Improving the image of the organisation in the eyes of customers and implementation of perspective plans

33. *The Report of National Commission on Labour,* op.cit., 106.

34. The Third Five Year Plan, 259.

35. Punekar, Deodhar and Sankaran (1980). *Labour Welfare, Trade Unionism and Industrial Relations,* Bombay: Himalaya Publishing House, 94.

36. *Report of the Central Banking Enquiry Committee.,* Vol. 1, Part 1, 258.

37. *The Report of the National Commission on Labour,* op.cit., 88.

38. *Report of the Royal Commission on Labour,* op.cit., 27.

39. Dale Yoder, (1960). *Personnel Principles and Policies,* Bombay: Asia Publishers House, 16.

40. *Report of the Committee on Labour Welfare,* (1969) op.cit., 63.

41. Moorty, M.V. and Narayana, B.L. (1965). *Participation of Workers in Welfare Work,* Visakhapatnam: Gupta Brothers.

42. *Report of the Committee on Labour Welfare* (1969) Delhi: Government of India, 252.

43. Vaid, K.N. (1970) op.cit.

Industrial Relations

In the preceding chapter an analysis was presented on wages and employee welfare. This chapter is an attempt to portray the nature and quality of industrial relations in Vijaya and Sangam dairies. The employees' perceptions on existing practices in both dairies are presented and trade union particulars are given in a tabular form. Industrial disputes, collective bargaining, employee participation in decision-making and grievance redressal are highlighted. The Voluntary retirement scheme is also discussed in this chapter.

Industrial relations describe "relationships between managements and employees or among employees and their organisations, that characterize or grow out of employment."[1] The International Institute of Labour Studies has defined it in a more comprehensive sense as to mean "social relations in production".[2]

Nature of Industrial Relations

The primary concern of the management and the workers is to make the organisation a success. This requires that the parties maintained harmony and peaceful relations. The interests of both are interdependent and they can subserve the interests of society at large. The parties can share the gains of increased productivity if they work as partners.

Establishment and maintenance of harmonious relations between labour and management is a pre-requisite

Twenty-six (8.5%) respondents have applied to the job in response to newspaper advertisement. A similar percentage of respondents have directly applied to the organisation. In case of five per cent respondents, the relatives' influence came handy to enter into the organisation.

Table 3.2: Agency Responsible for Getting the Job

Reasons	*Frequency*	*Per cent*	*Cumulative Per cent*
Employment exchange	224	73.4	73.4
Newspaper advertisement	26	8.5	82.0
Applied directly	26	8.5	90.5
Relatives influence	16	5.2	95.7
Through unions	3	1.0	96.7
Others	10	3.3	100.0
Total	305	100.0	

Selection

Selection is the process of picking individuals (out of the pool of job candidates) with requisite qualifications and competence to fill jobs in the organisation. A formal definition of selection is that "it is the process of differentiating between applicants in order to identify (and hire) those with a greater likelihood of success in a job.[10]

Vijaya and Sangam dairy units pay adequate attention in the selection of their employees. They believe that the efficiency of units depends upon the abilities and competencies. Though there is a scope to select candidates on the basis of local pressures, they appear to counter these pressures and give importance to the abilities of the candidates. It is noticed that in the initial stages the units did not follow systematic procedures while hiring personnel. However they have given importance to the general abilities, physical fitness, job knowledge and the potential of the candidates. In case of non-managerial employees they are placed on probation for two years. These employees are rotated from job to job and given exposure to all operations involved in milk processing and manufacturing of milk products. Where it is found that the candidates' job knowledge, or the skill level is adequate they are given in plant training; they are closely observed in their work by their supervisors and at times the supervisor offers necessary guidance and other inputs to the workers.

Vijaya dairy was the first to be started of the two. Sangam dairy came into existence after ten years. Vijaya dairy, after two years of its inception, wanted to streamline the selection procedures. In this regard they reviewed all the processors, procedures and practices related to selection and regularisation of services of employees. It is a requirement in public sector undertakings that the lower level employees are to be recruited and hired from the candidates sponsored by employment exchange. This practice facilitates adoption of rule of reservation, apart from making a fair and proper selection without yielding to the pressures associated with selection. The same practice has been followed by both the units. In consonance with this practice, the employees who joined the units initially were asked to register their names in the local employment exchange and get their names sponsored by it. There upon their services have been regularised subject to the satisfactory performance of their duties during the probationary period.

One important aspect we noted here is that Vijaya unit wanted to depute some employees depending on the requirement to Sangam dairy when it started its activities in the Guntur district. But their employees prefer to remain in Vijaya unit and expressed reluctance to go to another location and work there. As a result most of the human resource requirement was met by Sangam unit by deploying personnel from the milk procurement centres in the villages and milk chilling centres. Such personnel were given the required training to make them effective on their jobs.

As for managerial personnel the units found more scientific procedures with regard to their recruitment and selection. The management of the units is aware that in formative years, the dairy units want to establish themselves the required talented, experienced and dynamic personnel. The advertisement is the most preferred method of recruitment to generate applications from the right people. Written test followed by interview is common for selecting the right people. Some of the supervisors and the managers have been sent to Anand, a leading dairy centre in India, to attend different training programs. The National Dairy Development Board (NDDB) identified Anand as an harbinger of this industry with the necessary technology and expertise people. If any centre wishes to start a dairy unit the necessary technology and the expertise is made available from the centre apart from installing the plant, offer necessary knowhow for these centers. For example, the present managing director of Sangam dairy was originally deputed by NDDB who subsequently preferred to continue in this plant by resigning his job at Anand.

Table 3.3: Mode of Selection

Selection	*Frequency*	*Per cent*	*Cumulative Per cent*
No response	1	0.3	0.3
Test	43	14.1	14.4
Interview	223	73.1	87.5
Medical fitness	5	.1.6	89.2
Other	33	10.8	100.0
Total	305	100.0	

Above table 3.3 shows that majority of the respondents have been selected through "Interview"and more than fourteen per cent have been selected by "written test". About eleven per cent of respondents have been selected by other method while the remaining stated that they have been selected on facing medical fitness.

PLACEMENT

Placement is a decision to place a selected individual in a job to which he is most suitable. In selection the task is to match people with the positions. In placement the task is to match positions with people so that each individual is assigned to that position where he is likely to make the best use of his abilities consistent with the requirements of his total working group. Selection is best done where the number of applicants is large relative to the number of available jobs. Placement is best done where the number of available jobs is large relative to the number of selected individuals.[11]

At the time of employment, selection and placement are often inseparable parts of a single process. As a rule, a small company has only a few vacancies at any one time, and consequently it selects people for specific jobs. In large companies, however, where there are a number of vacancies, selection and placement may become distinct processes.

Placement problems arise when large-scale transfers or promotions are made or when some people rendered surplus in one part of the organisation are being placed elsewhere in the organisation or when executive trainees on completion of their general training programme are being assigned to jobs in production, sales, marketing or some other functional area and so on. In such situations the individual is already 'employed' and the placement decision is then made to assign him to the job for which he is considered to be best qualified.

In making placement of individuals the principle that each individual should be placed on that job for which he has the greatest ability should not be rigidly followed because this may result in some jobs being filled by unqualified persons. The aim should be to realize the abilities and talents of the largest number of individuals. This may involve some workers being assigned to jobs for which their talents are secondary. But the composite assignments collectively are optimum. In both the dairy units assigning the right person for the right job is ensured. At times, where the skill or experience of the candidate is inadequate, he is given training. This training is often on the job type where the candidate is closely supervised and coached. The supervisor has a concern to see that the new employee adjusts to the job to which he is assigned.

INDUCTION

Before newly hired employees are trained for a specific job, they should be welcomed as new members of the organisation. The first day of employment is long remembered by most people. Initial impressions and information count heavily in the latter attitudes towards the job and the company. Proper induction is therefore an integral part of the training process. Helping new employees to feel at home more quickly enables them to get the full benefit of specific job training.[12]

Employee induction and training are important procedures in building an effective work team that can reach a high level of productive efficiency.

Table 3.4: Induction

Response	*Frequency*	*Per cent*	*Cumulative Per cent*
Yes	103	33.8	33.8
No	202	66.2	100.0
Total	305	100.0	

From the above table 3.4 it can be clear that nearly two third of respondents had not taken induction training whereas more than one-third of respondents had taken induction training.

PROBATION

In case of non-managerial and supervisory categories, every person appointed in a new post in both the dairy units is placed on probation for a period of one year from the date of appointment. But in lower levels, the probation period of an employee ranges from 3-6 months. In probation period the employee is provided training for doing the job effectively. The management may extend the probation period for 6 months at a time as considered necessary subject to a maximum of one year. Once the probation of the employee in Sangam Dairy is declared to have satisfactory completed, his services will be regularised and he is placed in a time scale. He is also eligible for all other benefits which are extended to permanent employees.

During the probation period if an employee avails leaves other than casual leave, the period of probation will be extended to cover the period of availed leave. During the period of probation an employee is liable to be terminated from services at any time without assigning any reason by giving one month notice or in lieu of that one month wages.

Table 3.5: Probation Period

Probation	*Frequency*	*Per cent*	*Cumulative Per cent*
3 months	158	51.8	51.8
6 months	34	11.1	63.0
One year	113	37.0	100.0
Total	305	100.0	

Table 3.5 shows that probation period was three months as stated by more than half of the respondents. Thirty-seven per cent of the respondents stated that their probation period was one year. Whereas the remaining said that it was six months.

PROMOTION AND TRANSFERS

Promotion may be defined as an upward movement or advancement of an employee in an organisation to another job, which commands better pay or wages, better status or prestige and higher challenges, and responsibilities and opportunities. According to Scott and Clothier,[13] "A promotion is the transfer of an employee to a job which pays more money or one that carries some preferred status".

A transfer is a lateral movement of employees from one position or department or plant to another, generally without involving any significant change in compensation, duties, responsibilities and status.

For any promotion or transfer, what is needed is a device to evaluate the performance of the employee. If the performance of an employee is rated as consistently good, he is considered for promotion. Transfer is generally used to meet the exigencies of a situation and is a management prerogative.

Changes in various job positions from time to time help in matching the man and the job and this is one kind of training. The job changes include promotions, transfers and job dislocation as demotion, discharge, lay off, suspension etc.

Significantly no promotional opportunities exist in the selected dairy units for the lower level cadre workers and clerical employees working in the office. It is very rare that a technical operator in the processing plant gets an opportunity for promotion as senior operator or dairy operator grade-I. There are cases where they had no opportunity at all for promotion throughout their career. For example a dairy attendant who joined as such retired in the same post after serving for 33 years.

In the study, it is revealed that almost all employees are working in the same post for about 15 to 25 years and more. Most of them are retiring from the same post as when joined. There is a stagnation for promotions in the non-managerial cadre. Since there are no promotions in spite of long service, the employees are given increments in the time scale, even after reaching the highest in this scale, is allowed to draw annual increments.

The basis for promotion in the organisation is seniority as far as the policy is concerned. But the organisation also follows the criteria of seniority-cum-performance in some cases. It is a deviation from the policy when asked about this deviation, it is informed that management takes performance also into consideration in the cases where there is more than one employee in the same level of seniority in the same grade for promotion.

Transfers in this dairy are made both internal and external; internal transfer refers to transfer within the organisation. External transfers include transfer from one place to the other connected with the dairy activities. It is not uncommon to find that transfers are also given as punishments to the employees. It takes the form of shifting the employee from an urban locality to an interior rural village. This is the strategy adopted by the management in the co-operative and public sector to handle the problematic employees because taking disciplinary action it is a legal process whereas transferring an employee is the privilege of the management.

In case of managers the promotion avenues are much better when compared to their brethren in non-managerial cadre. An assistant dairy manager is promoted as deputy dairy manager who in turn is promoted as dairy manager. The criteria followed for promotion in their case are seniority-cum-merit. A panel of members consisting two board of directors, one representative of NDDB, Managing Director/ General Manager and Chairman, will look into the cases of promotion. The panel carefully considers such aspects as the length of service, initiative, application, performance of work, creativity, decision-making abilities of the candidates for promotion. The following guidelines have been formulated which govern the transfer of managerial employees.

1. Generally transfer should be ordered only in the month of May and June.

2. The employee should be ordinarily transferred in less than two years.

3. Employee on promotion will not be retained in the same place.

4. No employee irrespective of cadre to which he belongs should be allowed to work in the same place for more than 5 years under any circumstances.

Table 3.6: Transfer

Transfer	*Frequency*	*Per cent*	*Cumulative Per cent*
Yes	124	40.7	40.7
No	181	59.3	100.0
Total	305	100.0	

Table 3.6 shows that majority of respondents (59.3%) did not. get any transfer, whereas 40.7 per cent got transfer in their career.

Table 3.7: Promotion

Promotion	*Frequency*	*Per cent*	*Cumulative Per cent*
Yes	112	36.7	36.7
No	193	63.3	100.0
Total	305	100.0	

The data relating to the promotional opportunities that employees get in the sample units is presented in table 3.7, which reveals that nearly two-third of respondents (63.3 percent) had never any chance of promotion. Whereas more than one-third of respondents (36.7 percent) have had the opportunity of getting promotion in the organisation.

Promotion is one of the important variables where by an employer can keep his workforce contented by ensuring promotions periodically. The employer would do well to have a provision of adequate avenues of promotion to his employees at reasonable intervals by virtue of their merit and not only by seniority but also the responsibility accompanied by change of little and an increase in pay. The number of promotions received by the respondents is shown in table 3.8.

Table 3.8: Promotions Received by Respondents

Response	*Frequency*	*Per cent*	*Cumulative Per cent*
One	60	19.7	19.7
Two	36	11.8	31.5
Three	15	4.9	36.4
Four	1	.3	36.7
Without any promotion	193	63.3	100.0
Total	305	z100.0	

From table 3.8 it can be seen that majority of respondents have stated that they have not received any promotions. Only one-fifth of the respondents have received single promotion. Nearly twelve per cent of respondents (11.8) have received two promotions and about five per cent cf the respondents have received three promotions.

Level of Satisfaction on Recruitment and Selection-Item Analysis

To evaluate the overall opinions of the respondents towards recruitment and selection functions, an effort has been made to quantify the responses by using the method of summated ratings.

At the first stage, a set of items were selected and they were given responses on four point scale. Then each response was given score ranging from 1 to 4.

After constructing the tool it was pre-tested with a small sample of 60. The scores were summed up and analysed for its reliability. It was found that except one item, all the items had very high correlation coefficient with the total scores. The item which had low coefficient of correlation was dropped and the final tool was prepared.

Recruitment and selection are the operative functions of every human resource manager. An effective recruitment programme necessitates a well-defined policy, systematic procedures, proper techniques and methods for generating applications from prospective employees and selecting the right candidates. The acquisition of new employees is an important and complex task. The purpose of a sound recruitment and selection process is to choose individuals who are most likely to perform successfully in a job from those available to do the job.

To know the level of satisfaction on recruitment and selection of the respondents, 11 statements are selected from various research studies. (Rudhra Basava Raj (1969),[14] Lallan Prasad (1973),[15] Jacob (1973),[16] G.C.Patro (1989),[17] Ram Prasada Rao (1980),[18] Rao V.S.P (1991).[19] These statements have four point response pattern, i.e. Excellent, Good, Average and Poor. These responses are given the scores 4, 3, 2, and 1 respectively and summated. The score analysis table is given below.

Table 3.9: Level of Satisfaction on Recruitment and Selection

Score	*Frequency*	*Per cent*	*Cumulative Per cent*
11.00	5	1.6	1.9
20.00	6	2.0	3.6
22.00	13	4.3	7.9
23.00	1	.3	8.2
24.00	1	.3	8.5
25.00	1	.3	8.9
26.00	11	3.6	12.5
27.00	7	2.3	14.8
28.00	4	1.3	16.1

29.00	3	1.0	17.0
30.00	13	4.3	21.3
31.00	10	3.3	24.6
32.00	22	7.2	31.8
33.00	36	11.8	43.6
34.00	12	3.9	47.5
35.00	10	3.3	50.8
36.00	30	9.8	60.7
37.00	33	10.8	71.5
38.00	22	7.2	78.7
39.00	8	2.6	81.3
40.00	27	7.9	89.2
41.00	14	4.6	93.8
42.00	10	3.3	97.0
43.00	5	1.6	98.7
44.00	4	1.3	100.0
Total	305	100.0	

There are 11 statements and the scores range is 44 and 11:

No. of Statements	11
Response Pattern	4, 3, 2, 1 (Scores)
Maximum Score	44
Minimum Score	11

Further, to find out the variables affecting the level of satisfaction data were cross tabulated. First of all the frequency table of level of satisfaction on recruitment and selection was regrouped on the basis of First and Third quartile values and then results were presented.

As shown in the Table 3.10 that majority (57%) of respondents were moderately satisfied on recruitment and selection practices whereas nearly 40 per cent of respondents had low level of satisfaction. Other respondents were highly satisfied.

Table 3.10: Recruitment and Selection

Quartile values	*Frequency*	*Per cent*	*Cumulative Per cent*
High (31)	11	3.6	3.6
Moderate (31-37)	174	57.0	60.7
Low (38+)	120	39.3	100.0
Total	305	100.0	

Is level of satisfaction on recruitment and selection associated with the sex of the respondents? To find out the answer data relating to the sex of the respondents and their satisfaction levels have been cross tabulated. The results of the analysis are presented in Table 3.11.

Table 3.11: Recruitment and Selection by Sex

Sex	*Level of satisfaction on recruitment and selection*			*Total*
	Low	*Moderate*	*High*	
Male	11	151	106	268
Female		23	14	37
Total	11	174	120	305

$X^2 = 1.736$ df = 2 p = .420 Conti. Coeff = .075

It is evident from the table that the level of satisfaction of a majority of the respondents from both the sexes was moderate. However, further analysis reveals that comparatively large proportion of male respondents' satisfaction on recruitment and selection was found to be high. Very few of the male respondents' satisfaction shows low level whereas the female not scored at all. To test whether there is any significant association between the two variables, chi-square test was used. The results show that the association is statistically not significant. Sex has no bearing on satisfaction of recruitment and selection process.

Is recruitment and selection associated with the educational background of the respondents? To find out the answer, data relating to the educational background of the respondents and their recruitment and selection have been cross tabulated. The results of the analysis are given in Table 3.12.

Table 3.12: Recruitment and Selection by Educational Background

Educational Background	*Level of satisfaction on recruitment and selection*			*Total*
	Low	*Moderate*	*High*	
Elementary level		10	5	15
High school level	2	69	42	113
Intermediate	3	45	18	62
Graduation	6	34	33	73
Post graduation/ Professional		19	22	41
Technical		1		1
Total	11	174	120	305

$X^2 = 16.805$ df = 10 p = .079 Conti. Coeff = .229

It can be inferred from table 3.12 that a majority of the respondents' educational background, level of satisfaction on recruitment and selection have been moderate. However, further analysis reveals that most of the respondents have High School (113), Intermediate (62) Graduation (73) and Post-Graduation/Professional (41) educational background. An insignificant score of one is identified with technical qualification of the respondents. To test whether there is any significant association between the two variables, chi-square test was used. The results show that the association is statistically not significant. Hence the employees' educational background does not tell us about their level of satisfaction on recruitment and selection.

Respondents level of satisfaction on recruitment and selection is associated with the indebtedness or not has to be found by answering the questions relating to the indebtedness, data on respondents indebtedness and their level of satisfaction on recruitment and selection were cross tabulated. The results of the analysis are shown in Table 3.13.

Table 3.13: Recruitment and Selection by Indebtedness

Indebtedness	*Level of satisfaction on recruitment and selection*			*Total*
	Low	*Moderate*	*High*	
Yes	6	97	63	166
No	5	77	57	139
Total	11	174	120	305

X^2 =.302 df = 2 p = .860 Conti. Coeff = .031

It is indicated from table 3.13 that more than half of the respondents who have indebtedness, their level of satisfaction on recruitment and selection was 'moderate'. This is followed by 'high' level of satisfaction. Eleven respondents were scored to low level satisfaction on recruitment and selection. To test whether there is any significant association between the two variables, chi-square test was used. The results show that the association is statistically not significant. Hence, it is evident that respondents' indebtedness does not tell us about their level of satisfaction about recruitment and selection practices.

Is satisfaction level of recruitment and selection associated with the number of dependents of the respondents? To find out the answer, data relating to the number of dependents of the respondents and their satisfaction level on recruitment and selection have been cross tabulated. The results of the analysis are presented in Table 3.14.

Table 3.14: Recruitment and Selection by Number of Dependents

Number of Dependents	*Level of satisfaction on recruitment and selection*			*Total*
	Low	*Moderate*	*High*	
0.00		4		4
1.00	1	9	8	18
2.00		38	25	63
3.00	4	41	35	80
4.00	4	56	31	91
5.00	2	20	20	42
6.00		6	1	7
Total	11	174	120	305

X^2 =12.208 df = 12 p = .429 Conti. Coeff = .196

It is understood from Table 3.14 that a majority of the respondents' dependents satisfaction level on recruitment and selection was moderate. Further analysis shows that most of the respondents having two to five dependents, and their level of satisfaction was moderate. Another ten respondents having three to five dependents, the level of satisfaction in their case is 'low'. Interestingly more than one-third of the total respondents are highly satisfied even though majority of them have two to five dependents. To test whether there is any significant association between the two variables, chi-square test was used. The results show that the association is statistically not significant. Thus it is clear that the employees satisfaction level does not tell us about relationship between recruitment and selection and the number of dependents.

Is the level of satisfaction associated with the rural/urban background of the respondents? To find out the answer, data relating to the rural/urban background of the respondents and their level of satisfaction about recruitment and selection have been cross tabulated. The results of the analysis are presented in Table 3.15.

Table 3.15: Recruitment and Selection by Rural/Urban Background

Rural/Urban	*Level of satisfaction o. recruitment and selectic*			*Total*
	Low	*Moderate*	*High*	
Rural	11	143	108	262
Urban		31	12	43
Total	11	174	120	305

X^2 =5.455 df = 2 p = .065 Conti. Coeff = .133

As depicted in the Table 3.15 that the level of satisfaction in a majority of the respondents from both the rural/urban background has been moderate. However, further analysis reveals that more than one-third of the total respondents (108 rural, 12 urban) have "high" level satisfaction. Obviously eleven respondents with rural background have a 'low' satisfaction level. To test whether there is any significant association between the two variables, chi-square test was used. The results show that the association is statistically not significant. Hence the employees background either rural or urban does not tell us about their level of satisfaction on recruitment and selection practices in the sample units.

Whether the level of satisfaction is associated with the organisation of the respondents or not has to be found. Data relating to the organisationwise respondents and their satisfaction levels have been cross tabulated. The results of the analysis are indicated in Table 3.16.

It is evident from Table 3.16 that a majority of the respondents from both the organisations, and their level of satisfaction is moderate. Comparatively most (69) of the Sangam Dairy respondents scored 'high' than Vijaya Dairy (51). To test whether there is any significant association between the organisation and the satisfaction level on recruitment and selection, chi-square test is used. The results show that the association is statistically significant. In general in both the organisations majority of the respondents have moderate level of satisfaction, particularly in Sangam Dairy the respondents are highly satisfied with their recruitment and selection policies and practices.

Table 3.16: Recruitment and Selection by the Organisation

Organisation	*Level of satisfaction on recruitment and selection*			*Total*
	Low	*Moderate*	*High*	
Vijaya Dairy	6	123	51	180
Sangam Dairy	5	51	69	125
Total	11	174	120	305

$X^2 = 23.428$ df = 2 p = .000 Conti. Coeff = .267

It is further noticed that the employees of sample units are satisfied with their recruitment policy, selection procedure, induction and transfer policy.

Is the level of satisfaction on recruitment and selection associated with the category of the respondents? To find out the answer, data relating to the categorywise respondents and their satisfaction levels have been cross tabulated. The results of the analysis are presented in Table 3.17.

Table 3.17: Recruitment and Selection by Category

Category	*Level of satisfaction on recruitment and selection*			*Total*
	Low	*Moderate*	*High*	
Managerial	2	37	16	55
Non-managerial	9	137	105	250
Total	11	174	120	305

$X^2 = 3.022$ df = 2 p = .221 Conti. Coeff = .099

It is evident from table 3.17 that the level of satisfaction of a majority of the respondents from both the categories is moderate. Further analysis reveals that comparatively large proportion of non-managerial (105) respondents scored high, whereas the proportion of managerial category in this regard is 16. To test whether there is any significant association between these two variables, chi-square test is used. The results show that the association is statistically not significant. Thus the category of the respondents does not have a bearing on the satisfaction level on recruitment and selection methods.

Is the level of satisfaction on recruitment and selection associated with the caste of the respondents? To find out the answer data relating to the caste of the respondents and their levels of satisfaction has been cross tabulated. The results of the analysis are presented in Table 3.18.

Table 3.18: Recruitment and Selection by Caste

Caste	*Level of satisfaction on recruitment and selection*			*Total*
	Low	*Moderate*	*High*	
Open category	11	126	86	223
Backward classes		40	22	62
Scheduled caste		8	12	20
Total	11	174	120	305

$X^2 = 8.120$ df = 4 p = .087 Conti. Coeff = .161

It can be understood from Table 3.18 that in case of majority (174) of the respondents from all the castes, the level of satisfaction on recruitment and selection was moderate. However, further analysis reveals that 120 respondents (OC-86, BC-22, SC-12) are highly satisfied. Indeed, the BC and SC respondents could not get score to low. Whereas OC (11) respondents could score to low. It means that reservation category respondents appear to be satisfied on the recruitment and selection practices of dairy industry. To test whether there is any significant association between the two variables, chi-square test was used. The results show that the association is **statistically not** significant. Hence the employees' **caste OC, BC and SC do** not tell us about their level of satisfaction.

Is the level of satisfaction on recruitment and selection associated with the age of the respondents? To find out the answer, data relating to the age of the respondents and their level of satisfaction were cross tabulated. The results of the analysis are presented in Table 3.19.

Table 3.19: Recruitment and Selection by Age

Age	*Level of satisfaction on recruitment and selection*			*Total*
	Low	*Moderate*	*High*	
27 - 43 years		33	44	77
44 - 51 years	5	89	52	146
52 - 57 years	6	52	24	82
Total	11	174	120	305

$X^2 = 18.444$ df = 4 p = .001 Conti. Coeff = .239

It is evident from Table 3.19, the level of satisfaction a majority of the respondents from all the ages on recruitment and selection has been moderate. It is further indicated that more than one-third respondents are 'highly' satisfied. While majority of the respondents in the age group of 44.57 had moderate and high level of satisfaction, only 11 respondents in this age group expressed low level of satisfaction. To test whether there is any significant association between the two variables, chi-square test was used. The results show that the association is statistically significant.

In both dairies all the younger age respondents in the age group of 27-43 expressed their satisfaction regarding their recruitment and selection policies.

Is the level of satisfaction on recruitment and selection associated with the gross salary of the respondents? To find out the answer, data relating to the gross salary of the respondents and their recruitment and selection were cross tabulated. The results of the analysis are presented in Table 3.20.

Table 3.20: Recruitment and Selection by Gross Salary

Gross Salary (in Rs.)	*Level of satisfaction on recruitment and selection*			*Total*
	Low	*Moderate*	*High*	
3900-7400		38	41	79
7401-11000		88	53	141
11001-70000	11	48	26	85
Total	11	174	120	305

$X^2 = 35.227$ df = 4 p =.000 Conti. Coeff = .322

It is seen from Table 3.20 that the level of satisfaction in a majority (174) of the respondents' gross salary, has been moderate. This is succeeded by 'high' level of satisfaction scored by about 120 respondents. In case of very few (11) respondents whose gross salary is between eleven thousand to seventy thousand, the level of satisfaction is low. These employees might be the managers and functional heads of the dairy units. To test whether there is any significant association between the two variables, chi-square test was used. The results show that the association is statistically significant. From the above results, it is clear that there is a significant association between the employees gross salary and their level of satisfaction. Most of the dairy employees have been satisfied due to the obvious reason of revised salaries. This amount of gross salary is on par with that of state government employees. Hence, the respondents were satisfied with their recruitment and selection practices of the sample units.

Is the level of satisfaction on recruitment and selection associated with the net salary of the respondents? To find out the answer data relating to the net salary of the respondents and their level of satisfaction have been cross tabulated. The results of the analysis are exhibited in Table 3.21.

Table 3.21: Recruitment and Selection by Net Salary

Net Salary (in Rs.)	*Level of satisfaction on recruitment and selection*			*Total*
	Low	*Moderate*	*High*	
1800-3800	3	29	41	73
3801-6700	2	101	55	158
6701-16000	6	44	24	74
Total	11	174	120	305

$X^2 = 18.807$ df = 4 p = .001 Conti. Coeff = .241

From Table 3.21 it can be understood that the level of satisfaction with recruitment and selection for a majority of the respondents has been moderate. Another 120 respondents scored to 'high' level of satisfaction. To test whether there is any significant association between the two variables, chi-square test was used. The results show that the association is statistically significant. Thus, it is clear that the employees' net salary as a bearing on the level of satisfaction on recruitment and selection. Most of the employees in sample units have been availing the co-operative stores and getting loans from the banks. The amount is being deducted from their salaries. Even net salarywise, they are satisfied regarding the existing recruitment and selection practices.

There would be the association between recruitment, selection and income (net salary and gross salary) as the employees have overall satisfaction since the organisation provide them the income with which the employees are satisfied. With regard to association between age, recruitment and selection it would be the higher the age, the higher the balance of expectations. In reality this might lead to satisfaction of the organisational variables such as recruitment and selection. Organisation-wise, it is found that the respondents of Sangam dairy are more satisfied than that of its counterpart. It could be because of the organisational reasons such as the Sangam dairy has continued to employ people whereas Vijaya dairy has stopped recruitment and the selection and the latter has been suffering from the problem of excess manpower even after offering voluntary retirement scheme.

Based on the above analysis presented in this chapter it can be concluded that the recruitment and selection has been associated with the net salary, gross salary, age and organisation.

REFERENCES

1. Werther, William B. and Davis, Keith (1993). *Human Resources and Personnel Management.* New York: McGraw-Hill, Fourth Edition, 195.

2. Flippo Edwin, B (1980). *Personnel Management.* New York: McGraw Hill, 131.

3. Schuler, Randall S. et al., (1989). *Personnel/Human Resource Management.* New York: West Publishing Co., Third Edition, 106.

4. Stoops, Rick (1982, December). "Recruiting as a Sales Function", *Personnel Journal,* 890.

5. Heneman, Herbert, G III et al, (1986). *Personnel/Human Resource Management,* Irwin: Third Edition, 224.

6. The National Commission on Labour reported that except for the labour demanding specialised skill, the small industrial centres recruited labour mostly from the surrounding areas. Govt. of India, The Report of the National Commission on Labour (1969), Ministry of Labour and Employment, New Delhi.

7. Oranti, D.A. (1955), Jobs and Workers in India. Institute of International Industrial and Labour Relations, Ithaca: Cornell University, 37.

8. Sriniva, M.N. (1975), March 15). Social Environment and Managements Responsibilities, *Economic and Political Weekly,* Vol. X, No. 11, 489.

9. Umaramaswamy (1983), *Work, Union and Community—Industrial Man in South India.* Delhi: Oxford University Press.

10. Thomas, H. Stone (1989). *Understanding Personnel Management,* CBS College Publishing, 173.

11. Tripathi, P.C. (1996). *Personnel Management and Industrial Relations,* New Delhi, Sultan Chand & Sons, 160-161.

12. Paul, Pigors and Charles, A Miyers. (1981). *Personnel Administration A Point of View and Method.* New York: Other McGraw-Hill International Statements Editions in Related Field Kogakusha, 263.

13. Scott, Clotheir and Spriegal, (1951). *Personnel Administration,* 208.

14. Rudra, Basavaraj (1969). *Personnel Administration in India.* Puna: Vaikunta Mehta Institute of Co-operative Management.

15. Lallan, Prasad (1973). *Personnel Management and Industrial Relations in Public Sector.* Mumbai: Progressive Publishers.

16. Jacob, K.K. (1973). *Personnel Management in India.* Udayapur: S.J.C. Publishers.

17. Patro, G.C. (1989). *Human Resource Management.* New Delhi: Discovery Publishing House.

18. Ram Prasada Rao (1990). *Human Resource Management in Municipalities.* New Delhi: Discovery Publishing House.

19. Rao, V.S.P. (1991). *Human Resource Management in Small Industries.* New Delhi: Discovery Publishing House.

Human Resource Development

The preceding chapter presented the recruitment, selection, promotion and transfer policies followed by the analysis of level of satisfaction of sampled employees on these aspects. The present chapter makes an attempt to analyse the HRD practices and the analysis of respondents on various aspects of HRD implemented in the organisations.

People make organisations grow, and in order to facilitate that organisations should also make their people grow continuously.[1] Although HRD systems had been in existence in some form in the country earlier, a professional outlook to HRD started only in early seventies. Perhaps the first company in India to implement an integrated HRD system in the early seventies is Larsen and Toubro Ltd., towards the end of seventies the professional spirit of HRD spread to few other organisations. In the public sector, organisations like State Bank of India, B.E.M.L., have taken the lead in implementing new HRD processes.

William James of Harvard University estimated that employees could retain their jobs by working at mere 20-30 per cent of their potential. He believes that if these employees were properly motivated, they could work at enhanced level of 80-90 per cent of their capabilities.[2] Behavioural concepts like motivation and enhanced productivity could be used for such improvements in employee output. Training could be one of the means used to achieve such improvements through the use of learning resources.

In the past organisations were satisfied with 'training' as a tool of developing the skills of employees to meet the job requirement. Organisations began realising the limitations of training in developing abilities and competencies. In order to create a "development climate" which will help in developing and harnessing the human resources, they started exploring other mechanisms. It is this need for paying attention to other tools of development that led many organisations to set up new departments of HRD.

THE CONCEPT OF HRD

The concept of HRD is still in an evolutionary stage, and many authors could not grasp fully the true implications of the concept. Many personnel managers and organisations tend to view HRD as synonymous with training and development. Several organisations in the country renamed their training departments as HRD departments. Likewise, some organisations renamed their personnel departments as HRD departments.

The concept of HRD was formally introduced by Leonard Nadler in 1969 in a conference organised by the American Society for Training and Development. HRD, according to Nadler refers to "those learning experiences which are organised, for a specific time and designed to bring about the possibility of behavioural change". Among the Indian authors, T.V. Rao worked extensively on HRD. He defines HRD as "a process by which the employees of an organisation are helped in a continuous planned way to:

(i) Acquire or sharpen capabilities required to perform various functions associated with their present or expected future roles;

(ii) Develop their general capabilities as individuals and discover and exploit their own inner potentials for their own and/or organisational development purposes;

(iii) Develop an organisational culture in which superior subordinate relationship, team work

> and collaboration among sub-units are strong and contribute to the professional well-being, motivation and pride of employees.[3]

HRD is imperative to any organisation that wants to be dynamic and growth-oriented or to succeed in a fast-changing environment. Organisations can grow and become dynamic only through the efforts of human resources. Personnel policies can keep the morale, and motivation of employees high but, these efforts are not enough to make the organisation dynamic and to take it in new directions.

HRD and the Organisation

HRD is generally focussed in larger organisations, and there are some identifiable reasons for this, through any organisation—no matter what the size actually provided some kind of HRD. For a particular organisation, the HRD programme may be insignificant in terms of the organisation's overall budget. One may not even be able to find HRD in the table of organisation, company phone book, or other observable documents.

Even in a small organisation, however, somebody is providing learning experiences for new employees. It may be a very brief on-the-job experience, the coaching of one employee by another, or a supervisor telling an employee to read the manual that comes with some newly arrived equipment.

Irrespective of the size of an organisation, if we look around we will probably discover more HRD in operation than we think of. Some HRD activities are conducted without a specific managerial decision, or even without the knowledge of management. Even these clandestine HRD operations can contribute to the success of the organisation.[4]

Training

In a rapidly changing environment, the need for training for people to reach peak performance in their jobs, hardly needs any emphasis. "The rate of technology and managerial obsolescence is growing at an exponential rate. It is no longer considered valid to discuss if training is necessary. The debates are more on how to conduct training and how to make it more effective and enduring."[5] In fact, training and development is a necessary part of organisational life, because no system of recruitment and selection is so flaw-less that it yields a body of employees who can (a) immediately perform the tasks for which they are hired, and (b) acquire new skills as needed.[6] An organisation's most valuable form of capital is a well-educated and well-trained workforce and realising this, many organisations in India, belatedly at least, are committing themselves to the training and development of their workforce and executives.[7]

Training in Small Industry

In a small scale unit, the owner has the responsibility for developing and conducting the training programmes, aimed at providing opportunities for employees to acquire job-related skills and knowledge. All such programmes should aim at improving employee knowledge and skills so that they can keep themselves abreast of many changes that take place in competing sectors. If the owner is able to provide continuous training to his employees, it prepares the employees to assume more challenging tasks and enables them to grow vertically. This, in turn, would result in higher employee morale and greater production.

Unfortunately, many small business owners tend to overlook training function and take too much for granted.[8] The costs involved seem to be too prohibitive. They also resent the consequent dislocation to their production schedules. Some times, the fear that trained would not stay on the jobs for long, also acts as a deterrent. Again, after receiving training, employees may demand more wages and if it is negative, may quit the jobs.[9] Such psychological fears and emotional objections have prevented many a small business owner from undertaking systematic training programmes for their employees.

Training and development programmes are necessary in any organisation for improving the quality of work of the employees at all levels, particularly in a world of fast changing technology, changing values and environment.

Training is a short-term process utilising a systematic and organised procedure by which non-managerial personnel acquire technical knowledge and skills for a definite purpose. It refers to instructions in technical and mechanical operations like operations of some machine. It is designed primarily for non-managers. It is for a short duration and it is for a specific job-related purpose.

Development is a long-term educational process utilising a systematic and organised procedure by which managerial personnel get conceptual and theoretical knowledge.[10] In other words it refers not to technical knowledge or skills in operation but to philosophical and theoretical educational concepts. It involves broader education and its purpose is long-term development.

Need for Training

(i) Employment of inexperienced and new labour requires detailed instructions for effective performance on the job.

(ii) People have not only to work, but work effectively with the minimum of supervision, minimum of cost, waste, and spoilage and to produce quality goods and services.

(iii) Increasing use of fast changing techniques in production and other operations marquises training into newer methods for the operatives.

(iv) Old employees need refresher, training to enable them keep abreast of changing techniques and the use of sophisticated tools and equipment.

(v) Training is necessary when a person has to move from one job to another because of transfer, promotion or demotion.

Assessment of Training Needs

Training is an essential input in providing learning opportunities to employees of an organisation to enable them to optimally contribute towards meeting the short-and long-term objectives of the organisation. Thus, all the activities pertaining to training must be related to the specific needs of both the organisation and the individual employees. The specificity with which training needs are stated will be for effectiveness of the training effort as it will assist in evaluating firstly, the extent to which the skills required for a particular task or role have been acquired and utilised in improving one's performance; and the extent to which the individual interests, aspirations and potentials have been met and realised for ensuring job satisfaction and employee growth.[11]

Adhocism in the choice of training programmes and in formulating training strategies are likely to cause more frustration than satisfaction among organisation members as they may not be able to utilize their newly acquired learning on their jobs. Hence, there is a need to develop realistic plans for training and development of employees, execute them and follow them up with continuous monitoring and evaluation. The first phase in the planning process is the identification of specific training and development needs which involves the following:

Methods of Training

As a result of research in the field of training, a number of programmes are available. Some of these are new methods, while others are improvements over the traditional methods. The training programmes commonly used to train operative and supervisory personnel are discussed below. These programmes are classified into on-the-Job and off-the-Job Training Programmes.[12]

On-the-Job Training Methods

This type of training, also known as job instruction training, is the most commonly used method. Under this method, the individual is placed on a regular job and taught the skills necessary to perform that job. The trainee learns under the supervision and guidance of a qualified instructor. On-the-job training has the advantage of giving first hand knowledge and experience. under the actual working conditions. On-the-job training methods include job rotation, coaching, job instruction or training through step-by-step and committee assignments.

(a) Job Rotation

This type of training involves the movement of the trainee from one job to another. The trainee receives job knowledge and gains experience from his supervisor or trainer in each of the different job assignments. Though this method of training is common in training managers for general management positions, trainees can also be rotated from job to job in workshop jobs. This method gives an opportunity to the trainee to understand the problems of employees on their jobs and respect them.

(b) Coaching

The trainee is placed under a particular supervisor who functions as a coach in training the individual. The supervisor provides feedback to the trainee on his performance and offers him some suggestions for improvement. Often the trainee shares some of the duties and responsibilities of the coach and relieves him of his burden.

(c) Job Instruction

This method is also known as training through step by step. Under this method, trainer explains the trainee the way of doing the job, job knowledge and skills and allows him to do the job.[13] The trainer appraises the performance of the trainee, provides feedback information and corrects the trainee.

(d) Committee Assignments

Under the committee assignment, group of trainees are given assignment and asked to solve an actual organisational problem. The trainees solve the problem jointly. It develops team work.

Off-the-Job Methods

Under this method of training, trainee is separated from the job situation and his attention is focussed upon learning the material related to his future job performance. Off-the-job training methods are as follows.

(a) Vestibule Training

In this method, actual work conditions are simulated in a classroom. Material, files and equipment which are used in actual job performance, are also used in training. This type of training is commonly used for training personnel for clerical and semi-skilled jobs. The duration of this training ranges from days to a few weeks.

(b) Role Playing

It is defined as a method of human interaction that involves realistic behaviour in imaginary situations. This method of training involves action, doing and practice. The participants play the role of certain characters, such as the production manager, mechanical engineer, superintendent, maintenance engineer, quality control inspector, foreman, worker and the like. This method is mostly used for developing interpersonal interactions and relations.

(c) Lecture Method

The lecture is a traditional and direct method of instruction. The instructor organizes the material and gives it to a group of trainees in the form of a talk. To be effective, the lecture must motivate and create interest among the trainees. An advantage of lecture method is that it is direct and can be used for a large group of trainees.

(d) Conference or Discussion

It is a method in training the clerical, professional and supervisory personnel. This method involves a group of people who pose ideas, examine and share facts, ideas and data, test assumptions, and draw conclusions, all of which contribute to the improvement of job performance. Discussion has the distinct advantage over the lecture method as the discussion involves two-way communication and hence feedback is provided. The participants feel free to speak in small groups. The success of this method depends on the leadership qualities of the person who leads the group.

(e) Programmed Instruction

In recent years this method has become popular. The subject-matter to be learned is presented in a series of carefully planned sequential units. These units are arranged from simple to more complex levels of instruction. The trainee goes through these units by answering questions or filling the blanks. This method is expensive and time consuming.

Evaluation of Training

In order to assess the extent to which training programmes have achieved the purposes for which they are designed, it is necessary to evaluate various activities that have culminated in the implementation of the training package. Such an evaluation exercise would provide relevant information not only about the effectiveness of training but also about the future design of other training programmes. It is through the process of evaluation that training specialists can monitor the training programmes and update, modify and innovate in future training programme. The evaluation of the outcome and consequence of training also provides useful data on the basis of which relevance of training and its integration with other functions of management can be established.[14]

Employee development, which involves improving and increasing the abilities of employees, is required for the success of organisations.[15] Development begins with the orientation programme and continues to change. When there is a Personnel Department, the responsibility for planning and implementing formal employee development programmes usually is delegated to it. Otherwise, employee development is conducted informally by various individuals and groups.

The primary activities involved in employee development are orientation, training in job skills, and cultivation of managerial skills. Other activities related to employee development are evaluating performance, counselling and communicating organisational policies and procedures.

HRD in Dairy Industry

Development function has to do with increasing of skill, knowledge, behaviour and infusing the result kind of attitude. HRD function remained largely a neglected area in initial years of both the units. They were confined mostly to deputing some higher level to places like Anand, Erode, Bombay, Bangalore and Hyderabad. These activities were meant for cattle rearing, increasing the yield in milk, dairy technology aspects such as preserving milk, aseptic packaging, quality control and marketing of milk products. There was neither a cogent policy nor regular training activity in these organisations at the stage.

But during the last decade or so the HRD activity has received importance. It has been realised that the activities must be organised on the basis of need and in a systematic way at all levels of employees. In general HRD is regarded as an integral aspect of the personnel department and the department is entrusted with the responsibility of organising HRD function.

The HRD activities of Sangam dairy and Vijaya dairy are organised in a three tier system—village level, unit level and federation level. Villages form the grass root level of the co-operative milk societies. The membership of the villagers is mobilised and they are encouraged to become members of the society. They constitute an important aspect of dairy industry in the sense that the milk is supplied by them for processing at the district level. The farmers are given guidance about the cattle rearing. They are also educated on various aspects of dairy technology like fodder for the cattle, maintenance of their health, promotion of hygiene, increase in milk yield and their role in the organisational set-up co-operative societies. In this regard a good number of training programmes are organised for the farmers aiming at their participation and qualitative improvement in their contribution for effective functioning of society. A manager is appointed for this purpose at Sangam dairy who along with his supporting staff goes to the rural areas and organize the training programmes at this level.

At the district level where the milk processing units are located attention is paid to cover both managerial as well as non-managerial employees under various training programmes. As regards the non-managerial employees, on the job-training becomes the key aspect. As soon as an employee is hired, he is placed under the guidance of a supervisor, his performance on the job is closely supervised and monitored by the supervisor. The employee is given feed-back about his performance and if necessary coaching is given to overcome his deficiencies and improve his performance.

In Sangam dairy a training centre is established where the supervisors, technical staff, clerks, workers, helpers and dairy attendants are given training. This is mostly in the nature of off-the-job training. If expertise in the organisation in the unit is not adequate they can bring outside expert to train. It is noticed that an employee is given training not only in the narrow area of his job but also helped to acquire skills and knowledge in the related traits of the job. By this the concept of multiskilling is applied and an employee, after receiving his training, is able to perform the jobs of related trades. The researcher found that the efforts of the centre, though appreciable are not adequate and they need to be further strengthened. In Vijaya dairy also a training centre is in the formative stage and has just started to organize the training programmes for its employees.

It is also the practice of the units to send the employees to premier centres of dairy industry in the country for advanced training by utilising the services of different experts.

At the state level where the federation operates, it is not uncommon for the units to depute administration staff to Hyderabad where training is offered in different aspects of effective management of co-operative as well as different aspects of industrial relations like grievance redressal, workers participation in management, communications, leadership development, productivity improvement etc. Through discussions with various functionaries in the dairy units, the researcher got the impression that a congenial HRD climate needs to be created in the units. For this purpose the total support of the top management as well as the co-operation of the staff at the middle level is needed.

The type of training activities undertaken by the Vijaya dairy and Sangam dairy are presented in Tables 4.1 and 4.2 respectively.

As mentioned in Table 4.1 various training programmes are being organised in Vijayawada, Hyderabad, Bangalore, Bombay, Madras, Ahmedabad, Anand, Erode, Baroda, and Allahabad. The training programmes include animal insemination, animal husbandry, co-operative training, short-course on dairy development, input training for organisation and society, motivation for women, quality control training, internal training, cooperative management training extention at NDD institution-building development, dairy office management, HRD course, operation and maintenance as aseptic filling machines, in plant training, English training, first-aid training, power maintenance, APS, tinseemers and dairy technology. The duration of the

Table 4.1: Training Programmes with the Place and Duration

Sl.No.	*Programme*	*Place*	*Period*
1.	Animal Insemination	Ahmedabad	110 days
2.	Animal Husbandry	Anand	Two months
3.	Co-operative Training	Bomaby	11 days
4.	Short-course on Dairy Development	Bangalore	3 months
5.	Input Training for Organisation and Society	Anand Erode	One month
6.	Motivation for Women	Erode	Two months
7.	Quality Control Training	Bangalore	One month
8.	Internal Training —Vijayawada	KDMPCU Ltd	One month
9.	Co-operative Management Training	Anand	One month
10.	Extension at NDD Institution Building Development	Erode	15 days

Table 4.1: Contd...

Sl.No.	*Programme*	*Place*	*Period*
11.	Quality Control Training (at a period of Joining)	KDMPCU Ltd.,	1 month
12.	Dairying Office Management	Hyderabad	21 days
13.	HRD Course	Hyderabad	2 or 3 months
14.	Operation and Maintenance as Aseptic Filling Machines	Baroda	40 days
15.	IDDB	Allahabad	2 years
16.	In Plant Training	Bangalore	1 month
17.	English Training	Hyderabad	20 days
18.	First-aid Training—Vijayawada	KDMPCU Ltd	3 months
19.	On Powder Maintnance	NDDB, Anand	25 days
20.	APS	Baroda	-
21.	Tinseemers	Madras	1 week
22.	Dairy Technology	Hyderabad	3 months

Table 4:2: The Perspective Plan for Training Programmes in Sangam Dairy

Sl.No	*Name of the Programme*	*Duration*	*Batch size*	*2000-01*	*2001-02*	*2002-03*	*2003-04*
1.	Veterinary first-aid and Artificial Insemination)	45 Days	20	60	60	60	60
2.	V.D.C Training	12 Days	20	20	20	40	40
3.	Institutional Building and clean milk production	3 Days	20	160	160	180	180
4.	Refresher Course in A.I and first-aid	6 Days	20	40	40	40	40
5.	Farmers Inductions programme	1 Day	50	600	600	600	600
6.	M.C.M. Training Programme	2 Days	20	300	300	300	300
7.	Management and Accounts of MPCS	5 Days	20	100	100	100	100
8.	Woman Presidents	3 Days	10	30	30	30	30
				1310	1310	1350	1350

above training programmes vary from one week to two years depending upon the nature of the programme.

As revealed from the table 4.2 the perspective planning includes 8 training programmes i.e. veterinary first-aid and artificial insemination, VDC training, institutional building and clean milk production, refresher course in animal insemination and first-aid, farmers induction programmes, MCM training programmes, management and accounts of MPCS and women presidents. The total number of trainees to be deputed for the above programmes yearwise are 1310 (2000-01), 1310 (2001-02), 1350 (2002-03) and 1350 (2003-04). The duration of the programmes vary from one day to 45 days. As indicated in table 4.2 the management contemplated to provide the farmers induction programmes of one day duration and MCM training programmes of two days duration for 600 and 300 farmers respectively as per the perspective planning.

The table 4.3 gives the actual number of training deputed programmewise and yearwise and the corresponding expenditure incurred for each programme during 2001-02.

Table 4.3: Training Budget During the Year 2001 to 2002

Training Programme	*No. of employees sent*	*Centre and place*	*No. of days*	*Expenditure incurred in Rs.*
Improvements in work and work culture	4	SRDTC, Erode	5	12000
Evaluation of food packaging materials and system	1	Chennai	2	1800
Frozen semen production handling	1	Mattupatti, Kerala	16	2250
Marketing practices for success	3	IRMA, Anand	6	5250
Lead Auditor programme under ISO 9001-2000	1	IIQM, Jaipur	5	18000

During the year 2001-02 only ten trainees were deputed as against 410 as per the estimated perspective plan. Only five programmes were materialised out of the eight programmes contemplated in the perspective plan. The five programmes for which trainees were deputed during 2001-2002 include improvements work and work culture, evaluation of food packaging materials and system, frozen semen production handling, marketing practices for success, and lead Auditor programme under ISO 9001 to 2000. The expenditure incurred by the management programme-wise for the above programmes during 2001-02 was Rs. 12,000, Rs. 18,000, Rs. 2,250, Rs. 5,250 and Rs. 18,000 respectively. The duration of the training programmes varied from two days to 16 days. As observed by the researcher, in addition to the above programmes the management also provided farmers induction training programme and MCM training programme.

Table 4.4: Training Organised by the Company

Response	*Frequency*	*Per cent*	*Cumulative per cent*
Yes	91	29.8	29.8
No	214	70.2	100.0
Total	305	100.0	

The above table reveals that majority (70.2%) of the respondents have not received any training organised by the company while nearly thirty per cent of the respondents received training.

Table 4.5: Vocational training for employee wards

Response	*Frequency*	*Per cent*	*Cumulative per cent*
Yes	26	8.5	8.5
No	279	91.5	100.0
Total	305	100.0	

It can be inferred from Table 4.5 that an overwhelming majority of the respondents expressed that their wards have not received any vocational training and nearly one-tenth of the respondents' wards only underwent vocational training.

Table 4.6: Opportunities Given to the Students

Response	*Frequency*	*Per cent*	*Cumulative per cent*
Excellent	110	36.1	36.1
Good	85	27.9	63.9
Average	47	15.4	79.3
Poor	63	20.7	100.0
Total	305	100.0	

Table 4.6 shows that more than one-third of the respondents stated that "excellent" opportunities are given to the students in this organisation. This is followed by twenty-eight per cent of respondents who held that the opportunities are "good". Another 15.4 per cent of respondents felt "average" and more than one-fifth per cent opined that the opportunities given to the students are "poor".

Table 4.7: Training and Development Programmes for Employees

Response	*Frequency*	*Per cent*	*Cumulative per cent*
Excellent	7	2.3	2.3
Good	20	6.6	8.9
Average	68	22.3	31.1
Poor	210	68.9	100.0
Total	305	100.0	

As shown in Table 4.7, a majority (68.9%) of the respondents opined that opportunities for employee training and development are "poor". More than twenty-two per cent respondents' opinion is "average"; nearly seven per cent of the respondents' opinion is "good" and the rest of them stated that the training and development programmes for employees are "excellent"

Table 4.8: Opportunities to Make Use of the Skills Learned

Response	*Frequency*	*Per cent*	*Cumulative per cent*
Excellent	8	2.6	2.6
Good	46	15.1	17.7
Average	132	43.3	61.0
Poor	119	39.0	100.0
Total	305	100.0	

Table 4.8 presents the opinion of the respondents on the opportunities to make use of the skills learned in the training. More than two-fifth of the respondents felt 'average' while nearly forty per cent as 'poor'. A little more than fifteen and nearly three per cent of the respondents opined as good and excellent respectively. 43.3 per cent of the respondents stated that the opportunities they have is average.

Performance Appraisal

The performance appraisal system in an organisation is designed involving both the organisation and the personnel to improve their capabilities. The elements of performance management include: purpose, content, method, appraiser, frequency and feedback. The appraisal process involves determining and communicating to an employee how he or she is performing the job and establishing a plan of improvement. The information provided by performance appraisal is useful in three major areas: compensation, placement and training and development.[16] Appraisal helps to identify those with a potential for greater responsibility; and assists in deciding on an equitable compensation system. The methods of performance appraisal include rating scale, critical incident, marking methods and management by objectives. Several common errors have been identified in performance appraisal. Leniency occurs when rating is grouped at the positive end instead of being spread throughout the performance scale. The central tendency occurs when all or most employees are ranked in the middle of the rating scale. The halo effect occurs when a manager allows his or her general impression of an employee to influence judgment of each separate item in the performance appraisal. A sound appraisal system involves assessing employee performance on a regular basis. Performance appraisal can be done by superiors who rate subordinates and self-appraisal. A suitable performance appraisal system has to be designed keeping in view the culture and requirements of an organisation.

Performance Appraisal for Non-Managerial Employees

In both dairies, for non-managerial employees the performance will be assessed by the immediate supervisor in terms of regularity in duties, the tenor and alertness in his work, spirit of team work, working relations with fellow employees, obedience to the authorities, responsibility in his duties, his abilities and potentialities.

Performance Appraisal for Managerial Employees

There are different systems of performance appraisal for different cadres of managerial personnel. For general manager/managing director and senior managers the self-appraisal system is adopted.

The general manager/senior managers will assess their performance by themselves in terms of targets, accomplishments, constraints, utilisation of capacities, strong points, shortcomings and suggestions. Self-appraisal format is prepared including the above components which is to be filled in by the general manager/senior managers.

Performance Appraisal by the Reporting Authority

In this system the performance of the managerial personnel will be assessed by the reporting authority in terms of accomplishment, administration, thinking and relationships. There is four point merit rating namely "A" – outstanding; "B" – Very good; "C" – Average; "D" – Unsatisfactory for each of the components of the performance appraisal. The format prepared for performance appraisal is to be filled in by the reporting authority.

Potential Appraisal

The senior manager will assess the potentialities of subordinate managerial personnel in terms of their knowledge of work, initiative, judgement, and common sense, expression, acceptance of responsibility, ability to get things done, resourcefulness, capacity for further development, ability to develop and train others, ability for planning, organising, and capacity for handling people, cooperation, sociability, and character. There are four points of merit rating namely outstanding, very good, average, and unsatisfactory. For each of the above components there is a format for potential appraisal. The format prepared for the potential appraisal includes the above components and it is to be filled in by the reporting authority.

The respondents were asked about their views on the criteria—both performance and behavioural traits—used for assessing the performance.

Table 4.9: Criteria of Performance Appraisal

Response	*Frequency*	*Per cent*	*Cumulative per cent*
Excellent	3	1.0	1.0
Good	67	22.0	23.0
Average	58	19.0	42.0
Poor	177	58.0	100.0
Total	305	100.0	

As shown in the above table majority of the respondents (58%) felt that the criteria of performance appraisal are "poor". They felt the elements of the criteria are mostly related to behaviour traits rather performance traits. Important aspects like, quantity of work and quality of work skills, initiative, attitude do not figure in the criteria. 22 per cent of the respondents opined as "good" and 19 per cent of the respondents felt they are "average" On the said statement only one per cent stated as "excellent".

The performance appraisal system should be open and transparent and must be objectively done. One way of promoting this is that employees must have the intention for filling the criteria for appraisal. After the appraisal, another aspect is that a post-appraisal interview is to be held in which the appraisal and appraisee discuss the results and the appraise is rendered consulting to improve performance keeping these aspects in view the respondents were asked about their views.

Table 4.10: Transparency and Objectivity of the Appraisal System

Response	*Frequency*	*Per cent*	*Cumulative per cent*
Excellent	6	2.0	2.0
Good	52	17.0	19.0
Average	67	22.0	41.0
Poor	180	59.0	100.0
Total	305	100.0	

Table 4.10 depicts that single largest (59.3%) group of the respondents expressed that the transparency and objectivity of the appraisal system is poor. 22 per cent of the respondents expressed as "average" and 17 per cent of them expressed as "good", only 2 per cent of the respondents felt it is "excellent".

As stated earlier the management has realised the importance of developing its human resources. But its thinking has to take concrete shape and attain professionalism. It conducts same training programme but not on a continuing basis. The respondents were asked about their views in this respect.

Table 4.11: Making Use of Appraisal Results for Employee Development

Response	*Frequency*	*Per cent*	*Cumulative per cent*
Excellent	9	3.0	3.0
Good	60	19.7	22.6
Average	44	14.4	37.0
Poor	192	63.0	100.0
Total	305	100.0	

As shown in table 4.11 it can be inferred that majority of the respondents felt the efforts of the management in this regard are "poor". The management does not seem to realize training efforts either to identifying the needs of the employees nor is used as a means of their promotion and career development. Nearly one-fifth (19.7 per cent) of them stated as "good". Another 14.4 per cent respondents viewed as "average". But these responses have mostly stemmed from managerial category. The remaining 3 per cent of them stated as "excellent".

Table 4.12: Response on Self-appraisal

Response	*Frequency*	*Per cent*	*Cumulative per cent*
Yes	55	18.04	18.04
No	250	81.96	100.0
Total	305	100.0	

When the respondents were asked about the self-appraisal system in the dairy units, interestingly 18.04 per cent i.e. all the 55 managerial employees preferred self-appraisal system. But the non-managerial category preferred only appraisal by superiors.

Career Planning and Development

For effective HRD the corporate growth plans are not to be kept as a secret. These plans are made known to the employees. This is because the HRD philosophy assumes that people work better when they are trusted and they see meaning in what they are doing. So all staff know at least broadly the plans of the company.[17]

Such knowledge is also used for preparing the employees for change wherever such change is planned. The employees themselves facilitate the change. Sometimes before the change is introduced it is discussed at various levels. This also increases employee commitment.

To cope with the growing demands of the organisation the company continuously faces challenges to keep the talent readily available. Also at the individual level every employee would like to know the possibility of his own growth and career opportunities. This is done by every senior in helping his junior to plan his career. All seniors have more information about the growth, plans of the company and it is their responsibility to pass this on to their juniors and assist them in planning their careers in the company. Sometimes the planning may not become a reality, but they are all aware that if it does become a reality they are prepared to do a good job in their new roles.

Career Planning and Development in Dairy Industry

As per the units under study, career planning and development is not paid much attention. Partly the nature of industry is such that opportunities for individual growth in terms of promotions are very limited. The management also does not appear to have any policy in this regard. It is observed that among the non-managerial employees, they hardly get any chance even after serving a long time instances are not lacking where employees joined in a particular job and stagnate in the same position for decades. For example if a dairy attendant joins as such he has to retire in the same job even after putting over 20 years of service. If a person joins as a clerk in the grade of junior assistant he will at best become a senior assistant after many years of service. The employees at the junior level are allowed one additional annual increment to compensate partly for the lack of promotional opportunities. The researcher in the course of discussion with employees has observed that there is widespread dissatisfaction on this count.

The managerial employees are better in this respect. Managers working in production department, quality control and animal husbandry appear to enjoy some opportunities to get promotions and to climb the managerial ladder. Opportunities are open to these managers only to become either general manager/managing director.

REFERENCES

1. Rao, T.V. and Pereira, D.F. (1988). *Recent Experience in Human Resources Development.* New Delhi: Oxford and IBH Publishing Co, iii.

2. Arun Monappa and Mirza Saiyadain (1986). *Personnel Management.* New Delhi: Tata McGrow Hill Publishing Company, 138.

3. Rao, T.V. and Pereira. op. cit, 4.

4. Nadler, Leonard. *Corporate Human Resources Development.* New York: Van Nostrand Reinhold Company, 5.

5. Billimoria, R.P. (1987, July-August). "Training Perspectives" Newer Concepts and Methodologies. *Indian Journal of Training and Development*, 1.

6. Dubrin, A.J. (1981). *Personnel and Human Resource Management.* New York: D.Van Nostrand Co. 151.

7. Nazimuddin Ahmed (1987, January 26 - February 8) *"Speaking of Executive Development Business India,* 83-84.

8. Kline, John B. Stegall, Donald P. Steinmetz, Lawrence L. (1982). *Managing the Small Business,* Homewood Illinois : Richard D. Irwin Inc. 393.

9. Sashi, Bala (1984). *Management of Small Scale Industries.* New Delhi: Deep and Deep, 273.

10. Das, Gupta. A. (1974). *Business and Management in India.* Delhi: Vikas Publishing House.

11. Venkata Ratnam, C.S and Srivastava, B.K. (1974). *Personnel Management and Human Resources,* Tata McGraw Hill Publishing Company Limited, 150.

12. Subba Rao, P. (2002). *Essential of Human Resource Management and Industrial Relations.* Mumbai: Himalaya Publishing House, 264.

13. Holley, William. H and Jennings. Kenneth M. *Personnel Management,* CBS College.

14. Yoder, Dale and Standohar, Paul D (1982). *Personnel Management and Industrial Relations,* Eagle Wood Cliffs; Prentice Hall: Ibid, 158.

15. Byars, Lloyd. L. and Rue, Leslie W. (1979). *Personnel Management,* Concepts and Applications Philadelphia: W.B. Saunders Company, 169.

16. Sarma, A.M. (1998). *Personnel and Human Resource Management.* Mumbai: Himalaya Publishing House, 146.

17. Ravishankar S. and R.K. Mishra. (1985). *Management of Human Resources in Public Enterprises.* New Delhi: Vision Books Pvt., Ltd., 22.

5

Wages and Employee Welfare

Wages and employee welfare are important issues in the subject of HRM. Having presented HRD practices in the preceding chapter, an attempt is made in this chapter to analyse wage and salary administration in selected dairies and welfare facilities provided to the employees in these dairies followed by the analysis of the view point of respondent employees on wages and welfare.

In a cash-nexus economy, the significance of wages cannot be overemphasised. What happens to wages is of critical concern to everyone. To the employee, wages represent income, to the employer they represent cost and to the Government they signify potential tax. Wages are the largest source of purchasing power of labour, hence, changes in wages have an important bearing on the level of economic activity.[1] Moreover, wages constitute one of the important factors around which most of the labour problems revolve.[2] In the organised sector, the worker is conscious of his rights, politically awakened and is ready to protest to secure his rights.[3] In the unorganised sector, the situation is deplorable. Wages in the manufacturing establishments in the unorganised sector are around one-half of those in the organised sector.[4] Experience in small industry shows distressing facts about employee remuneration and benefits.[5]

In view of the above, an attempt is made in the chapter to examine the wages and employee welfare in sample units. Wage concepts, wage structure, factors influencing wage determination by the various studies, employee welfare administration in the dairy units, respondents' perceptions, responses, and their level of satisfaction are discussed in the following pages.

WAGE CONCEPTS

In the realm of wages, six important concepts have been identified. They are (i) statutory minimum wage (ii) bare or basic minimum wage (iii) minimum wage, (iv) fair wage, (v) living wage and (vi) need based minimum wage.[6]

Statutory minimum wage refers to the wage fixed under the provisions of the Minimum Wages Act, 1948 to protect the interests of workers employed in unorganised sector or scheduled employments. This is meant for elimination of exploitation and sweated conditions of workers.

Basic minimum wage is used in judicial pronouncements. It refers to bare subsistence meant to cover the bare physical needs of worker and his family. No industry has right to exist unless it is able to pay its workers at least a bare minimum wage.[7]

The concept of minimum wage, fair wage and living wage were defined by the Committee on Fair Wages appointed by the government in 1948. Minimum wage, according to the committee, must provide not merely for the bare sustenance of life but for the preservation of the efficiency of worker. For this purpose, the minimum wage must also provide for some measure of education, medical requirements and amenities.[8]

The fair wage was something which falls between a minimum wage and a living wage. The committee on Fair Wages stated that while lower limit of fair wage must obviously be the minimum wage, the upper limit is equally set by what may be called 'the capacity of industry to pay'. Between these two limits the actual wages will depend on (a) the productivity of labour, (b) the prevailing rates of wages in the same or similar occupation, (c) the level of the national income and (d) the place of the industry in economy.[9]

Living wage, according to Justice Higgins of Australian Common Wealth Court of Conciliation in the Harvester case, must provide for "the normal needs of average employee, regarded as human being living in a civilised community". According to the committee on fair wages, living wage represented the highest level of the wage and naturally, it could include all amenities which a citizen living in a modern civilised society was entitled to expect when the economy of the country was sufficiently advanced and the employer was able to meet the expanding aspirations of his workers.[10] From this it appears that in India it will take decades when the working class could hope to get living wages.[11] Till then it only remains as an ideal.[12]

Need-based minimum wage concept was evolved in India by the 15th session of the Indian Labour Conference held in 1957. It was agreed at the conference that the minimum wage must be need-based and should ensure the minimum human needs of worker and his family. Such wage should cater to the needs of a standard family consisting of three consumption units. While calculating the quantum of wage, it should consider the food, clothing and shelter requirements of the standard family. In addition, the wages should also cover fuel, lighting, and other miscellaneous expenditure. The conference enjoined on all the wage fixing authorities like wage boards etc., to take into account the norms suggested by Indian Labour Conference in calculating the needs of worker's family.

Laying down a sound wage system and its implementation is one of the most complex assignments in an industrial organisation. It is a dynamic and complex field involving many workable principles and procedures. Over a period of years, the wage payment system has taken different shape and acquired multi-dimensional character due to the rapidly changing technology and socio-economic transformation of the society. Employees began to compare their inputs and outcomes with those of others and expected just and equitable pay. It gave rise to innumerable disputes and frictions, particularly with regard to the relative pay to be assigned to certain jobs or occupational groups in organisations. Consequently, different patterns of wage payment and methods of wage fixation began to assume an important role in the management of personnel in enterprises.

The government and the community at large are vitally interested in wage levels because of a large number of industrial disputes and work stoppages revolving around the question of wages, bonus and allowances. Government is also concerned with wage standards, which affect the social climate of the country as well as such important parts of the economy as employment prices and inflation, national productivity, and the ability of the country to export enough goods to pay for its imports and so keep its international receipts and payments in balance. The government also employs a large number of workers and have, therefore, a direct interest in wage structure. In many developing countries, indeed, the government is the biggest employer.

Wage administration deals with techniques and procedures for designing and maintaining salary structures, rewarding staff, and exercising wage control. The basic aim of wage administration is to attract, retain and motivate employees by developing and maintaining competitive and equitable wage structure. Beach[13] visualizes four objectives of wage and salary administration.

First, compensation seeks to accomplish a labour market function of allocating human resources among different enterprises in terms of perceived attractiveness of jobs as revealed in the rate of pay and related wage supplements. Second, carefully-designed compensation systems facilitate control of wages and salaries and labour costs. Third, the financial compensation system seeks to maintain satisfaction of human resources reducing voluntary separations and complaints and grievance stemming from inadequate and inequitable wages, as perceived by the employees. An effective wage and salary administration system is likely to give the feeling that the remuneration is fair and that no favoritism has been shown in its fixation. Fourth, the financial compensation system purports to induce and reward improved performance and forms an effective motivator.

A wage survey is a way of collecting and analysing information on the policies, practices, and methods of wage payment from selected organisations in a given geographic location or particular type of industry so that comparisons can be made. Wage surveys are the primary method used to ensure external equity in an organisation's wage and salary system. Data may be gathered from a variety of sources.

The steps involved in wage survey procedure[14] may be outlined as follows:

Planning the Survey

1. Determining purpose of the survey,
2. Determining the area to be surveyed;
3. Determining the firms to be included in the survey;
4. Determining the jobs to be included in the survey;
5. Developing a method of insuring job comparability;
6. Determining information to be obtained;
7. Making the schedules;
8. Determining the survey method;
9. Selecting a staff.

Wage comparisons provide the key facts relied upon by labour and management in many negotiations. This is particularly true after a new wage movement is under way. Comparison with wages in other companies or in other industries are usually the core of the material considered in collective bargaining.

Wage comparisons are important to the employer, to the employee, and to the union. Wage comparisons are particularly important to unions. As Ross notes "They measure whether one union has done as well as the others. They show whether the negotiating committee has done a sufficiently skillful job of bargaining. They demonstrate to the union members whether they are getting money's worth for their due. A favourable comparison ('the best contract in the industry') becomes an argument for the re-election of officers, a basis for the solidification and extension of membership, and an occasion for advancement within the official hierarchy. An unfavourable comparison ('the best we could do under the circumstances') makes it likely that the rank and file will become disgruntled, rival leaders will become popular, and rival unions will become active."[15] Comparative pay structures have an important effect on the company's costs and, therefore, on its ability to compete effectively in the product market.

The National Council of Applied Economic Research has studied the occupational wage differentials in some of the industries, viz. cotton textile, sugar, iron and steel, tea, and automobile manufacturing. It has attempted to depict the differentials in earnings of men, women and children in the context of place, cadre, plant and industries. Inter-industry and inter-state differentials have been dealt within this study. The main study undertaken by it has two aims. First, to present the existing state of wage differentials, and second, to analyse what has been happening to wage differentials over the years. It has taken the help of the statistics of the Government of India, Reports of the Central Wage Boards, and other agencies.

Principles of Wage Formulation

A sound compensation system should encompass factors like adequacy of wages, social balance, supply and demand, fair comparison, equal pay for equal work measurement.[16] The concept of adequacy has two aspects, the internal and external. The internal component is concerned with the fair wage concept and hence has a link with the adequacy in relation to the given job, employee basic needs, apart from ensuring a decent standard of living. The external aspect has a relation to the comparable jobs in other industries. The wage compensation for a particular job should not be less than the level at which it is paid else where.

Wage Policy

Wage policy according to I.L.O refers to "legislation or Govt. action, calculated to effect the level or structure of wage, or both, for the purpose of attaining specific objectives of social and economic policy".[17] Wage policy is a determinant of the shares of the rival claimants of the product of industry and national dividend.[18]

In India a fair deal in wage compensation began after independence. Payment of a fair wage to labour fair return on capital employed and reasonable reserves for maintenance and expansion of the undertaking were emphasised in the Industrial Truce Resolution (1947).[19] The Industrial Policy Resolution (1948) also emphasised the promotion of fair wages. The successive five year plans also emphasised adoption of fair wage concept and stated that the wage rise should be effected in those sectors where it is very low. At the same time the plans also emphasised that improvement in wages should result mainly from increased productivity which implies not merely more efficient work on the part of labour, but also by better output plans, improvement in management practices and the like.

As regards wage policy in dairy industry, it is in consonance with the national wage policy (NWP) as enunciated in the five year plans and other policy documents of the government. According to the principles of co-operative sector, dairy units also believe in compensation system based on 'fair wage' concept. The Andhra Pradesh Dairy Development Co-operative Federation (APDDCF) adopts the fifth pay commission scales of pay to their milk unions since the federation plays government role. Hence the federation implements revised pay scales to all the dairy units.

Wage and Salary Administration in Dairy Industry

One of the most important and difficult problems of the management is that of determining the rate of the monetary compensations i.e. control of wage and salary levels. The main objectives of such wage and salary device is to give an incentive to greater employee productivity and to maintain a satisfactory public relations image.

Broadly speaking compensation refers to a wide range of financial and non-financial rewards or payments. Thus wages, salaries and many other benefits and services include paid vacations, sick leave, medical insurance etc. Monetary payments may be regarded as direct compensation and employee benefits as indirect compensation.

Initially Government used to bear half of the expenditure. After disinvestment as it is a cooperative dairy of the milk producers under the control of Federation, Federation played the role of the Government. At present the dairy itself is bearing the whole expenditure without any involvement of the third party.

Recently the salaries were revised in 1999 and the arrears were paid to the employees. The revised pay scales of the employees of both the dairies, designation-wise, are presented in Table 5.1.

As revealed from Table 5.1 it is observed that the scales of pay designation-wise are the same in both the dairies except the variation in the nomenclature of only one cadre. Though the two carry the same scale of pay there is change in the designation of these two positions in the two dairies. The nomenclature of General Manager in Vijaya dairy is changed to Managing Director in Sangam dairy.

In both the dairy industries, there are three cadres of managerial personnel. The managerial posts, are divided into three cadres as per the scales of pay. The highest pay scale Rs. 10250 to Rs. 16525 is drawn by General Manager/ Managing Director up to senior managers, followed by scale

Table 5.1: Wages in Dairy Industries Scale of Pay

Sl.No	Designation	Scaled Pay
1.	General Manager	10250-350-11650-450-13900-525-17050
2.	Deputy general Manager	9400-300-9900-350-11650-450-13900-525-16525
3.	Deputy General Manager (Prod)	-do-
4.	Deputy Director	-do-
5.	Special Officer	-do-
6.	Sr. Accounts Officer	-do-
7.	Sr. Manager (Mct)	-do-
8.	Personnel Officer	6950-200-7150-250-8400-300-9900-350 11650-450-13900-525-14425
9.	Welfare Officer	-do-
10.	Quality Control Officer	-do-
11.	Dairy Manager	-do-
12.	Dairy Manager (Tech)	-do-
13.	Asst. Dairy Engineer	-do-
14.	Safety Officer	-do-
15.	Asst. Director (Vety)	-do-
16.	Sales Manager	-do-
17.	Deputy Material Mgr	-do-
18.	Asst. Director (P&I)	-do-
19.	Asst. Engineer Civil	-do-
20.	Manager(Gr-I)	-do-
21.	Medical Officer	-do-
22.	Manager (Gr-II)	5980-170-6150-200-7150-250-8400-300-9900-350-11650-450-12100
23.	Milk Procurement Officer	-do-
24.	Assistant D.M.	-do-
25.	Assistant Q.C.O.	-do-
26.	Asst. Mg (Bi-Produ)	-do-
27.	Assistant Manager (Prod)	-do-
28.	Asst. Mgr (QC)	-do-
29.	Asst. Mgr (Mkt)	-do-
30.	Vety. Asst. Surgeon	-do-
31.	Fodder Dev. Officer	-do-
32.	Asst. Accounts Officer	-do-

Sl.No	Designation	Scaled Pay
33.	Asst. Manager (FMP)	-do-
34.	Bio-Chemist	-do-
35.	Asst. Mgr (Admn)	-do-
36.	Asst. Mgr (Stores)	-do-
37.	Jr. Engineer (Mech) APs	
38.	Jr. Enginer (Ele) Aps	-do-
39.	Jr. Engineer (Pre-pack)	-do-
40.	Foreman	-do-
41.	Supervisor (Civil)	5000-150-5300-170-6150-200-7150-250-8400-300-9900-350-10600
42.	Market Superintendent	-do-
43.	Co-op Soc. Registrar	-do-
44.	Account Supervisor	-do-
45.	Junior Mgr	-do-
46.	Transport Supervisor	-do-
47.	Processing Supervisor	4190-120-4550-150-5300-170-6150-200-7150-250-8400-300-8700
48.	Dairy Operator	-do-
49.	Quality Control Supr.	-do-
50.	Chargemen Trans.	-do-
51.	Plant Chargemen	-do-
52.	Supervisors	-do-
53.	Sr. Assistant	-do-
54.	U.D. Accountant	-do-
55.	Asst. Comp. Prog	-do-
56.	Shift-In-charge	3550-100-3950-120-4550-150-5300-170-6150-200-7150
57.	Plant Mech	-do-
58.	Trans Mech.	-do-
59.	Dairy Operator (Gr-II)	-do-
60.	Boiler Operator (Gr-I)	-do-
61.	Electrician Gr-I	-do-
62.	Sr. Driver	-do-
63.	Jr. Driver	3290-80-3450-100-3950-120-4550-150-5300-170-6150-200-6550
64.	Jr. Asst./ LDA	-do-

Sl.No	*Designation*	*Scaled Pay*
65.	Telephone Operator	-do-
66.	Storekeeper	-do-
67.	Steno	-do-
68.	Typist	-do-
69.	Boiler Operator Gr-II	-do-
70.	Electrician Gr-II	-do-
71.	Maistry (Civil	-do-
72.	Plant Operator	-do-
73.	Asst. Mechanics	-do-
74.	Tinker	-do-
75.	Welder	-do-
76.	Winder	-do-
77.	Roneo Operator	-do-
78.	Turner	-do-
79.	Tire Mech.	-do-
80.	Marketing Asst.	-do-
81.	RMRD Clerk/Weighing Clerk	-do-
82.	Sales Assistant	-do-
83.	Shift-In-charge	-do-
84.	Timekeeper	-do-
85.	Field Assistant	-do-
86.	Lab Assistant	-do-
87.	Record Assistant	2870-60-3050-80-3450-100-3950-120-4550-150-5300-170-5470
88.	Store Attendant	-do-
89.	Office Clerk	2750-60-3050-80-3450-100-3950-120-4450-150-5150
90.	Jr. Typist	-do-
91.	Office Attendant	-do-
92.	Security Guard	-do-
93.	Cleaner	-do-
94.	Scavenger	-do-
95.	Field Helper	-do-
96.	Time Scale Dairy Attendents/ Plant Worker	-do-
97.	Contingent Workers	Consolidate pay of Rs. 1000 per month)

of Rs. 6950 to Rs. 14425 from personnel officer to Manager grade I and Rs. 5980 to Rs. 12100 from milk procurement officer to junior engineer. Besides the basic pay, the managerial cadres are being paid other components of compensation. Moreover they are also paid other perks of monetary and non-monetary benefits.

The non-managerial personnel are divided into six cadres as per their scales of pay. The highest scale of pay of non-managerial personnel is Rs. 5000 to Rs. 10,600 at the level of supervisors followed by Rs. 4190 to Rs. 8700 drawn by dairy operator up to assistant computer programmer, Rs. 3550 to Rs. 7150 from plant mechanic to senior driver, Rs. 3,290 to Rs. 6,550 from junior driver to lab assistant, Rs. 2870 to Rs. 5470 from record assistant to store attendant, Rs. 2750 to Rs. 5150 from junior typist to worker. Besides the basic pay they are also paid incentives in the form of allowances, maximum bonus, LTC and other benefits. The contingent workers are drawing consolidated pay of Rs. 1000 per month.

Bonus

The employer is required to pay a part of profits as bonus to the employees. Bonus is regarded as a deferred payment. In a way, it is assumed that it bridges the gap between the present wage the worker is getting, and the wage which he should have got (living wage). It has become a statutory obligation to the employer under the Payment of Bonus Act, 1965, to pay bonus to the employees. The Act stipulates that the quantum of bonus is determined between a minimum of 8.33 per cent (of basic wage) and a maximum of 20 per cent through negotiations between the parties. All the industrial establishments covered under this Act are required to pay a minimum of 8.33 per cent whether the company earns profit or not after the infancy period.

Bonus Payment in Dairies

Earlier both the dairies have been paying bonus to their employees. From 1985 onwards Vijaya Dairy has stopped payment of bonus due to losses whereas Sangam Dairy has continued the payment of minimum 8.33 per cent of bonus to their employees. The data of yearwise payment of bonus in Sangam Dairy since 1995-96 is presented in Table 5.2.

Table 5.2: Bonus in Sangam Dairy During 1995-2002

Year	*Payment of bonus in Rs.*
1995-96	11,65,538
1996-97	9,90,457
1997-98	11,60,507
1998-99	5,84,559
1999-00	6,12, 500
2000-01	3,15,000
2001-02	1,84,128
2002-03 (estimated)	5,50,000

The table 5.2 depicts yearwise payment of bonus from April 1995 to March 2002 in the Sangam dairy. It is observed from the table in the years 1995-96, 1997-98, there is maximum payment of bonus. Due to staff turnover there is decline in the payment of bonus in the years 2000-2001 and 2001-02. During the current year the estimated payment of bonus is Rs. 5,50,000.

The following tables analyse the perception of the respondents of both dairies.

Table 5.3: Salary Commensurate with the Qualifications and the Efforts Done by the Respondents

Response	*Frequency*	*Per cent*	*Cumulative Per cent*
Yes	179	58.7	58.7
No	126	41.3	100.0
Total	305	100.0	

The table 5.3 shows that majority of the respondents' salary is commensurate with their qualifications and their efforts put in the organisation whereas the other respondents expressed contrary opinion.

Table 5.4: Salary Compared with other Industries

Response	*Frequency*	*Per cent*	*Cumulative Per cent*
High	65	21.3	21.3
Same	174	57.0	78.4
Low	66	21.6	100.0
Total	305	100.0	

It is interesting to see from Table 5.4 that majority of the respondents perceived their salary vis-a-vis the salary in other industries as either 'high' or 'same'. The percentage of respondents under these two levels of responses constitute 78.4 per cent. Only 21.6 per cent felt that their salary is lower than their counterparts in similar industries.

Table 5.5: Salary is Sufficient to Meet Basic Requirements

Response	*Frequency*	*Per cent*	*Cumulative Per cent*
Yes	175	57.4	57.4
No	130	42.6	100.0
Total	305	100.0	

The table 5.5 shows that majority of the respondents' salary is sufficient to meet their basic requirements, whereas the remaining respondents expressed that their salary is adequate.

From table 5.6 it can be concluded that more than two-third of the respondents are not eligible for incentives/perks, whereas the rest of the respondents are eligible. Only the managerial personnel are entitled for the perks.

Table 5.6: Eligibility for Incentives/perks

Response	*Frequency*	*Per cent*	*Cumulative Per cent*
Yes	90	29.5	29.5
No	215	7C.5	100.0
Total	305	100.0	

Table 5.7: Satisfaction with Bonus Payment

Response	*Frequency*	*Per cent*	*Cumulative Per cent*
Yes	65	21.3	21.3
No	240	78.7	100.0
Total	305	100.0	

It can be inferred from table 5.7 that more than three-fourth of the respondents are not satisfied with bonus payment, whereas the rest of the respondents are satisfied. This is obvious because the Sangam Dairy pays of minimum rate of 8.33 per cent and Vijaya Dairy does not pay any bonus at all on the plea that it is incurring losses year after year.

EMPLOYEE WELFARE

The term 'labour welfare' describes a modern concept conveying a specific programme for the well-being of workers. It is assumed that, while workers are citizens, the nature of their work, the level of their wages and education, their position in the employing organisation and the demands of modern industries, put them in a peculiar position calling forth special attention. In the beginning, when machines were invented, men and women workers were required to adapt themselves to the needs of the machines. This took some time, and in the process of adjustment, workers suffered much bodily and experienced mental agony. It was slowly realised that workers were human beings and that they were more valuable than machines. The new trend is, therefore, to adjust the machines and the workers. The story of labour welfare all over the world, is a story of this adjustment—adjustment of the machines and working conditions to the human needs of workers.[20] To some extent workers themselves have made this adjustment; partly it has been brought about by legislation; and intelligent employers have voluntarily in some measure provided for this adjustment.

Employers offer welfare services and benefits to attract and retain their employees. Employee welfare offers organisational advantages such as attracting good employees, increasing employee morale, and reducing labour turnover. The benefits offered to employees often times closely conform to the compensation and welfare philosophy of the organisation.[21] However, many organisations do not get the returns of the investment they expect because employees often place a minimal value on the welfare facilities they receive. This perception may be explained in part by the management's failure to communicate adequately to employees the value of welfare services to the organisation and its workforce. It is also important to analyse the costing aspects of welfare services in terms of their affordability. Though benefit programmes are generally expensive, they are an important means toward specific organisational objectives when well-conceived.

Social Security is one of the pillars on which the structure of welfare state rests and it constitutes the hard core of social policy in most countries. It is through social security measures that the state attempts to maintain every citizen at a certain prescribed level below which no one is allowed to fall. It is "the security that society furnishes, through appropriate organisation, against certain risks to which its members are exposed".[22] These risks are, essentially, contingencies against which the individual of small means cannot effectively provide by his own ability or foresight alone. Beveridge, while explaining the purpose of social security said, "The term special security is used to denote the security of an income to take the place of earnings when they are interrupted by unemployment, sickness or accident, to provide for retirement through age, to provide for loss of support by the death of another person, and to meet an exceptional expenditure, such as those connected with birth, death, and marriage".[23] Thus, social security measures seek to relieve individuals of anxiety as to what they would do in the case of loss or stoppage of income. The feeling of confidence so gained enables them to apply themselves to work wholeheartedly.[24]

Employee Welfare Policy in Dairy Industry

Vijaya and Sangam dairies provide a comprehensive package of employee services and benefits. The policy document—Dairy Development Co-operative Federation of Andhra Pradesh states that it is the intention of the organisation to promote the well being of its employees[25] by providing a number of welfare amenities through consultation with the dairy employees unions. With every settlement the management concludes with employees unions, the scope and coverage of employee services get extended. The dairies spend considerable sums of money for promotion of the well-being of employees. It tends to look upon welfare work as a means of securing, preserving and promoting the efficiency and improving the quality of life of workforce.

Welfare amenities in the dairies can broadly be classified into two categories i.e. statutory and non-statutory welfare amenities. For convenience and for a study in detail the researcher proposes to discuss welfare amenities under the above heads.

Statutory Welfare Facilities in Dairy Industries

For every organisation to survive, it has to attend the basic needs of the workers initially i.e., food and shelter. Further in order to get more work done by them, they have to be satisfied mentally. For this purpose, the new idea of providing welfare facilities to the workers was introduced by "Robert Owen", an industrialist from Scotland. He believed that the workers' performance was influenced by the total environment of working conditions and human treatment.

The employees in India are statutorily required to comply with the provisions of various welfare amenities. As mentioned in Chapter 5 of the Factories Act, 1948, the amenities include, washing facilities, facilities for storing and drying of clothing, facilities for sitting, first-aid appliances, shelters, rest rooms and lunch rooms, canteen, crèche, supply of drinking water, provident fund, payment of gratuity, leave with pay, workmen's compensation and ESI.

Washing Facilities

The Royal Commission on Labour clearly stated that the provisions of working facilities to all employees should be there in the factory premises. The commission recommended that the employees engaged in dirty process, suitable place for washing and water should be made available compulsorily.

Section 42 of the Factories Act lays down that in every factory (a) adequate and suitable facilities for washing shall be provided and maintained for the use of workers therein (b) separate and adequately screened facilities shall be provided for the use of male and female workers, and (c) such facilities shall be conveniently accessible and shall be kept clean.

The units under study are milk processing dairies which maintain cleanliness in the premises, that necessitates the appropriate provision of washing facilities by the management. In both dairies washing facilities are provided for this purpose.

Facilities for Storing and Drying of Clothing

Section 43 of Factories Act stipulates suitable provision for keeping the clothes not worn during working hours and for drying the wet clothes. This facility requires the provision of separate rooms, pegs, lockers or other arrangements.

Strictly speaking, almost all the employees of both dairies, who are working in workshop, processing section, and engineering department require the provision of facility for storing and drying of clothes. The management of Vijaya and Sangam dairies provided this facility to the employees up to their satisfaction.

Facility for Sitting

Section 44 of the Act specifies that in every factory suitable arrangements for sitting shall be provided and maintained for all workers obliged to work in a standing position, in order that they may take advantage of any opportunities for rest which may occur in the course of their work.

The management of Vijaya and Sangam dairies provided the stools and chairs for employees for sitting purpose in processing section, workshop and engineering section wherever there is necessity to sit a while, at the same time to observe the working of the machinery.

First-aid Appliances

According to Section 45 of the Factories Act, every factory must provide and maintain first-aid boxes or cupboards equipped with the prescribed contents. The number of such boxes must be not less than one for every 150 workers and they should be kept under the charge of a responsible person who holds a certificate in first-aid treatment recognised by the state government. These should be readily accessible during all working hours. In case there are more than 500 workers, an ambulance room of the prescribed size and containing the prescribed equipment is to be provided under the charge of qualified medical and nursing staff.

The above facility is made available in both the units. In Vijaya dairy there is a qualified doctor along with nursing staff who conduct medical check up for the employees once in every six months, it is observed that the management has also provided ambulance as required under the provisions of the Act. It is noticed that the Sangam Dairy has provided first-aid room and the ambulance van in addition to the qualified doctor and compounder. The doctor is available during the working hours from 10.30 AM to 5.00 PM on par with the timings of the administrative staff. On an average daily 25 employees consult the doctor for various complaints mostly for purpose of insurance claims. There is also provision for the reimbursement of medical bills in certain cases.

Shelters, Rest Rooms and Lunch Rooms

According to Section 47 of the Factories Act, every factory employing more than 150 workers must provide adequate and suitable shelters or rest rooms and a lunch room with provision for drinking water where workers can eat meals brought by them. But, in case a canteen is maintained, it will be regarded as part of this requirement.

Both the dairies under study are maintaining canteens for the benefits of employees and hence these units need not provide separate lunch rooms for their employees. At Vijaya and Sangam dairies shelters and rest rooms are provided with all facilities.

In Sangam Dairy the employees usually have their lunch in rest rooms whereas in Vijaya Dairy the rest rooms are provided with 29 beds. Moreover in every department there are rest rooms with cloak room facility to keep their belongings.

Canteen

The Labour Investigation Committee[26] of 1946 has emphasised the role of canteen in providing benefits to workers from the point of view of health, efficiency and well being. The canteens, provided by the employers, can provide nutritious items to the workers at lower prices and help the workers maintain and improve the efficiency. As such, canteen movement must be accepted by the state as a definite change and the running of canteens must be accepted by the employers as a national investment.[27] Recognising the importance of the canteen in India the government of India has made it a legal binding on the employers to provide the canteen facility in any specified factory where in more than 250 employees are ordinarily employed.

The labour investigation committee[28] was very clear in stating the objectives that must be pursued by a canteen of the industrial establishment. These were to introduce an element of nutritional balance into otherwise deficient unbalanced diet element of the worker, to provide cheap and clean food and an opportunity to relax in comfort near the place of work, to save time and trouble to workers on account of exhausting journey to and from work after long hours in the factory.

Canteen Management in Vijaya and Sangam Dairies

Both the dairies are running the canteen on 'no profit no loss' basis. In Vijaya dairy the canteen is maintained and administered by management by constituting a committee with equal representation of workers and management. Whereas in Sangam dairy the canteen is maintained by the two existing trade unions on rotation basis, each maintaining the canteen for a period of six months. In Vijaya dairy the purchase, preparation, and sales are supervised by canteen committee representatives whereas in Sangam dairy the above supervision is done by trade union representatives. The canteens of both the dairies are subsidised by the managements. The monthly expenditure on subsidy for the canteens in Vijaya and Sangam dairies are Rs. 70,000 and Rs. 42,500 respectively.

Canteen Working Hours

The canteen working hours in both dairies are presented in table.

Table 5.8: Canteen Timings

Sl.No.	*Timings*	
	Vijaya	*Sangam*
1.	7.00 A.M - 9.00 A.M	7.00 A.M - 8.15 A.M
2.	10.00 A.M - 11.00 A.M	-
3.	12.30 P.M - 1.30 P.M (Lunch)	1.00 P.M - 2.00 P.M (Lunch)
4.	-	3.30 P.M - 4.30 P.M
5.	-	7.00 P.M - 8.00 P.M
6.	-	0.00 A.M - 2.00 A.M

The table 5.8 reveals that the working hours of the canteens in both the dairies are not uniform. The Sangam dairy canteen works round the clock to provide canteen service to the employees in the three shifts. Whereas in Vijaya dairy the canteen works in the morning from 7 A.M to 1.30 P.M. Though the Vijaya dairy works in three shifts, the canteen facility is not available for the employees working in other timings. But employees who work in the night shifts are supplied with tea free of cost.

Canteen Items and Prices

The canteen items and prices for both the dairies are presented in table 5.9.

It is observed from table 5.9 that canteen items and prices in both the dairies are similar in certain respects and also vary in some other respects. The prices of canteen items in both the dairies vary except in respect of tea and coffee. The tiffin items in Sangam dairy range between 0.50 paise to 75 paise whereas in Vijaya dairy there is uniform price of 0.75 paise for all the Tiffin items except the oil items, which cost 0.40 paise. The price of the sweet items vary from 0.60 paise in Vijaya to 1.00 rupee in Sangam dairy. It may be mentioned here that if the rates in the canteens are compared with that of local hotels, they are much cheaper.

Table 5.9: Canteen Menu

Sl.No	*Items*	*Price for Employees in Rs. Ps.*		*Price for students and security Guards in Rs. Ps*
		Vijaya	*Sangam*	*Sangam*
1.	Meals (400) gm	3.00	3.00	8.00
2.	Meals (500) gm	-	4.00	10.00
3.	Idly	0.75	0.50	1.50
4.	Upma	0.75	0.50	1.50
5.	Tomato bath	0.75	0.75	2.50
6.	Dosa	0.40	0.75	2.50
7.	Chapathi	0.40	0.75	2.50
8.	Puri	0.40	0.75	2.50
9.	Gare	0.40	0.75	2.50
10.	Vada	0.40	0.75	2.50
11.	Sweet	0.60	1.00	2.50
12.	Mixture	-	0.75	2.50
13.	Coffee	0.75	0.75	2.50
14.	Tea	0.50	0.50	1.00

The table 5.10 shows yearwise canteen subsidy of the two dairies under study.

Table 5.10: Canteen Subsidy Yearwise from 1995 to 2002

Year	*Amount in Rs.*	
	Vijaya dairy	*Sangam dairy*
1995-96	-	4,23,726
1996-97	9,28,409.70	4,17,374
1997-98	9,27,642.55	4,30,618
1998-99	8,68,560.85	4,07,979
1999-2000	6,87,672.05	4,68,985
2000-01	6,70,415.55	5,14,275
2001-02	3,23,610.10	5,56,870

As revealed from table 5.10 year wise expenditure on canteen subsidy is shown in the table. In respect of Vijaya dairy, the data is not available for the years, i.e. 1995-96, regarding the expenditure of canteen subsidy. There is increase in the expenditure on canteen subsidy in Sangam dairy from Rs. 4,23,726 during 1995-96 to Rs. 5,56,870 during 2001-02. The expenditure on canteen subsidy in Vijaya dairy decreased from Rs. 9,28,409.70 during 1996-97 to Rs. 3,23,610.10 during 2001-2002. The decrease in expenditure may be due to the introduction of VRS.

Creche

Section 48 of the Factories Act, 1948 says that wherein more than 30 women workers are ordinarily employed, they shall be provided with a crèche for the use of children of working women employees below the age of six years.

It is noticed that in both dairy units, employees have children above 6 years age and hence the creche facility is not availed by the women employees.

Welfare Officer

Section 49 of the Factories Act, 1948 stipulates that in every factory wherein 500 or more workers are ordinarily employed, the employer shall employ welfare officer.

As the number of workers employed is more than 500 in the daries under study, welfare officer is to be appointed. It is observed that since 1995 onwards welfare officer's post is vacant. In both the daries a senior person of the Personnel and Administration Department looks after the duties of the welfare officer.

Leave with Pay

The dairy units framed leave rules similar to the state government employees, which are applicable to different categories of its employees. A close examination of leave facilities reveals that they are more beneficial than it is required under the provisions of the Factories Act.

Leave Facilities for Office Staff

The existing leave facilities for the office staff in both the dairies include casual leave (15), optional holidays (5), earned leave (30 out of which 15 can be encashed), medical leave (20 half pay leave). Festival holidays and national holidays can also be availed as per the Act.

Leave Facilities for Production and Field Staff

The production and field staff are entitled for 30 casual leave in addition to weekly off. But the public holidays are not allowed for them. They have similar leave facilities in respect of earned leave, medical leave as in the case of office staff.

Earned leave encashment is allowed for the employees of both dairies twice in a year, i.e January 1st and July 1st every year. In Sangam dairy the employees working in any four declared festival holidays will be paid double the wages.

The table 5.11 shows year-wise expenditure on earned leave encashment in both the dairies.

Table 5.11: Earned Leave Encashment from 1995 to 2002

Year	*Amount in Rs.*	
	Vijaya dairy	*Sangam dairy*
1995-96	-	11,87,589
1996-97	44,49,274	15,47,361
1997-98	39,50,967	17,88,823
1998-99	42,58,022	20,54,870
1999-2000	86,38,603.50	23,62,402
2000-01	61,54,804	31,35,856
2001-02	60,63,051	43,92,421

As shown in table 5.11 the expenditure in Sangam dairy has increased from Rs. 11,87,589 during 1995-96 to Rs. 43,92,421 during 2001-02. In Vijaya dairy the expenditure has increased from Rs. 44,49,274 during 1996-97 to

Rs. 60,63,051 during 2001-02. The Vijaya dairy incurred more expenditure in all years on earned leave encashment when compared to Sangam dairy because of more manpower strength.

Drinking Water Facilities

As per the statutory provisions of the Factories Act, the management is providing its employees with drinking water facilities at suitable places. Cool water is also provided through water coolers. It is observed that these water facilities are kept near the working place, urinals, latrines, spittoons and wherever necessary. The location of water points is found to be convenient and in conformity with the provisions of the Act.

Employee Provident Fund

All the employees of both the dairies are covered under Employees Provident Fund Act, 1952. The organisations deduct 10 per cent of the monthly salary of their employees towards Fund. The organisation contributes a matching amount towards Employee Provident Fund as per the Act. The employees contribution towards Provident Fund is

Table 5.12: Management Contribution to Provident Fund Account

Year	*Amount in Rs.*	
	Vijaya dairy	*Sangam dairy*
1995-96	-	41,95,983
1996-97	51,07,836.00	44,05,867
1997-98	59,25,154.00	56,44,358
1998-99	70,94,895.70	71,59,728
1999-00	88,35,653.70	88,90,891
2000-01	90,84,404.00	1,11,06,429
2001-02	1,06,61,681.00	1,12,77,525

Source: Compiled from the annual reports of Vijaya and Sangam dairies.

limited up to the pay of Rs. 2,500 even if the employee draws more than Rs. 2,500.

Table 5.12 shows the yearwise expenditure on account of managements contribution to provident fund account of its employees during 1995-96 to 2001-2002.

The table 5.12 shows yearwise expenditure of managements contribution to the provident fund account in both the dairies. The Vijaya dairy data is available from 1996-97 to 2001-02. In Vijaya dairy the expenditure is increased from Rs. 51,07,836.00 (1996-97) to Rs. 1,06,61,681 (2001-02). In Sangam dairy the expenditure has increased from Rs. 41,95,983 (1995-96) to Rs. 1,12,77,525 (2001-02).

Deposit Linked Insurance Scheme

As part of Provident Fund Act, deposit linked insurance scheme was introduced by the government in 1976. The main purpose of the scheme is to extend financial help to the legal heirs of the deceased employee. The legal heirs get a maximum amount of Rs. 10,000 under this scheme. The management is contributing 0.06 per cent of

Table 5.13: Management's Contribution under the Deposit Linked Insurance Scheme During 1995 to 2002

Year	*Amount in Rs.*	
	Vijaya dairy	*Sangam dairy*
1995-96	-	2,14,622.00
1996-97	57,914.50	2,02,746.00
1997-98	1,92,672.40	1,83,419.00
1998-99	3,43,613.25	2,10,356.00
1999-00	1,78,621.50	2,04,527.00
2000-01	2,74,003.00	3,19,609.00
2001-02	9,44,061.00	3,54,702.00

Source: Compiled from the annual reports of Vijaya and Sangam dairies.

the wages of every employee to the provident fund scheme every month.

The deposit linked insurance scheme is applicable to both the dairies under study. In the event of death of the employee, the managements of Vijaya and Sangam dairies arranged to pay immediately to the legal heirs of the deceased Rs. 30,000 and Rs. 62,000 respectively. The management of Sangam dairy is incurring an expenditure of rupees 4 lakhs per year on the scheme.

The table 5.13 shows yearwise management's contribution under the deposit linked insurance schemes of the two dairies. The Vijaya dairy data is available from 1996-97 to 2001-02. The expenditure under this head has increased from Rs. 57,914.50 (1996-97) to Rs. 9,44,061 (2001-02). In Sangam dairy the expenditure on this account has increased from Rs. 2,14,622 (1995-96) to Rs. 3,54,702 (2001-02).

Gratuity

Gratuity is paid at the time of separation of an employee from the company on account of retirement, death or discharge at the rate of 15 days wages for every

Table 5.14: Yearwise Payment of Gratuity from 1995 to 2002

Year	*Amount in Rs.*	
	Vijaya dairy	*Sangam dairy*
1995-96	-	12,36,357
1996-97	29,36,581	14,47,082
1997-98	28,70,976	15,50,951
1998-99	1,29,44,798	21,75,564
1999-00	98,26,324	16,66,616
2000-01	1,19,91,858	64,05,180
2001-02	67,61,534	1,09,37,116

Source: Office records of personnel and administration department of Vijaya and Sangam Dairies.

completed year of service (for calculation, the last month pay is taken into account).

In both the industries, the employees who render a minimum of 5 years service are eligible for gratuity. In case of death or employment injury the minimum 5 years service is not applicable. The maximum amount of gratuity is Rs. 1,00,000. Gratuity is calculated by pay + dearness allowance × 15/25 × number of years completed. The employees are given the wages of 15 days as gratuity per every completed year of service. The gratuity is applicable to the employees till they attain retirement i.e., 58 years; for the lowest cadre workers it is applicable till they attain 60 years.

The table 5.14 shows yearwise payments of gratuity by the two dairies. In Vijaya dairy the available data reveals that there is increase in the expenditure from Rs. 29,36,581 (1996-97) to Rs. 67,61,534 (2001-02). In Sangam dairy the expenditure is increased from Rs. 12,36,357 (1995-96) to Rs. 1,09,37,116 (2001-02).

Workmen's Compensation

When an employee meets with an employment injury arising out of and in the course of employment, he will be attended by medical officer immediately and will be shifted to hospital. If the injury is of serious nature, he will be granted disablement leave till he resumes duty. He will be paid at the rate of 100 per cent of his salary if he takes treatment as out-patient. After completion of treatment, his loss of earning capacity will be assessed by a medical board and he will be paid compensation amount worked out according to his loss of earning capacity.

In case of fatal accident, compensation will be paid to the dependents of the deceased employee as per the provisions of ESI Act irrespective of whether they crossed wage limit of ESI provisions. In case of non-managerial personnel who meet with employment injury, compensation is paid as per the provisions of Workmen's Compensation Act.

The amount of compensation paid to the employees by the Sangam dairy during the period 1995-96 to 2002 is provided in table 5.15.

Table 5.15: Compensation Paid to the Employee under the Workmen's Compensation Act during 1995-96 to 2002

Year	*Amount of Compensation paid in Rs.*
1995-96	-
1996-97	57,186
1997-98	52,826
1998-99	-
1999-00	1,73,602
2000-01	-
2001-02	-

The table 5.15 depicts year-wise expenditure for compensation payment to the employees under the Workmen Compensation Act. The compensation payment showed an increase from Rs. 57,186 (1996-97) to Rs. 1,73,602 (1999-2000). It is observed from the table during the years 1995-96, 1998-99, 2000-01 and 2001-2002 there seem to be no accidents since compensation payment was not shown against these years.

The table 5.16 presents yearwise payment of compensation to the deceased employees.

The table 5.16 reveals yearwise expenditure on compensation payment to the deceased employees by the two dairies. Vijaya dairy showed an increase in the expenditure from Rs. 4,13,233 (1996-97) to Rs. 9,35,468 (2001-02). In Sangam dairy the expenditure on this account decreased from Rs. 2,67,386 (1996-97) to Rs. 20,000 (2001-02) and it is further reduced to Rs. 10,000 during 1999-2000. It appears that number of deaths are minimum during the years 1999-2000 and 2001-02.

Table 5.16: Compensation to the Deceased Employees 1995-96 to 2002

Year	*Vijaya Dairy*	*Sangam Dairy*
1996-97	4,13,233	2,67,386
1997-98	1,90,748	3,19,865
1998-99	4,28,867	2,16,252
1999-00	2,74,541	10,000
2000-01	5,38,238	2,36,340
2001-02	9,35,468	20,000

Employees State Insurance

The ESI Act, 1948 encompasses certain health related eventualities that the workers are generally exposed to; such as sickness, maternity, temporary or permanent disablement, occupational disease or death due to employment injury, resulting in loss of wages or earning capacity—total or partial. Social security provisions made in the Act to counterbalance or negate the resulting physical or financial distress in such contingencies, are thus, aimed at upholding human dignity in times of crises through protection from deprivation, destitution and social degradation while enabling the society the retention and continuity of a socially useful and productive manpower.

The ESI scheme is based on the principle of 'pooling of risks and resources' in which every contributor, at any given point of time, emerges as a beneficiary or a benefactor and society at large is the net gainer. Employees, employers, State Govts. and the Corporation are the major stake holders in the system of organised and coordinated effort providing social protection to beneficiaries. The role of employers, in particular remains pivotal to the success of the scheme, be it surveys for coverage, implementation, registration of factories/ establishments, registration of employees, regular payment of contribution, facilitating inspections and timely action to ensure steady flow of benefits to the employees.

Coverage

The ESI Act, 1948 in the first instance, applies to non-seasonal factories using power in the manufacturing process and employing 10 or more persons and non-power using factories or establishments employing 20 or more persons for wages. The provisions of the Act are being implemented areawise by stages. The Act contains enabling provision under which the "appropriate government" is empowered to extend the provisions of the Act to other classes of establishments—industrial, commercial, agricultural or otherwise. Under these provisions most of the state governments have extended the provisions of the ESI Act to the establishments such as shops, hotels, restaurants, cinemas, motor transport agencies (employing 20 or more employees), power using beedi manufacturing units (employing 10 or more employees), state pencil manufacturing units etc.

The scheme has so far been implemented in 22 states and some union territories; the exceptions being a few states in the north-eastern region of the country

Employees of the aforesaid factories and establishments in receipt of wages not exceeding Rs. 6,500 P.M. are covered under the Act. By the end of March 2001, about 2,35,000 factories and establishments at about 680 industrial centers had been brought under the coverage of the ESI Act benefiting about 87 lakh insured persons and their dependent family members.[29]

The scheme is primarily funded by contributions raised from insured employees of covered factories and establishments and their employers in the implemented areas as a small but specified percentage of wages payable to such employees.

The rates of contribution were last revised by the Corporation from 1st January, 1997 and are still in vogue. These rates of contribution are:

1.	Employee's Contribution	- 1.75 per cent of the wages
2.	Employer's Contribution	- 4.75 per cent of the wages
	Total	- 6.50 per cent of the wages

Employees in receipt of an average daily wage of Rs. 40 or less, are exempted from payment of their share of contribution (w.e.f. 8.4.2000) but are entitled to all social security benefits under the scheme.

The state governments, as per provisions of the Act, contribute 1.5 per cent of expenditure on medical care on ESI beneficiaries in their respective states within the ceiling of Rs. 600 per insured person family unit per annum. Any expenditure over and above this ceiling is borne entirely by the state governments.

The contributions paid by employees and employers are deposited in a common pool known as the ESI fund that is utilised for payment of cash benefits to the insured persons and their dependents as well as for providing medical facilities to the beneficiaries. The administrative and other expenses of the corporation are also met from this fund.

Benefits to Employees

Under the ESI scheme the comprehensive and the need-based package of major social security benefits in cash and kind include

1. Medical Benefit - for self and dependents
2. Sickness Benefit - for self
3. Maternity Benefit - for self
4. Disablement Benefit
   - *(a)* Temporary Disablement Benefit - for self
   - *(b)* Permanent Disablement Benefit - for self
5. Dependents' Benefit - for dependants in case of death due to employment injury.

In addition, the scheme also provides benefits to insured workers. These are;

- *(i)* Funeral expenses – for self
- *(ii)* Rehabilitation allowance – for self

(*iii*) Vocational Rehabilitation – for self

(*iv*) Old age medicare – for self and spouse

(*v*) Medical bonus – for insured women and insured Persons wife

An interesting feature of the ESI scheme is that the contributions are related to the paying capacity as a fixed percentage of the employees wages, whereas social security benefits are provided according to entitlement without any distinction of class or status. Medical benefit is provided at uniform scale from day one of entering insurable employment.

The details of various benefits in cash, and kind that the insured persons or their dependants are entitled to are given in the succeeding pages.

The table 5.17 shows the yearwise expenditure on ESI facilities to Vijaya Dairy Employees.

Table 5.17: ESI

Year	*Expenditure Rs.*
1996-97	1,01,865.65
1997-98	69,770.65
1998-99	47,470.50
1999-00	40,995.50
2000-01	1,47,846.40
2001-02	3,23,320.37

The table 5.17 shows yearwise expenditure on ESI in Vijaya dairy. The expenditure has increased from Rs. 1,01,865.65 (1996-97) to Rs. 3,23,320.37 (2001-02).

Non-statutory Welfare Measures in Dairy Industry

Housing

Among the basic necessities of life, housing is very significant that comes next to food and clothing. Housing

Esi Benefits in Vijaya Dairy

Sl.No	*Benefit*	*Contributory conditions*	*Duration*	*Rate*
1.	*(a)* Sickness Benefit	Payment for at least 78 days in the relevant contribution period	91 days in any two consecutive benefit periods	Standard benefit rate (not less than 50 per cent of wages)
	(b) Extended sickness benefit for 34 specified long term diseases	Continuous employment for a period of two years and payment of contribution for at least 156 days in four contribution periods.	309 days duration has been extended beyond 400 day (91 days S.B. plus 309 days E.S.B.) to two years in deserving cases duly certified by a Medical Board	140 per cent of the standard benefit rate (But not less than 70% of the wages)
	(c) Enhanced Sickness Benefit (for undergoing sterilisation operation for family welfare).	Same as for Sickness Benefit at (a) above.	7 days for Vasectomy and 14 days for tubectomy extendable in cases of post-operative complication etc.	Twice the standard benefit rate but not less than full wages.

(Contd...)

Sl.No	*Benefit*	*Contributory conditions*	*Duration*	*Rate*
2.	Disablement Benefit (Employment injury or occupational disease)			
	(a) Temporary Disablement Benefit	No condition	Till the incapacity lasts	140 per cent of the standard sickness benefit rate (But not less than 70%) of the wages
	(b) Permanent Disablement	No condition	For life	Up to 140 per cent of the standard sickness benefit rate. Actual amount depends upon the loss of earning capacity of the worker as may be determined by a Medical Board
3.	Dependents' Benefit (for death due to employment injury or occupational disease)	No condition	To widow/widows for life or until re marriage. To legitimate or adopted son and to legitimate or adopted un-married daughter till age of 18 years to legitimate infirm son and to legitimate adopted son or adopted unmarried infirm daughter till infirmity lasts	140 per cent of the standard sickness benefit rate but not less than 70 per cent of the wages to be divided among the dependents in the prescribed ratio.

Sl.No	Benefit	Contributory conditions	Duration	Rate
4.	Maternity Benefit	Payment of contribution for 70 days in immediately preceding two consecutive contribution periods.	12 weeks of which not more than six can precede the expected date of confinement; 6 weeks for miscarriage and additional one month for sickness arising out of pregnancy related confinement, premature birth of child or miscarriage.	Double the standard benefit rate (not less than full wages)
5.	Medical Benefit	No condition (insured person and his family is eligible from the date of entry of insured person into insurable employment).	To start with for a period of 3 months or till the spell of treatment lasts whichever is later and thereafter based on payment of contribution	Full medical care (all) facilities including hospitalisation for insured persons and members of their family.

(Contd...)

Sl.No	*Benefit*	*Contributory conditions*	*Duration*	*Rate*
6.	Other Benefits			
	(a) Funeral Expenses	No condition (i.e. merely by virtue of being an insured person).		Actual expenditure on funeral not exceeding Rs. 2500 w.e.f. 1.10.2000
	(b) Rehabilitation allowance	No condition	For each day on which insured person remains admitted in Artificial Limb Centre for fixation/repair or replacement of artificial limb.	Double the standard sickness benefit rate but not less than full wages
	(c) Vocational and rehabilitation	Insurable employment upto 40 per cent permanent disablement and below 45 years age.	Till such training lasts at a recognised centre/institute	—
	(d) Medical benefit to retired and disabled insured persons	On payment @ of Rs. 10 per month in lumpsum for one year in advance	—	

Sl.No	Benefit	Contributory conditions	Duration	Rate
		(i) to insured persons who leave insurable employment on attaining the age of superannuation after being insured for not less than five years	Period for which contribution is paid	Full medical care for self and spouse only
		(ii) to insured persons who cease to be in insurable employment on account of permanent disablement due to an employment injury.	Period for which contribution is paid till attaining the age of superannuation.	Full medical care for self and spouse only.
	(e) Medical bonus	No condition other than insurable employment of self /spouse	Rs. 250 is paid as a lumpsum grant towards confinement expenses to an insured woman, wife of insured person.	At places where necessary medical facilities are not available under the ESI scheme.

(Contd...)

being a basic necessity, as also rightly pointed out by the committee on labour welfare, needs a very high priority in any scheme of national planning and industrial development. In developing countries like India, housing has been a social problem affecting all sections of population in some way or other. Since the health and efficiency of factory workers are affected by the type of houses they live in, inadequate and poor quality of housing, development of slums around the industrial areas are considered to be the attendant evils of industrialisation. The Royal Commission on Labour also remarked that the inadequate and poor quality of housing is the bane of urban industrial life. It further commented that in every industrial country. the problems associated with the housing of the working classes have increased as industry has developed and India is not an exception to that rule.[30] The labour investigation committee which reviewed the housing conditions in various urban areas of India felt that a clear long-term housing policy was essential for improving housing conditions of industrial workers.[31] In spite of several schemes, housing continues to be a problem because of industrialisation, urbanisation and migration. The capacity of workers has been limited to raise resources to solve this problem by themselves. As such, employers have got a role to play in providing housing facilities to their workers on their own accord. Further, the role of co-operative societies in providing houses to their member workers has helped them in a marginal way.

Housing at Vijaya Dairy

In view of the importance of housing accommodation to the employees Vijaya dairy has provided 98 quarters nearer to the dairy. For others who do not reside in the quarters 20 per cent of pay is paid as house rent allowance.

The table 5.18 indicates that type A quarter is meant for general manager. Officers are accommodated in B type quarters whereas junior managers are provided with C type quarters. Type D and E are allotted to workmen.

Table 5.18: Cadrewise Allotment of Quarters

Sl.No.	*Cadre*	*Type*
1.	General Manager	A
2.	Officers	B
3.	Junior Managers	C
4.	Workers	D & E

Housing loans are given to the employees who completed 5 years of service. The amount of loan is about 70 per cent of the basic pay and D.A. The loan is recovered in installments after completing the construction for which 9 per cent interest is charged.

Housing at Sangam

Management provided sixty-four quarters to the essential staff i.e. electricians, dairy engineers, production manager and administration staff etc. The particulars of the quarters are given in the table 5.19.

Table 5.19: Type of Quarters

Quarter Type	*Allotted to*	*No. of quarters*	*Nominal rent charged in Rs.*
A	Grade I officers	4	228.00
B	Grade II officers (Dairy Managers, Assistant managers, Dairy engineers, Assistant dairy engineers etc)	4	96.00
C	Supervisory cadre	16	82.00
D	Workers cadre	40	53.00

The quarters are classified into four types i.e. A, B, C, D. There are four A type quarters which are allotted to grade I officers, four B grade quarters allotted to type II officers, (Dairy managers, Assistant dairy managers, Dairy engineers and assistant dairy engineers), sixteen C type quarters allotted to supervisory cadre and forty D type quarters allotted to workers cadre.

The rent is fixed according to the type of quarter. i.e. Rs. 228 for A type, Rs. 96 for B type, Rs. 82 for C type and Rs. 53 for D type.

For the workers who do not have quarters facility, house rent allowance is paid to them. For employees coming from Tenali and surrounding areas 12.5 per cent of their basic pay is paid as house rent allowance. The employees coming from Guntur are entitled for 20 per cent of the basic pay as house rent allowance. In addition, the employees are paid conveyance of Rs. 150 per month.

Transport

The provision of adequate and cheap transport facilities to industrial workers residing at long distances from the place of their work is essential as such facilities relieve the workers from the strain and anxiety and provide relief and relaxation and reduce late arrival and absenteeism.

The importance of the transport facilities in a developing country like India hardly needs any emphasis in view of several factors such as the remoteness of industrial areas from the main centres of working population, growing urbanisation and growing tempo of industrialisation coupled with dispersal of industries. Transport is particularly a necessity to these workers who work in shifts and leave for home at odd hours when public transport facilities are not available. The study reveals that both the dairies do not provide transport facilities but they pay transport allowance of Rs. 40 to their employees.

Medical Facilities

The protection of health must be accorded a prime place because any unhealthy worker will become a chronic absentee and thus earns less which eventually will lead to low morale. As such, health of the worker is a matter of importance not only to the worker himself but to the employer as well as the state. A healthy worker is a better adjusted worker and will contribute to the efficiency and productivity of the organisation.[32]

In India, it is very necessary that the employers and the state should provide adequate facilities both in the form of preventive as well as curative measures so as to help the workers maintain good health. In India, the problems of health are more serious because of low income leading to malnutrition and living in slums exposing the workers to many infections.

As such, the programmes of health of industrial workers should be comprehensive and should include, according to National Commission on Labour,[33] measures for contributing to the establishment and maintenance of the highest possible degree of physical and mental well being.

Medical Facilities at Sample Units

An enquiry into various medical amenities provided by the two sample units has been made. This benefit is available in Vijaya dairy to an insured person which comprises free medical treatment in the case of sickness, maternity and any employment injury. The medical treatment is available in the ESI dispensary.

In Sangam dairy there is one MBBS lady doctor presently working on deputation from government. She is assisted by one compounder and one ambulance is also provided to the dispensary. If the employees suffer from major deceases like paralysis, cancer, heart and kidney diseases, the management provides financial assistance of Rs. 1,90,000. In case of accidents 'on duty' the organisation bears the entire expenditure for the treatment of injured employee and provide special leave to him. In case of accidental death of the employee 'on or off duty' the management grants Rs. 50,000 to the dependents of deceased employee.

The table 5.20 shows the year-wise medical expenditure of both dairies.

Table 5.20: Medical Expenses of the Dairies under Study during 1995 to 2002

Year	*Expenditure incurred in Rs.*	
	Vijaya dairy	*Sangam dairy*
1995-96	-	6,381
1996-97	8,37,283.50	57,051
1997-98	8,82,494.00	1,30,068
1998-99	8,67,982.00	3,880
1999-00	9,31,556.75	10,000
2000-01	9,53,825.95	-
2001-02	9,85,162.65	5,726

In Vijaya dairy the expenditure has increased from Rs. 8,37,283.50 (1996-97) to Rs. 9,85,162.65 (2001-02). The Sangam dairy showed the minimum expenditure of Rs. 3,880 during 1998-99 and the maximum expenditure of Rs. 1,30,068 during 1997-98. The Sangam dairy did not incur any expenditure under this head during 2000-01.

Medi-claim Insurance

This scheme was introduced by the Sangam dairy in 1998. Medical insurance presently known as 'medi claim' provides Rs. 50,000 coverage to employees and his wife and two children.

Out of Rs. 50,000 for the first Rs. 25,000 employee should bear 25 per cent and for the other Rs. 25,000 the employee should bear 10 per cent and for rest of entire amount insurance company gives the claim.

Yearwise expenditure on medi-claim insurance is presented in table 5.21.

As revealed from table 5.21 the expenditure on medi-claim increased from Rs. 8,35,174 (1999-2000) to 12,50,000 during 2001-02.

Table 5.21: Medi-claim Insurance

Year	Expenditure in Rs.
1999-00	8,35,174
2000-01	8,35,174
2001-02	12,50,000

Consumers' Co-operative Stores

The consumers' cooperative stores is of immense help to the workers if it functions properly. It eliminates the middlemen and can provide necessarily consumable articles at lower prices and help the workers to improve their standard of living. These stores can also distribute essential commodities maintaining the quality by preventing adulteration.

The co-operative stores can also indirectly help in changing the outlook of the workers by making them come out of self-centred to group centred activities. Such change in outlook may induce the workers to undertake many other common activities leading to mutual benefits. However, if trade unions could also educate their members about the necessity and benefits from such co-operative ventures, more cooperative activities could take place among the industrial workers.[34]

Functioning of Consumers' Co-operative Stores at Sample Units

Sangam dairy employees' mutually aided consumers co-operative stores limited has been established on 14th December, 1998. The promoter of this stores is Chandrasekhar who is the president in Bharat Dairy Mazdoor Sangam. The employees of Sangam dairy did not want to depend on the management for financial support. Hence they established the stores with a capital of Rs. 1,30,000 by raising contributions of Rs. 1,000 as share capital for each member. Now the membership is raised up to 350. During 2000-01 the society gave airbags worth of Rs. 150 to their share-holders as a dividend. The items are purchased from Tenali and Guntur. The stores is supplying kirana and fancy items to its members. The annual turnover of the stores is Rs. 9 lakhs. The sales are being made on cash or credit basis. If the sales are made on credit basis they deduct such amounts from the salaries. The management provided a room free of rent and electricity charges for accommodating the stores by the side of canteen. The sales are allowed for outsiders also. It collects eight to ten per cent profit on food items and four per cent profit on fancy items.

The main aim of stores is to maintain all the items including chappals, clothing, gas and dewali items etc. which are needed by the employees. It is proposed to serve items required for the canteen. The new members have to pay Rs. 100 as membership fees and Rs. 1000 as share capital.

The stores was registered with No. AMC/GNT/DCO/1998/435. The stores works from 9 AM to 7 PM. One joint committee was constituted with ten members from the trade union leaders and directors of the dairy. Every year two directors will become members on rotation basis. The Vijaya dairy is not maintaining any co-operative stores as observed from the study.

Co-operative Credit Societies

It is well known that most of the industrial workers in India suffer from indebtedness. It is shocking to know that the two-thirds of workers in the organisations are in debt and the extent of debt generally exceeds three months wages.[35] Not only are they unable to pay principal amount borrowed, but higher rates of interest at which they borrow has snow falling effect. This makes it impossible for workers to come out of the clutches of money-lenders, sometimes, finding himself in hopeless drinking and other illicit activities to forget his wrenched condition. It is obvious that unless the root cause of these undesirable liability i.e., indebtedness is removed, the economic well being of the industrial worker cannot improve.

It is in this connection that co-operative credit society among industrial workers can help them in meeting some of their urgent but heavy expenses without resorting to exploitative sources.

A worker who is obsessed with the problems of repayment can be hardly expected to be creative and efficient worker. Therefore, the employers must think of the ways and means of elimination of the indebtedness and encourage and help the formation and in the smooth running, of the credit societies. The central banking enquiry committee asserted that Employees, in their own interests, should pay greater attention to the provision of credit facilities for the employees and also should take active part in the supervision of societies started for their benefits.[36]

Co-operative Credit Society at Vijaya Dairy

Every employee who is a member of society can get Rs. 40,000 loan with a minimum interest. The maximum loan facility is Rs. 45,000 depending upon the pay drawing capacity of the members. Maximum number of employees who are members in the society are benefited by this loan facility.

Co-operative Credit Society at Sangam Dairy

Sangam Dairy Credit Society was established in the year 1987 with Regd. No. 510. The society collects Rs. 50 as thrift amount from the members. Presently the credit society has 314 members. It collects deposits from all the members. It gives 9.5 per cent cumulative interest on the deposits for every six months. Presently the deposits under the society amount to Rs. 18 lakhs. It gives loan for members and also for the fixed deposit holders at the rate of 10.5 per cent interest. The amount of loan depends upon their basic salaries subject to the maximum of Rs. 40 thousand. The management recovers the loan by way of deduction from the salaries and the deducted amount is sent to the society. So far the society has given loans to the members to the extent of Rs. 23 lakhs. The society, keeping 10 per cent of the deposits as share capital gives the remaining amount as loans.

The perception of the employees regarding cooperative awareness, participation and functioning is analysed in tables 5.22, 5.23 and 5.24.

Table 5.22: Co-Operative Awareness

Response	*Frequency*	*Per cent*	*Cumulative Per cent*
Yes	142	46.6	46.61
No	163	53.4	100.0
Total	305	100.0	

Table 5.22 shows that majority of the respondents do not have awareness about co-operative societies while the other respondents have awareness about the co-operative societies.

Table 5.23: Participation in Co-operative Societies Activities

Response	*Frequency*	*Per cent*	*Cumulative Per cent*
Yes	53	17.4	17.4
No	252	82.6	100.0
Total	305	100.0	

From table 5.23 it can be seen that most of the respondents did not participate in the co-operative societies activities whereas the rest of the respondents participated.

Table 5.24: Co-operative Functioning

Response	*Frequency*	*Per cent*	*Cumulative Per cent*
Good	67	22.0	22.0
Average	60	19.7	41.6
Poor	178	58.4	100.01
Total	305	100.0	

Table 5.24 reveals responses on co-operative functioning of the respondents. Majority of the respondents' response is 'poor' and another one-fifth of the respondents'

response is 'average'. The other 22 per cent of the respondents' response is 'good' on the said statement.

Workers Education

Education is the means to sharpen one's capacities and to channelise them into more creative direction. Increased awareness provides information regarding more alternatives and improves reasoning through education and helps in making better choice. As such an educated worker can make a better decision, understand quickly and imbibe the requisites of the job quickly. As such the importance of education for workers can never be overemphasised. However, no measures were evolved till many years after the independence to take up the workers education. No concrete steps were taken by government or employees or for that matter most of the unions to educate and enlighten the workers for a long time. This apathy continued for some years even after independence.[37]

There was hardly a committee on labour which did not emphasis the importance and the necessity of educating the workers in India. The Royal Commission on Labour very succinctly brought out the importance of education of workers in the following words.

Modern machine industry depends in peculiar degree on education, and the attempts to build it up with an illiterate body of workers must be difficult and perilous. We should emphasize the fact precisely, because of the importance of education industrial labour should receive special attention.[38]

Workers educational programme is not well organised in both dairies. Unit level classes are conducted in the organisation as part of workers education programme. Worker teachers are trained at the regional levels. Some refresher classes are also conducted.

Education for Employees

Employees who are sponsored by both the dairies for higher studies will be given special leave during the period of their studies besides all other facilities including salary as they are in service.

This system of imparting education to the employees is a motivational factor to the employees. Many of the employees in the organisation used this facility.

Children's Education

For employees' children who are studying in government recognised convents (if there is no recognised school within the radius of ½ km) the fees are borne by the management.

Recreational Facilities

A healthy body and healthy mind are closely connected. It is in this respect that recreational facilities are very important. Besides reducing strain, the recreation provides relaxation and encourages development of group feeling.[39] All this naturally helps in developing a fuller personality as recreation makes a worker psychologically happy by giving opportunity for self expression and relaxation. Various forms of recreation give the opportunities for cultural, physical and aesthetic development. For example, participation in fine arts inculcates the sense of culture and participation in games help them develop physically. Besides, participation in group activities help them understand the necessity of team work and discipline. As such, recreation has unique place in the life of people and life cannot be deemed complete without it. Malviya Commission[40] has this to say about recreation.

No special institution devised by human ingenuity for satisfaction of man's fundamental urges of self expression, recognition and new experience has served its originator so truly and so well as recreation.

Recreational Facilities in Sample Units

In Vijaya dairy the recreation club was formed by the representatives of the trade union. The general manager of the factory is the chairman of the club. All the sports material is purchased and supplied by the management. Now and then the cultural activities are also conducted. The factory is also sending the teams outside the district for games and sports. One colour T.V. is provided in the rest room for recreational purpose. Twice in a year, games, sports and recreational activities are being conducted among the workers and officers to inculcate the feeling of equity and to promote the inherent talents of the employees. Disc antenna facility is also provided for facilitating the factory employees. The management also provided library facility for its employees. The library is accommodated in a separate room with Telugu dailies, weeklies, monthly magazines and some important sports journals, and labour law books.

The management of Sangam dairy gives Rs. 1,00,000 per year to Nataka Kala Parishat formed by the employees for promoting cultural activities. The employees also participate in sports and 'drama' competitions conducted by APDDCF. The Nataka Kala Parishat conducted 33 programmes throughout Andhra Pradesh. It won many prizes and awards including golden Nandi, silver Nandi awards etc. For encouraging employee artists the management provides duty leave and traveling allowance to the participants. The Sangam dairy has also maintained library with daily newspapers, weeklies, and journals.

Leave Travel Concession (LTC)

There is a growing realisation on the part of the employees and employers that an occasional visit to holiday homes, renowned places, pilgrimages or sight seeing provide a sigh of relief for some time from the monotonous industrial life and an opportunity to learn and know more about men and matters. Hence several enlightened managements have started implementing the leave travel benefit as a labour welfare measure.

Every employee who has completed five years of continuous service is eligible for L.T.C. This facility can be availed by an employee once in a block of two calendar years for visiting home town and once a block of four years for visiting any place in Andhra Pradesh. Provision under this scheme includes reimbursement of actual fare from the place of duty to the home town or any other place of their choice as the case may be, by shortest route. The class of fare reimbursable is the one to which the employee is normally entitled according to his cadre.

The dairies have been spending considerable amount towards the LTC facility extended to the employees as can be seen from Table 5.25.

Table 5.25: Expenditure on Leave Travel Concession

Year	*Expenditure incurred in Rs.*	
	Vijaya dairy	*Sangam dairy*
1995-96	-	8,03,074
1996-97	9,35,634	98,711
1997-98	12,835	14,269
1998-99	1,694	3,95,197
1999-00	16,18,324	7,65,259
2000-01	5,39,938	4,13,711
2001-02	6,284	2,12,766

The table 5.25 shows yearwise expenditure on leave travel concession of both the dairies. The Vijaya dairy incurred maximum expenditure of Rs. 16,18,324 during 1999-2000 followed by Rs. 5,39,938 during 2000-01. In the year 1998-99 the least expenditure of Rs. 1,694 was incurred. The Sangam dairy incurred maximum expenditure of Rs. 8,03,074 during 1995-96 followed by Rs. 7,65,259 during 1999-2000, in the remaining years the expenditure has declined. In the year 1997-98 the least expenditure of Rs. 14,269 was incurred.

Uniforms to Employees

The Sangam and Vijaya dairies provide its employees with two pairs of uniform every year and also give a washing allowance of Rs. 20 for each employee per month. Stitching allowance for women employees is Rs. 30 and 250 for gents. Sangam dairy during the year 2001-02 spent Rs. 3,24,523 on distribution of clothes. Lorry drivers are provided with khaki uniform and swetters during the winter season.

Table 5.26: Cadre-wise Uniform Colour

Safety Officer	Grey
Dairy Worker	Blue colored shirt and dark blue colour pant
Dairy Manager	White Coats or Aprons
Quality Control Officer	White Aprons
Security	Dark blue pant and shirt

Cadre-wise grey uniform for safety officer is provided. Blue and white colours are provided to dairy workers, dairy manager and quality control officer. The security personnel are provided with dark blue pant and shirt.

Footwear

The facility of the supply of footwear to the employees is found in Sangam dairy only but not in Vijaya dairy. The Sangam dairy management supplies shoes to every employee.

Shoes and chappals distribution, their prices, number of pairs and expenditure incurred is shown in table. 5.27.

Table 5.27: Shoes and Chappals

Sl.No.	*Articles*	*No.of Pairs*	*Expenditure in Rs.*
1.	Leather Shoes	685	119190
2.	P.V.C. Type Shoes	201	16000
3.	Leather Chapels Ladies	27	18361
4.	Sandak Chappals	28	15681
	Total		138594

During the current year managements supplied 685 pairs of leather shoes costing Rs. 1,19,190. PVC type shoes (201 pairs) costing Rs. 16,000, sandak chappals (28 pairs) costing Rs. 15,681, and 27 pairs of leather chappals for ladies costing Rs. 18,361. The total expenditure incurred by the management for supplying shoes and chappals to the employees is Rs. 1,38,594.

Fixed Travelling Allowances

The field staff are entitled for fixed travelling allowance of Rs. 1000 per month.

Table 5.28: Fixed Travelling Allowance to Field Staff

Year	*Expenditure incurred in Rs.*	
	Vijaya dairy	*Sangam dairy*
1995-96	-	1,61,420
1996-97	5,61,923.05	1,75,310
1997-98	4,26,569.40	2,26,800
1998-99	5,79,122.95	2,36,050
1999-00	4,03,321.50	2,64,150
2000-01	5,81,005.50	3,54,775
2001-02	9,59,980	4,14,936

In both dairies travelling allowances are paid to field staff grade-wise. Grade-I cadre and Grade-II cadre staff may claim first class rail fare and deluxe bus for road travel respectively. Grade-III cadre is allowed 2nd class train fare and express bus fare for road travel.

The table 5.29 shows the various allowances for which the employees of both the dairies are entitled.

As shown in the above table 5.29 the employees of the both the dairies are entitled for various allowances. Employees are entitled for conveyance Rs. 150 per month risk allowance of Rs. 100 per employees working in powder, Ghee and processing sections, Rs. 20 for tetra pack employees, Rs. 10

Table 5.29: Allowances

Nature of Allowance	*Monthly Expenditure incurred in Rs.*	
	Vijaya Dairy Rs.Ps. Per month	*Sangam Dairy Rs.Ps. per month*
Conveyance	65 on wards	150
Risk allowance	60	100
Dust allowance		90
Night allowance	Two cups tea	4.25 NP per day
Cashier allowance		300
Special risk allowance		75
Duplicating allowance		20
Photostat allowance		20
Computer allowance		58
Veterinary office allowance		156
Riksha allowance	45	90
Washing allowance	20	50
Telephone operating allowance		75
Drivers special allowance		225
Stearing allowance for driver	75	75
Light vehicle stearing allowance	60	60
Medical allowance	550	
City Compensatory allowance	45	

for other categories of employees Rs. 60 for JPO/Do/SDO/BO/ and NMR employees, Rs. 50 for bull shed workers, Rs. 3 per day towards dust allowance, Rs. 4.25 paise per day towards night allowance, Rs. 300 per month as cashier allowance, Rs. 2.50 paise per day towards special risk allowance, Rs. 20 per month towards duplicating allowance, Rs. 20 per month towards Photostat allowance, Rs. 58 per month computer allowance, Rs. 156 per month towards veterinary office allowance, Rs. 3 per day riksha allowance, Rs. 50 per month towards washing allowance, Rs. 75 per month towards telephone operator allowance, Rs. 225 per month towards drivers special allowance, Rs. 75 per month towards stearing allowance for driver and 60 per month towards light vehicle stearing allowance.

Loans

The management in both the dairies extend loan facility to their employees for marriages, for female children Rs. 25,000 and for male children Rs. 15,000 at the rate of 13 per cent interest. The loan should be repaid in eight installments.

The management of both the dairies provide educational loan of Rs. 2000 per year without any interest to the children of employees. The loan is recovered in 10 equal monthly installments.

Workers Welfare Fund

The management of both the dairies constituted workers welfare fund for which the employees contribute Rs. 2 and the employer contribute Rs. 5 per month and thus making total contribution of Rs. 7 per month. The worker cadre is entitled for the benefit of welfare fund. This fund is remitted to the government, i.e. labour department of A.P. From out of this fund scholarships are awarded to the children of the employees for education purpose on merit basis. The amounts of scholarship for various classes, courses are 7th class Rs. 300 per year, 10th class Rs. 500 per year, BE/MBBS/MCA Rs. 2000 per year.

Household Articles and Vehicle Loans

The Vijaya dairy extends loans to its employees for purchasing household articles and vehicles. The loans are recovered from the employees in thirty installments.

In Sangam dairy the employees get the loans depending upon the cadre. Loans are given to the employees below supervisory cadre for purchasing cycles and mopeds. For supervisors loans are provided for purchasing motor cycles. The employer contributes 75 per cent of the cost for vehicles, the remaining 25 per cent of the cost is borne by the employees. These loans are recovered by the employer in 24 monthly installments.

Festival Advance

Festival advance of Rs. 2,000 and Rs. 1000 are extended to the employees without interest in Sangam and Vijaya dairies respectively. These loans are recovered from the employees in ten equal installments in both the dairies.

Other Benefits

In Sangam dairy milk is supplied to the employees at concessional rate of Rs. 13 per litre, the actual cost of per litre being Rs. 16, the maximum quantity of milk supplied to the employees at concessional rate is 1½ liter. The cost of the milk supplied to the employees at concessional rate will be deducted from the salaries.

Death Relief Fund Scheme

A unique scheme called "the death relief fund" has been introduced by Sangam dairy by obtaining special permission from the government of Andhra Pradesh. Since then the scheme is running successfully till today. The employees can join the scheme as members on voluntary basis by expressing their willingness through a written application.

The objective of the scheme is to help the family of deceased employee (while on duty) to meet the financial needs of the bereaved family to some extent. Under the scheme the members contribute one day salary in the event of death of any member and the amount so collected will be credited in the bank as fixed deposit. The interest amount is generally handed over to legal heirs. If the deceased member has parents alive, then the amount is shared between his parents and his wife and children. The ratio of the amount to be shared is decided by the death relief fund committee which is constituted with the managing director, the welfare officer (convener) and all presidents of the trade unions. Since there is no welfare officer in Sangam dairy, whoever looks after the duties of welfare officer will Act as the convener of the committee.

At present the amount accumulated under death relief fund is about Rs. 2,20,000, the membership strength being 860. The number of families which received death relief fund yearwise include 1992 (1), 1993 (1), 1994 (7), 1995 (4), 1996 (2), 1997 (7), 1998 (4), 1999(4), 2000 (3), 2001 (4) and the current year 2002 (3).

Wages and Employee Welfare—Item Analysis

To find out the overall opinions of the respondents towards employees welfare activities an effort was made to quantify the responses by using the method of summated ratings.

At the first stage, a set of items were selected and they were given 2/1/2/1/1/2/3 responses. Then each response was given score ranging from 1, 2, 3... etc.

After constructing the tool it was pre-tested with a small sample of 60. The Scores were summed up and analysed for their reliability. It was found that except one item, all the items had very high correlation coefficient with the total scores. The item which had low coefficient of correlation was dropped and the final tool was prepared.

Employee welfare is an implied responsibility of the employer. To motivate the employees on a continuous basis the employer has to provide various welfare facilities in any organisation.

To know the level of satisfaction on welfare facilities of the respondents, the researcher has selected 27 statements from various research studies. (Murthy M.V. and Narayana B.L. (1965),[41] Report of the Committee on Labour Welfare (1969),[42] Vaid K.N. (1970).)[43] These statements have the following response pattern i.e. yes/no; yes/no and Poor, Average, Good. These responses are scored in terms of 1, 2 and 3 respectively. The responses of respondents were converted into numerals and summated. The score analysis is given in table 5.30. The first column shows scores obtained by the respondents. The second column shows the number of respondents. For example, the first row shows 15 respondents (4.9%) obtained scores of 81.

Table 5.30: Employee Welfare

Employee Welfare	*Frequency*	*Per cent*	*Cumulative Per cent*
81.00	15	4.9	4.9
82.00	3	1.0	5.9
83.00	2	.7	6.6
85.00	3	1.0	7.5
91.00	6	2.0	9.5
92.00	1	.3	9.8
93.00	2	.7	10.5
94.00	1	.3	10.8
95.00	5	1.6	12.5
96.00	11	3.6	16.1
97.00	8	2.6	18.7
98.00	4	1.3	20.0
99.00	1	.3	20.3
100.00	6	2.0	22.0
101.00	4	1.3	23.6
102.00	1	.3	23.9
103.00	1	.3	24.3
104.00	10	3.3	27.5
105.00	2	.7	28.2
108.00	11	3.6	31.8
109.00	4	1.3	
110.00	2	.7	33.8
112.00	4	1.3	35.1

Employee Welfare	*Frequency*	*Per cent*	*Cumulative Per cent*
113.00	2	.7	35.7
114.00	5	1.6	37.4
115.00	.6	2.0	39.3
116.00	3	1.0	40.3
117.00	4	1.3	41.6
118.00	4	1.3	43.0
121.00	2	.7	43.6
122.00.	8	2.6	46.2
123.00	2	.7	46.9
124.00	2	.7	47.5
125.00	4	1.3	48.9
126.00	6	2.0	50.8
127.00	3	1.0	51.8
128.00	4	1.3	53.1
129.00	9	3.0	56.1
130.00	11	3.6	59.7
131.00	4	1.3	61.0
132.00	4	1.3	62.3
133.00	5	1.6	63.9
134.00	3	1.0	64.9
135.00'	5	1.6	66.6
136.00	5	1.6	68.2
137.00	3	1.0	69.2
138.00	6	2.0	71.7
139.00	1	.3	71.5
140.00	2	.7	72.1
141.00	5	1.6	73.8
142.00	5	1.6	75.4
144.00	2	.7	76.1
145.00	6	2.0	78.0

Employee Welfare	*Frequency*	*Per cent*	*Cumulative Per cent*
148.00	4	1.3	79.3
149.00	2	.7	80.0
150.00	1	.3	80.3
152.00	3	1.0	81.3
153.00	3	1.0	82.3
154.00	4	1.3	83.6
157.00	5	1.6	85.2
159.00	2	.7	85.9
171.00	1	.3	86.2
175.00	5	1.6	87.9
176.00	2	.7	88.5
178.00	2	.7	89.2
180.00	1	.3	89.5
183.00	2	.7	90.2
184.00	5	1.6	91.8
185.00	3	1.0	92.8
187.00	22	7.2	100.0
Total	305	100.0	

There are 27 statements and these scores ranges from 81 to 189.

No. of statements : 27

Respondent pattern : Yes and No is taken as 2 and 1 respectively, while poor, average, good are given the scores 1,2,3 respectively. Maximum scores $(2+2+3) \times 27 = 189$.

Further to find out what are the variables that affect the level of satisfaction, data has been cross tabulated. First of all the frequency table of level of satisfaction on employee welfare has been regrouped on the basis of first and third quartile values and then results have been presented.

Table 5.31: Employee Welfare

Quartile values	*Frequency*	*Per cent*	*Cumulative Per cent*
High (104)	131	43.0	43.0
Middle (104-142)	131	43.0	85.9
Low (143+)	43	14.1	100.0
Total	305	100.0	

As shown in table 5.31 most of the respondents are satisfied about the welfare facilities. Their levels of satisfaction are 43 per cent scored to high; likewise 43 per cent scored to moderate. Rest of the respondents' level of satisfaction is low. It can be attributed to their high expectations when compared to the actual facilities provided by the management.

On the whole most of the employees are satisfied with welfare facilities that is to say the management has positive attitude towards their employees welfare. This also implies the employer and employee relations are harmonious.

Is employee welfare associated with the sex of the respondents? To find out the answer, data relating to the sex of the respondents and their employee welfare have been cross tabulated. The results of the analysis are presented in Table 5.32.

Table 5.32: Employee Welfare by Sex

Year	*Employee welfare regrouped*			*Total*
	Low	*Moderate*	*High*	
Male	117	119	32	268
Female	14	12	11	37
Total	131	131	43	305

$X^2 = 8.639$ df = 2 p = .013 Conti. Coeff = .166

It is evident from Table 5.32 that 131 respondents from both sexes and their level of satisfaction on employee welfare is moderate. However further analysis reveals that comparatively larger proportion of male respondents' employee welfare is moderate. This is followed by equally scored to low level of satisfaction. 32 male respondents and 11 female respondents are highly satisfied about employee welfare facilities. To test whether there is any significant association between the two variables, chi-square test was used. The results show that the association is statistically significant. Hence the sex of the respondents indicates some significance with employee welfare.

From Table 5.32 more than one-third respondents scored to low level of satisfaction it may alert the management of the sample units to design and provide wider range of employee welfare facilities. As studies emphasised, for every six months, management is to feel the pulse of the employees, and provide facilities according to their requirements. Every employer should realise that investment on employee is a productive investment.

Is employee welfare associated with the educational background of the respondents? To find out the answer, data relating to the educational background of the respondents and their Employee Welfare have been cross tabulated. The results of the analysis are presented in Table 5.33.

It is evident from the table 5.33 that 131 respondents' educational background, and their level of satisfaction on employee welfare is moderate. Another 131 respondents scored 'low' level of satisfaction. Other 43 respondents are 'highly' satisfied. To test whether there is any significant association between the two variables, chi-square test was used. The results show that the association is statistically significant. Hence, the employees' educational background tells us about their level of satisfaction about employee welfare.

In general where the educational background is high, their level of satisfaction is low on benefits and services offered by the management. In the dairy units also the same trend has been noticed.

Table 5.33: Employee Welfare by Educational Background

Education Background	*Employee welfare regrouped*			*Total*
	Low	*Moderate*	*High*	
Elementary level	8	7		15
High school level	53	58	2	113
Intermediate	24	23	15	62
Graduation	24	33	16	73
Post-graduation/ professional	22	9	10	41
Technical		1		1
Total	131	131	43	305

X^2 = 36.905 df = 10 p = .000 Conti. Coeff = .329

Is employee welfare associated with the indebtedness of the respondents? To find out the answer, data relating to the indebtedness of the respondents and their employee welfare have been cross tabulated. The results of the analysis are presented in Table 5.34.

Table 5.34: Employee Welfare by Indebtedness

Indebtedness	*Employee welfare regrouped*			*Total*
	Low	*Moderate*	*High*	
Yes	76	67	23	166
No	55	64	20	139
Total	131	131	43	305

X = 1.264 df = 2 p = .531 Conti. Coeff = .064

It is indicated that from Table 5.34 that more than half of the respondents (166) have indebtedness among whom 23 respondents expressed high satisfaction and 67 respondents expressed moderate satisfaction about employee welfare. This is followed by low (76) level of satisfaction. To test whether there is any significant association between the two variables, chi-square test was used. The results show that the association is statistically not significant. That is the respondents' indebtedness does not tell us about their level of satisfaction.

As revealed from the above analysis the indebtedness of the employee has no effect on their satisfaction about employee welfare. If employee welfare is taken care of by the management the indebtedness will not effect the level of satisfaction of the employees. The employees whether indebted or not are happy with the welfare amenities.

Is employee welfare associated with the number of dependents of the respondents? To find out the answer, data relating to the number of dependents of the respondents and their employee welfare have been cross tabulated. The results of the analysis are presented in Table 5.35.

Table 5.35: Employee Welfare by Number of Dependents

Number Dependents	*Employee welfare regrouped*			*Total*
	Low	*Moderate*	*High*	
0.00	1	2	1	4
1.00	10	8		18
2.00	26	23	14	63
3.00	45	28	7	80
4.00	36	42	13	91
5.00	12	22	8	42
6.00	1	6		7
Total	131	131	43	305

$X^2 = 22.982$ df = 12 p = .028 Conti. Coeff = .265

It is understood from the table that in a majority of the respondents, number of dependents and their level of satisfaction on employee welfare is moderate. This is followed by low level of satisfaction. Whereas 43 respondents are highly satisfied on employee welfare. To test whether there is any significant association between the two variables, chi-square test was used. The results show that the association is statistically significant. From this it may be inferred that there is significant association between employee welfare and number of dependents of the respondents.

The above analysis tells that the number of dependents will influence the level of satisfaction about employee welfare. Employees with less number of dependents may have higher level of satisfaction about welfare amenities.

Is employee welfare associated with the Rural/Urban background of the respondents? To find out the answer, data relating to the Rural/Urban background of the respondents and their Employee Welfare have been cross tabulated. The results of the analysis are presented in Table 5.36.

Table 5.36: Employee Welfare by Rural/Urban Background

Rural/Urban	*Employee welfare regrouped*			*Total*
	Low	*Moderate*	*High*	
Rural	118	108	36	262
Urban	13	23	7	43
Total	131	131	43	305

$X^2 = 3.348$ df = 2 p = .187 Conti. Coeff = .104

It is evident from table 5.36 that the level of satisfaction and employee welfare in the case of 131 of the respondents from both the Rural and Urban background is moderate. This is followed by low level of satisfaction. 36 respondents from the rural and 7 respondents from urban scored high level of satisfaction. To test whether there is any significant association between the two variables, chi-square test was used. The results show that the association is statistically not significant. Hence the employees' background either rural or urban does not tell us about their level of satisfaction on employee welfare.

From the above analysis it may be understood that the rural or urban background has no differential impact on employee welfare. In other words the welfare amenities that are provided do not have their impact on the level of satisfaction between the Rural and Urban employees.

Is employee welfare associated with the organisation of the respondents? To find out the answer, data relating to the organisation of the respondents and their Employee Welfare have been cross tabulated. The results of the analysis are presented in Table 5.37.

Table 5.37: Employee Welfare by the Organisation

Organisation	*Employee welfare regrouped*			*Total*
	Low	*Moderate*	*High*	
Vijaya Dairy	78	81	21	180
Sangam Dairy	53	50	22	125
Total	131	131	43	305

$X^2 = 2.286$ df = 2 p = .319 Conti. Coeff = .086

It is evident from Table 5.37 that in the case of 131 of the respondents from both the organisations, the level of satisfaction on employee welfare is moderate. This is followed by low level of satisfaction by 131 respondents of both the organisations. 21 respondents from Vijaya Dairy and 22 respondents from Sangam Dairy scored high level satisfaction. To test whether there is any significant association between the two variables, chi-square test was used. The results show that the association is statistically not significant. That is whether the employees of Sangam Dairy or Vijaya Dairy does not tell us about their level of satisfaction on employee welfare.

From the above analysis one can understand that the employees of both the organisations are equally happy about the welfare amenities. That is to say irrespective of the organisations respondents expressed satisfaction about employee welfare.

Is employee welfare associated with the category of the respondents? To find out the answer, data relating to the category of the respondents and their Employee Welfare have been cross tabulated. The results of the analysis are presented in Table 5.38.

Table 5.38: Employee Welfare by Category

Category	*Employee welfare regrouped*			*Total*
	Low	*Moderate*	*High*	
Managerial	25	27	3	55
Non-Managerial	106	104	40	250
Total	131	131	43	305

$X^2 = 4.243$ df = 2 p = .120 Conti. Coeff = .117

It is evident from the table that the level of satisfaction of 131 respondents from both the categories on employee welfare is moderate. This is followed by low level of satisfaction by 131 respondents. 40 non-managerial and 3 managerial respondents are highly satisfied with employee welfare. To test whether there is any significant association between the two variables, chi-square test was used. The results show that the association is statistically not significant. That is whether the employees are of managerial or non-managerial category the category does not have its influence on the level of satisfaction on employee welfare.

It is obvious from the above analysis that both managerial and non-managerial employees are happy with the welfare amenities. That means irrespective of the category and cadre the employees have satisfaction about welfare amenities.

Is employee welfare associated with the caste of the respondents? To find out the answer, data relating to the caste of the respondents and their employee welfare have been cross tabulated. The results of the analysis are presented in Table 5.39.

Table 5.39: Employee Welfare by Caste

Caste	*Employee welfare regrouped*			*Total*
	Low	*Moderate*	*High*	
OC	83	105	35	223
BC	40	19	3	62
SC	8	7	5	20
Total	131	131	43	305

$X^2 = 17.687$ df = 4 p = .001 Conti. Coeff = .223

It is evident from table 5.39 that in the case of 131 of the total respondents from all the castes and the level of satisfaction on employee welfare is moderate. However further analysis reveals that again in the case of 131 respondents from all castes satisfaction is low. To test whether there is any significant association between the two variables, chi-square test was used. The results show that the association is statistically significant.

It can be inferred from the above analysis that caste has influence on the level of satisfaction about employee welfare. That means the higher castes that is OCs may have better satisfaction about welfare amenities than BCs and SCs.

Is employee welfare associated with the Age of the respondents? To find out the answer, data relating to the age of the respondents and their employee welfare have been cross tabulated. The results of the analysis are presented in Table 5.40.

It is evident from table 5.40 that in the case of a majority of the respondents from all the ages the level of satisfaction on employee welfare is moderate. It is followed by 131 respondents from all the age group having low level of satisfaction. To test whether there is any significant association between the two variables, chi-square test was used. The results show that the association is statistically not significant. That is the employees' age does not have any relation to employee welfare.

Table 5.40: Employee Welfare by Age

Age	*Employee welfare regrouped*			*Total*
	Low	*Moderate*	*High*	
27-43	31	33	13	77
44-51	57	76	13	146
52-57	43	22	17	82
Total	131	131	43	305

$X^2 = 15.924$ df = 4 p = .003 Conti. Coeff = .223

The above analysis reveals that there is no relationship between age and satisfaction about the welfare amenities. Irrespective of the age group the employees have expressed satisfaction about welfare amenities.

Is employee welfare associated with the gross salary of the respondents? To find out the answer, data relating to the gross salary of the respondents and their employee welfare have been cross tabulated. The results of the analysis are presented in Table 5.41.

Table 5.41: Employee Welfare by Gross Salary

Gross Salary (in Rs.)	*Employee welfare regrouped*			*Total*
	Low	*Moderate*	*High*	
3900-7400	44	35		79
7401-11000	55	53	33	141
11001-70000	32	43	10	85
Total	131	131	43	305

$X^2 = 26.314$ df = 4 p = .000 Conti. Coeff = .282

It is evident from table 5.41 that in the case of 131 respondents from all the employees the level of satisfaction on employee welfare is moderate. This is followed by low level of satisfaction whereas the other respondents are highly satisfied. To test whether there is any significant association between the two variables, chi-square test was used. The results show that the association is statistically significant. Hence the employee's gross salary has association with employee welfare.

From the above analysis it may be noted that the gross salary will influence the level of satisfaction of the employees about welfare amenities. The more the gross salary the more may be the satisfaction.

Is employee welfare associated with the Net Salary of the respondents? To find out the answer, data relating to the Net Salary of the respondents and their employee welfare have been cross tabulated. The results of the analysis are presented in Table 5.42.

Table 5.42: Employee Welfare by Net Salary

Net Salary (in Rs.)	*Employee welfare regrouped*			*Total*
	Low	*Moderate*	*High*	
1800-3800	31	33	9	73
3801-6700	73	56	29	158
6701-16000	27	42	5	74
Total	131	131	43	305

$X^2 = 18.807$ df = 4 p =.000 Conti. Coeff = .508

It is evident from table 5.42 that in the case of 131 of the respondents from all the employees' the level of satisfaction on employee welfare is moderate. This is followed by low level of satisfaction scored by 131 respondents. The remaining respondents scored high satisfaction. To test whether there is any significant association between the two variables, chi-square test was used. The results show that the association is statistically not significant.

The above analysis denotes that the net salary has no impact on the level of satisfaction of the employees about welfare amenities. The net salary may not influence the satisfaction of the employees about welfare amenities.

It is found that the level of satisfaction of male respondents is higher than the female. It may be because of the fact that both dairies do not provide any special welfare facilities to the female respondents other than the statutory benefits. In respect of educational background, the study found that the higher the levels of the education the lower the level of satisfaction on employee welfare. It may be because education brings more awareness and increases the level of aspiration. When the aspirations are not met, the dissatisfaction increases. It is further found that the higher the number of dependents of the respondents the lower the level of satisfaction with employee welfare. The rationale behind this might be the increased number of dependents of the employee may increase the expectations of the respondents as he has to meet the requirements of his dependents. With regard to association between caste background of the respondents on satisfaction with employee welfare, it is found that the level of satisfaction of open category (upper caste) is higher than that of others. It might be because of the status on the benefits they enjoy in the society, upper caste people may not expect more from the organisation.

Based on the above analysis presented in this chapter it can be concluded that the employee welfare has association with sex, educational background, number of dependents, caste and gross salary.

REFERENCES

1. Seal, K.C. (1965, July). 'A Critical Review of Research and Literature on Wages in India'. *Indian Journal of Industrial Relations,* Vol. 1, No. 1, 41-59.

2. Biswas, R.K. (1982, March). Concept of Wages Under Different Labour Laws. *Labour Gazette,* 761-772.

3. Suri, G.K. and Chellappa, H.V.V. (1973, July). 'Wage-cost-productivity Nexus and Incomes Policy'. *Indian Journal of Industrial Relations,* Vol. 9, No. 1, 69.

4. Papola, T.S. (1981). *Urban Informal Sector in a Developing Economy*. New Delhi: Vikas Publishing House Pvt. Ltd. Kashyap, S.P. and Himal Singh (1987, July) 'Urban Informal Sector. Issues Arising Out of Gujarat's Experience'. *Indian Journal of Industrial Relations,* Vol. 23, No. 1, 49.

5. Munshi, N.M. (1983). *'Personnel Management in Small Industry of Saurashtra'*. Unpublished Doctoral Thesis Submitted to Saurashtra University.

6. Government of India (1966). *Report of the National Commission on Labour,* 230.

7. In a Series of Adjudication Cases in Respect of Wage Disputes, the Courts have Laid down this Principle in Unequivocal Terms.

8. Government of India, (1969). *Report of the Committee on Fair Wages,* 9.

9. *Ibid.,* 11.

10. *Report of the National Commission on Labour* (1966). New Delhi: Government of India Publications, 236.

11. The Hindustan Times Vs. Their Workmen, AIR, 1963, S.C. 1322.

12. Express Newspapers Pvt. Ltd. Vs Union of India, 1958, S.C. 578.

13. *The Management of People at Work,* 643-644 and 652.

14. Belchar, David W and Heneman, Jr., Herbert G, "How to Make a Wage Survey", Technical Report Series No. 2, Industrial Relations Centre, University of Minnesota (1948, July). Quoted in David W. Belchar, *Wage and Salary Administration,* 45.

15. Ross, Arthur M. *"The Dynamics of Wage Determination under Collective Bargaining"*. 800.

16. Government of India (1973). *Report of the 3rd Central Pay Commission,* New Delhi: Minister of Finance.

17. International Labour Organisation, (1956). *Problems of Wage Policy in Asian Countries,* Geniva, 39.

18. Government of India, *Report of the National Commission on Labour,* op.cit, 220.

19. In the aftermath of the Industrial Unrest Immediately Prior to and after Independence, a Tripartite Conference was Convened by the Government in 1947, to Suggest Remedial Measures for Industrial Unrest. At this Conference an Industrial Truce Resolution was Adopted.

20. Moorthy, M.V. (1958). *Principles of Labour Welfare,* Visakhapatnam: Gupta Brothers, 1.

21. Sarma, A.M. (1998). *Personnel and Human Resource Management,* Mumbai: Himalaya Publishing House, 240.

22. International Labour Organisation (1942). *Approach to Social Security—An International Survey,* Geneva: the Auditor, 83.

23. William, Beveridge (1942). *Social Insurance and Allied Services,* Report Presented to Parliament by Command of His Majesty, London: H.M.S.O. 120.

24. Vaid, K.N. (1970). *Labour Welfare in India,* New Delhi: Sri Ram Centre for Industrial Relations, 251.

25. Government of Andhra Pradesh (1980). Andhra Pradesh Dairy Development Co-operative Federaion. Hyderabad : Department Publication, 6.

26. *The Report of the Committee on Labour Welfare,* Government of India, (1969) Delhi: 252.

27. *International Labour Organisation* (1947). Planning for Labour, 107.

28. *Report of the Labour Investigation Committee,* (1946). Government of India, New Delhi: 343.

29. Suman Swarup., (2001, September) *Employers Guide,* New Delhi. Employees' State Insurance Corporation, Director General.

30. *Report of Royal Commission on Labour in India,* (1929). Government of India, Delhi, 270.

31. *Report of the Labour Investigation Committee,* op.cit., 362.

32. Giri, V.V. (1962). *Labour Problems in India Industry,* (2nd edition), Bombay: Asia Publishing House, 299.

33. ***The Report of National Commission on Labour,*** **op.cit., 106.**

34. The Third Five Year Plan, 259.

35. Punekar, Deodhar and Sankaran (1980). *Labour Welfare, Trade Unionism and Industrial Relations,* Bombay: Himalaya Publishing House, 94.

36. *Report of the Central Banking Enquiry Committee.,* Vol. 1, Part 1, 258.

37. *The Report of the National Commission on Labour,* op.cit., 88.

38. *Report of the Royal Commission on Labour,* op.cit., 27.

39. Dale Yoder, (1960). *Personnel Principles and Policies,* Bombay: Asia Publishers House, 16.

40. *Report of the Committee on Labour Welfare,* (1969) op.cit., 63.

41. Moorty, M.V. and Narayana, B.L. (1965). *Participation of Workers in Welfare Work,* Visakhapatnam: Gupta Brothers.

42. *Report of the Committee on Labour Welfare* (1969) Delhi: Government of India, 252.

43. Vaid, K.N. (1970) op.cit.

6

Industrial Relations

In the preceding chapter an analysis was presented on wages and employee welfare. This chapter is an attempt to portray the nature and quality of industrial relations in Vijaya and Sangam dairies. The employees' perceptions on existing practices in both dairies are presented and trade union particulars are given in a tabular form. Industrial disputes, collective bargaining, employee participation in decision-making and grievance redressal are highlighted. The Voluntary retirement scheme is also discussed in this chapter.

Industrial relations describe "relationships between managements and employees or among employees and their organisations, that characterize or grow out of employment."[1] The International Institute of Labour Studies has defined it in a more comprehensive sense as to mean "social relations in production".[2]

Nature of Industrial Relations

The primary concern of the management and the workers is to make the organisation a success. This requires that the parties maintained harmony and peaceful relations. The interests of both are interdependent and they can sub-serve the interests of society at large. The parties can share the gains of increased productivity if they work as partners.

Establishment and maintenance of harmonious relations between labour and management is a pre-requisite for the stability and progress of industry. When good understanding prevails between them, each party tries to serve the other to the best of its ability. Workmen try to give their best and improve productive efficiency, and the management acknowledges its satisfaction and attractive working conditions. In such a state of relations marked by amity, there is little scope for grievances and disputes. But the maintenance of good labour management relations is very often a difficult job.

In a realistic sense, complete harmony, peace or co-operation can be elusive. The objectives of the parties are so different that only 'antagonistic co-operation' is possible in labour management relations.[3] "Despite the heavy accent in recent times on common good and virtue of industrial peace and harmony, the pursuit of opposite aims continues to cause strife."[4] Wage earners form trade unions to safeguard their interests and to register protest in an organised way. Unions assume the form of defense or combative mechanism aimed at meeting the exploitative tactics of employer. This evokes a reaction in employer who wants to serve his interests well by taking recourse to counter-defensive measures such as employers' association, economic pressures, hiring strike-breakers or invoking the help of police and in the interest' of law and order. Thus, the whole gamut of human relations arising from the sale of services by working for price and their working on the premises of the employers under their control forms the subject matter of industrial relations. These relations exist and grow out of employment and involve relationship between the employers and employees as well as their organisations.[5]

Role of State

Employment conditions in industry are not regulated merely by employees and employers, though both have a major role in it. State intervention in the regulation of labour management relations has been on the increase and, therefore, the role played by the state and its interaction with employers and employees legitimately forms part of industrial relations. What is intended in the present chapter is the study of the pattern of labour management relations that arise and the institutions and forums created by the parties to resolve these problems and to regulate the relations between them.

Industrial Relations Strategy in Dairy Industry

An attempt is made below to describe the industrial relations strategy in dairy industry based on the information collected from the managers of both dairies through interviews. The discussions revealed that the dairy units aim at improving productivity and profitability and also a fair deal to workers. Management of dairy units and employees' unions believe that industrial peace and harmony are the hallmark of optimum production. Both of them have agreed to maintain industrial peace and are committed to make efforts to ensure high level of performance with safety, health inputs and sustained efforts. The parties, recognised that future prosperity and efficiency of the undertaking rest heavily on the ability of the parties to work in co-operation to achieve higher productivity trends. The management gives importance to personnel and industrial relations matters. The personnel and industrial relations matters are entrusted to the personnel department. The company's personnel and industrial relations policy is to provide benefits to employees through negotiations. The parties would discuss their mutual issues through negotiations before they think of other methods to resolve their conflicts. The management has been favourably disposed in revising wage scales periodically taking into account the principles of equity and fairness and the capacity of the industry to pay. The management seeks to streamline and change the system of working of the organisation to make it sound and buoyant. Through discussion with the union, shop floor discipline has been tightened. Improving the image of the organisation in the eyes of customers and implementation of perspective plans (to improve competitive advantage) ensuring time, work and discipline, good housekeeping, elimination of wasteful practices are some of the serious problems the management has to contend with. The standing orders of the company are followed in observing discipline. The management conducts training programmes to help the employees to improve their skills and knowledge. Both management and union have agreed to restructure business operation to suit the technological and market requirements. The union agreed in principle for the introduction of work hours whereby an employee will do along with the job allotted to him, the jobs of the lower or higher category whenever required, similar to his nature of work. The major decisions affecting the workforce are being taken with due negotiations with the recognised union. The union functions, democratically with elected executives and the election is through a secret ballot. The company has extended check-off facility to the recognised union to collect union subscriptions.

Measures for Conflict Resolution in Dairy Industry

The measures that the parties adopt in dairy units for conflict resolution are presented systematically.

It can be understood by the researcher that both statutory as well as non-statutory measures are adopted in dairy units, either to prevent industrial conflicts or for their resolution.

The Industrial Disputes Act, 1947[6] was enacted with the objective of promoting cordial relations and expeditious settlement of industrial disputes.

Several authorities are created for the purpose of investigation and settlement of industrial disputes. They are (i) Works Committee, (ii) Conciliation Officers, (iii) Board of Conciliation, (iv) Court of Inquiry, (v) Voluntary Arbitration, (vi) Labour Courts, (vii) Industrial Tribunal and (viii) National Tribunal.

Pattern of Labour Management Relations in Dairy Industry

Labour management relations in dairy industry have never remained static. The quality of these relations have changed from time to time. It is appropriate to discuss these changes in terms of the concepts of Armed Truce, working harmony and union management co-operation as developed by Frederick Harbison and John Coleman.[7]

Armed Truce

According to this concept, management may decide to deal with the union on an "armed-truce" basis.[8] This is because the basic interest of the company and union are in conflict. The management's effort is to contain the union and to preserve managerial rights. Personnel programmes are used by the management to strengthen its position with employees. The union on its part tends to be aggressive and try to get 'something more' for the members in order to continue to have their support. In short, the parties are engaged in a kind of power struggle, each trying to dominate or outwit the other. While the management's concern is for preservation of its prerogatives, the union tries to preserve union security.

In dairy industry the earlier phase of labour management relations was marked by what may be broadly termed as "armed truce". Since inception till 1988 the relations between management and union in the plant had been marked by bitterness, animosity and even trial of strength. In the initial stages there were problems of union recognition and the plant witnessed the emergence of new unions from splitting the old ones. Significantly in both the dairy units all the trade unions have formed as joint action committee (JAC) to represent the issues relating to the total employees. This practice is being successful in both the dairy units.

Working Harmony

Under this 'model' the management may structure its dealings with the union so that working harmony may develop between them. This approach is based on the assumption by the management that it has an opportunity to help unions become responsible. The management often takes the initiative in seeking to establish friendly relationship based on fair dealing and understanding of each other's problems and interests. The management recognises union's need for security and tries to assure this by showing gesture which strengthens the union. The union, on the other hand, appreciates the company's need for reducing costs and increasing production in order to provide continued employment. Union management discussions centre round not on 'prerogatives' but on problems and the manner of solving them. There is sharing of information and management consulted workers through their union over wide range of company probemm.[9]

In Vijaya and Sangam dairies, since the beginning, trade union's attitude has been positive to represent the employees interest in an amicable manner. The management has started showing a desire to establish rapport with the union and discuss all common issues with the employees' representatives. As a result of the change in 'head and heart', the Vijaya dairy management has recognised A.P. Dairy Cooperative Employee and Workers Union (affiliated to INTUC) and the Sangam dairy management recognised GDMPCU employees union (affiliated to INTUC). They have showed desire to strengthen the hands of union and have close consultation with it. Interestingly both the recognised units have gradually been losing their hold on their members due to the changing environment of the state. In Vijaya dairy APDDC staff and workers union, which is affiliated to INTUC, continues to be the recognised union. Whereas in Sangam dairy a new union Telugunadu Staff and Workers Union has emerged as the recognised union. The earlier GDMPCU employees union affiliated to INTUC could not show good results and failed to come to the expectations of the members.

Another important feature is the formation of bipartite committees. Works committee, canteen committee, safety committee, production committee and quality control committee have been formed in both the units. They help in joint consultation and promotion of amity and good relations.

Union Management Co-operation

As per this 'model' management may decide to develop a programme of co-operation on production problems. This type of relationship is some what rare, often the need for it develops only when the survival of the firm is at stake or its competitive position weakening. Both management and union make a common cause to reduce cost and increase output and share the gains which result from such mutual efforts. This type of relationship can also be termed as 'Win-Win' relationship between the parties who work as partners in the joint enterprise and be benefited by sharing the gains resulting from mutual efforts. It may be noted that the relationship described above under different concepts is not very clear-cut. At any one time there may be elements of both armed truce and working harmony in a particular union management relationship. It is natural that over a period of time the nature of relationship changes as the parties develop more experience in dealing with each other. Sometimes new management representatives and new set of union officials who enter the picture may also bring about a change in the quality of relationship. This has happened in the case of dairy units under study.

In the initial stages the parties had difficulties in establishing orderly and systematic relationship. The parties, though unsuccessful, made attempts to settle their differences through negotiations. The parties even had number of joint sessions in an effort to sort out their issues. Because of lack of confidence and trust between them their efforts at negotiations could not bear fruit. As a result, they had to seek the help of conciliation officer to arrive at settlement.

The Role of Trade Unions

Trade Unions are a product of industrial society.[10] The main elements in the development of these unions in every country have been more or less the same. The setting up of large scale industrial units and the wide-spread use of machinery, opening of new lines of production, changes in living and working environments of workers and concentration of industries in large urban centres have all created a new class of 'wage-earners'.

To combat the evils of industrial competition and to ameliorate their conditions through improved bargaining power and status, the workers organised themselves into trade unions. Indeed, the regulation of employment conditions is the very raisond'etre of unionism.[11] Recognition by the community of this right to combine, organise for collective action and withhold labour when necessary, was a long and painful process everywhere. Unions have now come to symbolise workers' right to organise and to press their demands collectively and to go on strike if their claims are not accepted.

Trade Unions now play an important role in the industrial and social life of a country. They occupy a pivotal position in all the industrially advanced western countries. Even in countries which are newly experiencing rapid economic activity and trying to attain planned economic progress, trade unions occupy no less strategic position; and perhaps, their importance is even greater considering the dynamic role they play in contributing to increased productivity and accelerating the pace of industrial progress. The Trade Union Act, 1926 gave workers the right to form and register trade unions, to conduct trade disputes and promote the interests of their members through political, educational and civic means. The trade unions have since split and presently there are many national trade unions, besides a large number of regional ones with different ideologies.[12]

In the first three years after 1991 the union reaction was highly adverse to adjustment programme and the free market ideology of the new economic policies. Their strong reactions have affected industrial relations adversely in industry. This reaction was due to the negative impact on employment and National Renewal Fund (NRF) being totally utilised for providing golden handshake under the voluntary retirement scheme. The government contention all along has been that employment situation would have been worse without the new economic policies. The unions were also fearing of large scale introduction of new economic policies. The unions were also fearing of large scale introduction of new technology; which has really not happened in a big way. Now there has been considerable softening of the union's stand in view of the irreversibility of the structural reforms, the unions facing opposition from the government as well as their own members, their need to show to the country that they are also responsible citizens and the managements' attempts to develop their human resource in the wake of a competitive pressures. The landmark agreement and cooperation given by unions in the Indian Drugs and Pharmaceutical Ltd., units has shown that the union's stance has undergone a change. This trend needs to be intensified.

Trade Unionism in Dairy Industry

Trade union is an outcome of the factory system. While considerable work has been done on trade unions operating in large scale units, precious little is known about how trade unions operate in small scale units. Trade unions in dairy units under study, are playing crucial role to represent the issues of employees and achieving the benefits by representing in united manner in an amicable way. The trade union leaders are drawn from the rank and file of the employees and there is no outside leadership for the unions in the dairy units under study. As is the case with unions elsewhere in the country, the unions in dairy units also are found wanting in observing democratic principles in their functioning, neither regular elections are held to elect office bearers nor decisions are taken in the general body meetings. But the recognised union in Sangam dairy held elections in 2001 after a gap of many years. The managements discuss the issues with the union leaders by taking them into confidence and for amicable settlement. The unions also extend their co-operation to the managements by showing positive attitude towards the management. The existing trade unions and the particulars of their strength and affiliation are presented in the succeeding pages.

There are seven unions in Vijaya dairy affiliated to various political parties. Among them there is one recognised union namely, the Andhra Pradesh Dairy Co-operative Employee and Workers Union which is affiliated to INTUC. Some of the remaining unions are active though not recognised. As shown in the table 6.1 unions are affiliated to various national federations such as INTUC, AITUC, BKS, BMS, CITU and TNTUC (state level). The membership fees per month for the unions varies from Rs. 11 to 14. For the last 10 years, there have been no elections for the unions in Vijaya dairy. The researcher came to know that the reason is no union has come forward to challenge the present recognised union.

As clear from the table 6.2 there are seven trade unions in Sangam dairy. Among them there is only one recognised union namely, Telugunadu Staff and Workers Union which is affiliated to TNTUC. Upto 1990 employees' association was affiliated to INTUC and enjoyed the recognised union status. Subsequently some of the members left the organisation because the union was not successful in fulfilling the promises to regularize the NMRs in dairy. The rest of the unions are registered. They are affiliated to various national level trade unions i.e. INTUC, AITUC, CITU and BMS. Two of the unions, namely Sangam Mazdoor Union and SC/ST/BC Welfare Unions are independent. The membership strength of unions varies from 30 to 210, the membership fee ranging between Rs. 12 to Rs. 40.

Table 6.3 reveals that majority (62%) of the respondents are members of some union or other whereas

Table 6.1: Existing Trade Unions of Vijaya Dairy

Sl. No.	*Name*	*Affiliation*	*Reg.No.*	*Membership Fee*	*Claimed Membership*	*President of the Union*
1.	A.P.D.D.C Staff and Workers Union.	INTUC	B-22	Rs. 12	650	G.R.Prasad (Recognised union)
2.	A.P.D.D.C Karmika Sangh	INTUC	A-794	Rs. 14	450	Ch.Chitti Babu
3.	APDDC Federation and Working Union	AITUC	G-383	Rs. 11	70	K. Uma Maheswara Rao
4.	APDD Karmik Sangh	BKS	G-1748	Rs. 12	40	D.R.K.Raju
5.	APD Mazdoor Sangm	BMS	B-1281	Rs. 12	50	G.V. Rama Raj
6.	APDDC Employers and Workers Union	CITU	C-203		80	K.Venkateswara Rao
7.	National Workers And Staff Union	TNTUC	B-790	Rs. 12	250	Koneru Venkateswarlu

Table 6.2: Sangam Dairy—Trade Union Particulars

Sl. No.	Name of the union	Affiliation	Reg.No.	Strength	Membership Fee (in Rs.)	President of the Union
1.	GDMPCU Employees Association	INTUC	C-662	110	25	M. Chandra Sekhar Rao
2.	A.P.D.D.Co.F Ltd, Workers Union	AITUC	G-382	70	24	Mulaga Venkateswara Rao
3.	Telugunadu Staff and Workers Union	TNTUC	C-1084	210	40.	Janga Babu Rao (Recognised union)
4.	Sangam Karimka Samaikya	CITU	C-1879	30	12	T. Venkateswara Rao
5.	Sangam Mazdoor Union	Independent	C-2122	30	24	M. Lakshmaiah
6.	Bharatiya Dairy Mazdoor Sangh	BMS	C-973	150	24	Vasireddy Chandra sekhar
7.	SC/ST/BC Welfare Union	Independent		70	24	A. Rataiah

Table 6.3: Membership in Trade Union

Sl.No.	*Response*	*Frequency*	*Per cent*	*Cumulative Per cent*
1.	Yes	189	62.0	62.0
2.	No	116	38.0	100.0
	Total	305	100.0	

thirty-eight per cent of the respondents are not members of any union.

Table 6.4: Reasons for Joining the Trade Union

Reasons	*Frequency*	*Per cent*	*Cumulative Per cent*
Protection from management	36	11.8	11.8
Employee solidarity	28	9.2	21.0
To gain monetary benefits	18	5.9	26.9
To be a member of the group	96	31.5	58.4
Other reason	16	5.2	63.6
Not applicable	111	36.4	100.0
Total	305	100.0	

Table 6.4 shows that more than thirty-six per cent of the respondents have stated that they are not members of any union. Whereas nearly one-third of the respondents have taken the membership of some union because of their urge. Nearly twelve per cent of the respondents have joined the union to protect themselves from the management. Nearly ten per cent of the respondents joined for employee solidarity. Other six per cent of the respondents have joined the union to gain monetary benefits. The rest of the respondents have stated other reasons.

Table 6.5 indicates that majority of the respondents are ordinary members in the trade union. Whereas one-sixth of the members are the office bearers of the trade unions.

Table 6.5: Trade Union Membership

Membership	*Frequency*	*Per cent*	*Cumulative Per cent*
Ordinary member	158	83.9	83.9
Office bearer	31	16.1	100.0
Total	189	100.0	

The respondents were asked if they have taken part in strikes organised by the unions in dairy units since their inception. The views elicited from them are present in Table 6.6.

Table 6.6: Participation in Strikes and Demonstrations

Response	*Frequency*	*Per cent*	*Cumulative Per cent*
Yes	125	41.0	41.0
No	180	59.0	100.0
Total	305	100.0	

It can be seen from Table 6.6 that majority (59%) of the respondents have not participated in strikes and demonstrations even once. Whereas the remaining respondents (41%) have participated in these direct actions of unions.

Table 6.7: Exercise the Vote in Recent Union Elections

Response	*Frequency*	*Per cent*	*Cumulative Per cent*
Yes	125	41.0	41.0
No	180	59.0	59.0
Total	305	100.0	

Table 6.7 depicts that majority (59.0%) of them have not exercised their vote in union elections. It is in Vijaya dairy (41%) of them have exercised their vote in the recent

elections. In Sangam dairy elections were held in 2001 and these respondents belong to Sangam dairy.

Table 6.8: Payment of Union Subscription

Response	*Frequency*	*Per cent*	*Cumulative Per cent*
Yes	190	62.3	62.3
No	115	37.7	100.0
Total	305	100.0	

From table 6.8 it can be inferred that majority of the respondents are regular in payment of union subscription, while the other respondents are not regular in payment of the said subscription.

Table 6.9: Participation in Union Fund Raising Activities

Response	*Frequency*	*Per cent*	*Cumulative Per cent*
Yes	101	33.1	33.1
No	204	66.9	100.0
Total	305	100.0	

Table 6.9 indicates that two-thirds of the respondents have not participated whereas one-third of the respondents have participated in the union fund raising activities.

Table 6.10: Union Met the Expectations of its Members

Response	*Frequency*	*Per cent*	*Cumulative Per cent*
Yes	152	49.8	49.8
No	153	50.2	100.0
Total	305	100.0	

Table 6.10 narrates that more than half of the respondents are of the opinion that unions have failed to meet the expectation of its members. Interestingly nearly

half of the respondents have opined that the union has successfully met the expectations of its members.

Table 6.11: Preference to Leadership

Preference	*Frequency*	*Per cent*	*Cumulative Per cent*
Inside leadership	264	86.6	86.6
Outside leadership	41	13.4	100.0
Total	305	100.0	

It can be concluded that an overwhelming majority of the respondents prefer inside leadership whereas the rest of respondents prefer outside leadership.

Collective Bargaining

Like many other countries, in India collective bargaining has some impetus from various statutory and voluntary provisions. The Trade Disputes Act, 1929, the Bombay Industrial Relations Act, 1946, the Industrial Disputes Act, 1947, and the Madhya Pradesh Industrial Relations Act, 1960 provided a machinery for consultation and paved the way for collective bargaining. Among the voluntary measures, mention may be made of the different tripartite conferences, joint consultation machineries, code of discipline, implementation and evaluation committees, etc.

In the industrial sector, the textile industry in Ahmedabad claims to have been a pioneer in the field of collective bargaining. Although the idea was acceptable to many industrial centres, it had not been a common practice prior to 1947 except in certain places where it was experimented but there was absence of a uniformity in approach and practice.

Between 1946 and 1957 several industrial organisations in India have accepted the collective bargaining system. Notable among them are the multinationals. Prominent among such multinationals and indigenous companies are the Dunlop

Rubber Company Ltd. (1947), the Bata Shoe Company Ltd., (1948), the Indian Aluminium Company Ltd. (1951), the Imperial Tobacco Company Ltd. (1952), the Mysore Iron and Steel Works Ltd. (1953), the Mysore Paper Mills Ltd. (1955), the Tata Iron and Steel Company Ltd. (1955) and Hindustan Lever Ltd. (1955).[13]

In India Collective bargaining was traditionally conducted at plant level. Initially, the workmen were assisted and advised by outside political party leaders. But gradually the internal leadership was developed and the parties learned the techniques and strategies of collective bargaining. There is growing recognition, in India, among trade unions and managements, of collective bargaining as a device for resolution of industrial conflicts. This is evident from the growth of collective bargaining at the national, industry and plant levels.

Collective Bargaining in Dairy Units under Study

Collective bargaining in both units is adopted as a democratic method of settlement. Wages and salaries are fixed as per the state government employees (fifth pay commission). The other issues relating to monetary and non-monetary benefits, introducing new measures to restructure the organisation (VRS), improve the quality; marketing strategies in the competitive environment, participative work culture are introduced in consultation with the union. Bilaterally most of the issues were settled. Trade unions also show their integrity and responsibility to cope up with management and the management also encourages the trade unions to exercise their democratic practices. Trade unions together make a common cause from a joint action committee to show their solidarity and improve their strength at the bargaining table. Negotiations are first tried to resolve the issues and this healthy practice is followed in the dairy units.

Table 6.12 demonstrates the evaluation of the union influence on management in the recent scenario. Nearly

Table 6.12: Evaluation of Union Influence on Management

Union influence	*Frequency*	*Per cent*	*Cumulative Per cent*
Increasing	152	49.8	49.8
Decreasing	76	24.9	74.8
No change	48	15.7	90.5
Lost their influence completely	29	9.5	100.0
Total	305	100.0	

half of the respondents have opined that union influence on management has increased whereas nearly one-fourth of the respondents have expressed their opinion that union influence has declined. Interestingly more than fifteen per cent of the respondents have felt that there is no change in union position and the remaining respondents are of the opinion felt that unions have lost their influence completely in the current scenario.

Table 6.13: Effectiveness of Collective Bargaining

Response	*Frequency*	*Per cent*	*Cumulative Per cent*
Yes	162	53.1	53.1
No	143	46.9	100.0
Total	305	100.0	

Table 6.13 depicts that majority of the respondents have felt that collective bargaining is effective whereas the other respondents (46.9%) have expressed contrary opinion.

Industrial Disputes and Settlements

Conciliation

Conciliation method has been used frequently for settlement of disputes. Conciliation can be defined as the practice by which the services of a neutral third party are used in a dispute as a means of helping the disputing parties to reduce the extent of their differences and to arrive at an amicable settlement or agreed solution.[14] The purpose of this method is to expidite settlement of disputes and to terminate work stoppages if they have already occurred. In India, the Industrial Disputes Act, 1947 provides for conciliation as a method of settlement of disputes. Provision is made for appointment of conciliation officers and the Board of Conciliation. The conciliation officer, in conciliation proceedings tries to bring the two parties together and persuades them to arrive at a settlement. The board of conciliation consists of equal number of representatives of employers and employees and an independent chairman, who is appointed by the government.

In dairy industries conciliation plays an important role. The methods of collective bargaining and conciliation are so closely inter-related, it is not always clear about the distinction between operational process of the two methods. For example, when the negotiations are deadlocked, the conciliation officers' intervention helps the parties to resume negotiations between them and arrive at an agreement. Further, when an agreement is reached between the parties solely due to their mutual efforts, they tend to approach the. conciliation officer (Assistant Commissioner of Labour Vijayawada and Guntur) for signing the agreement under section 12(3) read with 18(3) of the Industrial Disputes Act, 1947 for having a binding effect on all the workmen of the establishment.

Settlement Under Section 12(13) in Sangam Dairy

Parties to the dispute settlement from the management is K. Rajan Babu, Chairman, P. Gopala Krishna, managing Director and T. Muralidhar, Manager (Personnel). From employees association (INTUC) representatives are Vijendra P., B. Ram Mohan Rao and Sankar Reddy.

The Sangam dairy employees association, the recognised trade union, submitted a charter of 19 demands through their letter dated 19-9-1998, a 12(3) settlement was entered between the management and the recognised trade union. The above letter referred to state that the settlement was seven years back and new settlements has to be arrived at on certain demand. Discussions were held on 2-12-98, 8-12-98, 17-12-98 and 25-1-99 with all trade unions representatives by Chairman, Managing Director and Manager (personnel).

The following understanding is arrived at and the powers were duly delegated to the Managing Director for enabling to arrive at a 12(3) settlement with the recognised trade union.

Whereas board vide B.R.No. 18(4) dated 11-2-1999, it was resolved that all 25 demands were approved accordingly as recommended to the Board and Managing Director.

The management and recognised trade union approached Assistant Commissioner of Labour (ACL) Guntur for admitting charter of demands into conciliation on 1-3-99 and ACL fixed joint meeting on 24-3-99 at 3 pm and further called both the parties on 6-8-99 at 3 pm and it was decided to admit the issue into conciliation. In the said conciliation meeting after having discussions, finally both the parties arrived at a common understanding and arrived to an amicable settlement under Sec. 12(3) of ID Act before the conciliation officer on 16-08-99 as follows:

Demand 1: Both agreed for speedy action in preparation of staffing pattern since it is long pending and for filling up of all vacancies.

- Steps for filling up vacancies would be taken after approval of the parties by the supervisory board.

Demand 2: Employees completing 45 years of age and continuing in the same cadre without getting even one promotion in the vacant post, an additional increment should be given.

- 24th year increment preponed to 18th year.

Demand 3: Dairy operator posts have to be restored and promotional changes should be provided to worker cadre.

- Management agreed to examine at the time of approval of staffing pattern.

Demand 4: Abolition of existing contract system in the dairy to utilize the capacities of workmen to the optimum level.

- Management agreed that the surplus will be utilised in place of contract labour.

Demand 5: Preparation of job charts and to provide standards of working in various capacities.

- Management accepted.

Demand 6: Monthly washing allowances to be enhanced from Rs. 30 to Rs. 75 since rates of detergent were raised.

- Management agreed to enhance washing allowance from Rs. 30 to Rs. 35 only with effect from 01-04-1999.

Demand 7: Stitching charges to be enhanced from Rs. 150 to Rs. 300 (gents) and Rs. 20 to Rs. 40 (females).

- Management agreed to enhance rates from Rs. 150 to Rs. 200 for males and Rs. 20 to Rs. 25 for females with effect from 01-04-1999.

Demand 8: The night shift allowances to be enhanced from Rs. 4 to Rs. 10 per day.

- Management agreed to enhance for Rs. 4 to Rs. 4.25 w.e.f 01-04-1999

Demand 9: Risk allowance to be enhanced Rs. 50 to Rs. 100 for working in registrations, boilers, boosters, dust and computer centers.

- Management agreed to enhance the rates as per the APDDC Federation rates.

Demand 10: Medical allowances to be enhanced from Rs. 675 to Rs. 2,000.

- Management agreed to implement the medi-claim policy.

Demand 11: Marriage advances to be enhanced from Rs. 10,000 to Rs. 25,000.

- Management agreed to enhance from Rs. 10,000 to Rs. 20,000 at the rate of 8 per cent interest.

Demand 12: Increase of festival advance from Rs. 1,000 to Rs. 2,000.

- Management is already implementing the same.

Demand 13: Interest on vehicle loan may be minimised upto 8 per cent.

- Management agreed to minimize from 14 per cent to 13 per cent only.

Demand 14: HRA rate to be enhanced from 10 per cent to 12.5 per cent.

- Management did not agree with the demand of the union.

Demand 15: Separate toilets for male and female for production, administration, procurement and inputs division employees.

- Management agreed to provide toilets separately as demanded.

Demand 16: Toilets, fans, furniture to be provided at rest room.

- Management agreed.

Demand 17: Auditorium to be repaired and to provide better recreation facilities.

- Management agreed.

Demand 18: Special pay for drivers to be enhanced from Rs. 100 to Rs. 175.

- **Management agreed to enhance the special pay to drivers on par with the federation.**

Demand 19: Conveyance allowance to be enhanced from Rs. 15 to Rs. 20 who are residing in Guntur and Rs. 12 to Rs. 20 who are residing in Tenali.

- Management agreed to enhance contingency allowance for Guntur and turned down the enhancement of conveyance allowance at Tenali.

Settlements in Vijaya Dairy u/s 18(1) of the ID Act

Settlement 1: Parties to the Dispute

1. Workers and employees of milk products factory Vijayawada represented by AITUC.
2. Vijaya dairy represented by General Manager.

Whereas the workers and employees of milk products factory, Vijayawada represented by AITUC staged Dharna in front of the factory every day from 25/10/1995 on the following demands.

1. Enquiry into the alleged corruption
2. Payment of leave travel concession
3. Payment of bonus
4. Lifting-up of restrictions on the sanctioning of earned leave
5. Abolition of the procedure of deduction of casual leave for the late marks by carry forward to next month
6. Solving the problems of A.P.S. Staff.

Whereas the management with a view to maintain industrial peace and tranquility convened joint meeting on 9-11-1995 at 9 pm. On behalf of the management five members were present and on behalf of the employees five members were present. After protracted discussion held between the parties, the management finally has come to a settlement with the union on the demands raised by them as follows.

Demand 1: Enquiry into against the alleged corruption

The management agreed to bring the points of irregularities and corruption to the notice of the chairman for investigation. (The personnel officer is directed to take action).

Demand 2: Payment of leave travel concession

The management agreed to implement the points noted in the circular of head office to admit the clients on those guidelines. (The personnel officer is directed to follow-up action).

Demand 3: Payment of bonus

As there are instructions from the cooperative department not to pay bonus/ex-gratio by the reference 215 dated 30-8-95 read with G.O.Ms.No.113 Animal Husbandry. (dairy-II) department dated 23-8-95 for a period of two years or till such time the accumulated losses are wiped out whichever is earlier. In view of the above G.O. both parties agreed to follow the orders if any received from head office.

Demand 4: Lifting-up of restrictions on the sanctioning of earned leave

The management agreed to take up the issue with the head office and directed the P.O./Sr. Accounts Officer to follow the existing rules on the demand.

Demand 5: Abolition of the procedure of deduction of casual leave for the late marks by carry forward to next month

The management agreed to permit the office staff to attend office late for valid reasons three times in a month provided that the period of absence does not exceed one hour including the grace times of 10 minutes. For every three subsequent late attendances or less during the month one day casual leave will be deducted from the casual leave account. The deduction shall be made during the calendar year for the late attendance without permission. This will come into effect from 1-1-1996.

Demand 6: Solving the problems of A.P.S. Staff

The chairman has agreed to discuss the matter separately with the representatives of the Asceptic Package Section (APS) staff within a week.

Demand 7: Limits of deduction from the salaries

During the course of deliberation, the union raised another demand on the limits of deduction from the salaries. The management agreed to allow deduction up to 50 per cent of gross wages including festival advance and departmental deductions etc., and 75 per cent of gross wages in case of employees cooperative credit society loans only up to 31-3-1996 or until further order.

The union and the management mutually agreed to file memorandum of settlement arrived under section 18(1) of ID Act, 1947 before the concerned conciliation officer to have the impact of statute that is 12(3) and to have an opportunity to apply for all the workmen.

Settlement 2: Consumption of Excess H.S. Diesel Oil

Instructions were issued for recovery of the cost of excess HSD oil consumed by certain drivers, than the quantity fixed to the allotted routes. On this certain representations were received from the trade unions and the drivers for waival of the present kilometer rating system for the assessment of diesel oil consumption, since the vehicles have become very old and the norms fixed are redundant.

In view of the above, the management has decided to re-examine the issue and fix fresh norms taking all the related and relevant factors into consideration.

Therefore the orders issued are kept in abeyance till the fresh norms are fixed and the senior accounts officer M.P.F., is requested to stop the recovery and refund the amount already recovered from the drivers in this regard.

The union and the management mutually agreed to file memorandum of settlement arrived under section 18(1) of ID Act, 1947 before the concerned conciliation officer to have the impact of statute that is 12(3) and to have an opportunity to apply for all the workmen

Settlement 3: Payment of pay revision commission arrears and enhancement of stitching charges and other allowances.

The Krishna District Padi Parisharma Karmika Sanghala Samakhya Milk Products Factory has submitted its demands to the Management relating to:

1. Payment of pay revision commission arrears and
2. Enhancement of stitching charges and other allowances.

The demands were cited in a letter to the Andhra Pradesh Dairy Development Corporation Federation, Hyderabad, and the response came on 3-1-2000.

It was ordered to take necessary action for payment of pay revision commission arrears, enhancement of stitching charges and other allowances as requested. The union and the management mutually agreed to file memorandum of settlement arrived under section 18(1) of ID Act, 1947 before the concerned conciliation officer to have the impact of statute that is 12(3) and to have an opportunity to apply for all the workmen

Settlement 4: Payment of Interim Relief

The workers demanded for the payment of Interim Relief amount. All trade unions of Krishna District Milk Product Cooperative Limited have made a cycle rally from milk product factory to sub-collector's office in Vijayawada and submitted the representation to the sub-collector. Then, the trade unions demonstrated a "dharna" on 22-9-1998 from 11.00 a.m. to 11.30 a.m. for the aforesaid reason.

As a result, the management accepted to pay the interim relief @ 11 per cent to the employees.

The union and the management mutually agreed to file memorandum of settlement arrived under section 18(1) of ID Act, 1947 before the concerned conciliation officer to have the impact of statute that is 12(3) and to have an opportunity to apply for all the workmen.

Adjudication

This is a case of deciding seniority K. Rama Krishna Rao S/o Venkata Subba Rao, native of Vadlamudi, Guntur district and Smt. K. Lalitha Kumari W/o Ashok Kumar superintendent, Sangam dairy, Vadlamudi are the parties to the dispute regarding their seniority. Both the parties worked in AP dairy development corporation (APDDC). In the year 1978 in feeder balancing dairy, Vadlamudi was separated from APDDC and entrusted to Guntur district milk producers cooperative union. The employees working earlier in Guntur region of APDDC were absorbed in the separated unit by name Sangam dairy on application. K. Rama Krishna Rao who was appointed initially in the APDDC in the year 1971 who was absorbed in the sangam dairy on application was taken as LDC whereas K. Lalitha Kumari who initially employed in the APDDC in the year 1973 was absorbed in Sangam dairy on application as UDC on 16/9/78. Therefore Rama Krishna Rao raised a dispute before the management of Sangam dairy stating that he was initially appointed in the APDDC in the year 1971 whereas K. Lalitha Kumari was appointed initially in the year 1973 in the APDDC. He requested the management of Sangam dairy to consider his seniority over K. Lalitha Kumari and appoint him as UDC and to revise the seniority list giving the place over K. Lalitha Kumari in the seniority list.

The management of Sangam dairy duly taking into consideration of the contention of K. Rama Krishan Rao and having satisfied with the seniority maintained in APDDC appointed K. Rama Krishna Rao as UDC with effect from 27-9-79 and placed him in the seniority list as serial number one, and serial number three was assigned to K. Lalitha Kumari.

Lalitha Kumari the first respondent was aggrieved by the orders of management. The petitioner raised a dispute before the conciliation officer, later it was referred to labour court for adjudication. The respondent petitioner was appointed as typist in 1978 and she was initially appointed in the APDDC dairy in 1973. Whereas the appellant, i.e. Rama Krishna Rao who was appointed as LDC in the year 1975 and he was initially appointed in the year 1971 in APDDC. The appellant raised industrial dispute aggrieved by the refixation of seniority putting the petitioner/first respondent above him, on the ground that the seniority fixed could not be changed by the concerned authority.

The said dispute was registered as ID. No. 133/84 by the Labour Court, Guntur. The Labour Court Guntur in its award dated 1-3-1989 held that the seniority list dated 8-3-1983 was not valid in as much as seniority of the appellant had been fixed on 15/9/1981 appointing the appellant as UDC, with effect from 1-8-1978 and his seniority therefore can't be disturbed in the absence of any order to that effect questioning the said award. A writ petition was filed by the first respondent/petitioner. The learned single judge held that the finding of the labour court was illegal and that the representation of the first respondent petitioner was properly considered and decided by the management according to the policy decision. The learned council for the appellant urged that the Managing Director of Sangam dairy considering his representation passed the order dated 27-9-78 duly revising the seniority of the appellant as UDC with effect from 1-8-1978 and accordingly the seniority list was prepared in the year 1981 which was not questioned by the respondent one and therefore it has become final. The said seniority list could not be changed by the management merely on the ground of policy decision by making the first respondent as senior to him. The learned council for the first respondent re-iterated his agreements that have been advanced in the writ petition, i.e. that the petitioner/respondent one had been appointed as UDC on 16/9/78 and on the date the appellant was only LDC having been appointed as such on 1-8-78 and that the

appellant was appointed as UDC only on 27-9-1978 and therefore he is junior to her in the Sangam dairy. He further contends that the data of initial appointment of the appellant in the APDDC will have no effect on the seniority to be fixed between them in the service of Sangam dairy. It is not in dispute that the appellant was initially appointed in APDDC two years prior to the appointment of first respondent. It is relevant to notice that the Sangam dairy was under the control of APDDC. In 1978 a unit of the corporation was entrusted to GDMPCO union. It was there after called as Sangam dairy. The employees of the corporation who are willing to be absorbed permanently in Sangam dairy were formally directed to apply for appointment in Sangam dairy. Accordingly they were appointed and since then they were deemed to be in the service of Sangam dairy. Though the appellant and the first respondent were treated as employees of Sangam dairy from the date of their appointment in the Sangam dairy and the fact cannot be lost sight of that both of them were earlier employees of APDDC.

It is true that the first respondent has been appointed UDC whereas on the date the appellant was only working as LDC. The contention of the learned council of the appellant was that on his application the Managing Director ought to have appointed him as UDC and that it was not done. The managers of Sangam dairy considering the grievance as genuine passed the orders on 27-9-1978 changing the seniority of the appellant w.e.f. 1-8-1978 as UDC. The main argument of learned council for the appellant is that once his seniority was given w.e.f. 1-8-1978 as UDC that has to be maintained for all purposes. The impugned seniority list putting the first respondent senior to him is not based on any order of the management of Sangam dairy.

Hence the Labour Court was right in upholding the seniority list dated 1-8-1993 was bad. Learned council for the first respondent has tried to show but in vain. In the absence of any such order the action of the management in preparing the impugned seniority list is invalid. The management who is empowered to appoint a person prospectively has also got power to appoint him even retrospectively. In the exercise of such power the appellant was appointed with retrospective effect as UDC duly recognising his earlier appointment in the APDDC. Fixation of seniority in the absence of rules should be guided by the date of appointment of an employee.

In view of the orders passed by the Managing Director, Sangam dairy dated 27-9-78 showing the appellant as having been appointed as UDC earlier to the first respondent, there is no escape from holding that the appellant is senior to the first respondent. The learned single judge is therefore is correct in holding that the impugned seniority list fixed as for the policy of the management was sustainable. The seniority of the person is a vested right on the same cannot be deprived of merely on the ground of policy. Therefore the divisional bench held that the seniority list dated 8/3/1983 did not correctly represent seniority between the appellant and first respondent and it is accordingly quashed. The award passed by the Labour Court is in accordance with the law and it is hearby upheld.

Strikes in Dairy Industry

The tenor of labour management relations can be vividly understood when we analyse strikes in the dairy units in terms of their genesis, attitudes of the parties, the issues resolved and the mode of settlement. An attempt is made in the following pages to make a brief account of all the seven strikes which have occurred in the units under study since inception. The instances of strikes are presented below.

Strikes in Vijaya Dairy

Strike-1: The employees of Vijaya Dairy on 30-06-1994 under the leadership of joint action committee (JAC) undertook cycle rally followed by one day token strike demanding the employment of the dependents of the deceased employees. The demand was conceded by the management and as a result 37 members secured employment.

Strike-2: The employees of Vijaya Dairy on 11-01-1995 organised tool down strike under the leadership of Joint Action Committee demanding festival advance. The administration initially promised but not implemented the same. The strike led to the police interference and the commissioner of police D.T. Naik intervened for resolving the conflict. Finally the Chairman of Vijaya Dairy, Mandava Janaki Ramaiah agreed for sanctioning the festival advance.

Strike-3: The joint action committee of the trade unions of the Vijaya Dairy made representation to the management about their demands namely:

1. Payment of dearness allowance arrears from 01-07-1995 to 01-01-1996.
2. To confer autonomous status to the dairy under the new Act.
3. Payment of VRS at the rate of 3 months salary for every completed year of their service.

Since the management did not respond to the demands of the employees, the unions undertook dharna at gate on 28-09-1996. The management invited the leaders of the joint action committee for negotiations and finally agreed to pay D.A arrears, and to give autonomous status but they have agreed for sanctioning VRS benefit only at the rate of 45 days salary for every completed year of their service but not as per the demand.

Strikes in Sangarn Dairy

Strike-1

During 1989 in the Sangam dairy the unions affiliated to INTUC (GDMPCO Union Employees Association) BMS (Bharatiya Dairy Mazdoor Sangam) and AITUC (APDDCOF

Ltd, Workers Union) went on strike for 15 days on issues of illtreatment of the workers by the management. The union leaders K. Nagi Reddy (INTUC), V. Prabhunadh (BDMS) and Sri N. Joshi (AITUC) who are the leaders in the agitation were terminated from their service. Subsequently the political parties intervened and settled the dispute. Consequently the leaders were re-instated in the service. However, two of the leaders left the organisation for not being satisfied with the attitude of the management. One of the leaders is still continuing in the service.

Strike-2

At the inception of the Sangam dairy the GDMPCO Union Ltd Employees Association affiliated to INTUC was established in 1979 and it was later recognised in 1992. The Employees Association was formed due to the harsh behaviour of the management towards the workers. Moreover in the initial stages the management of Sangam dairy was not providing minimum statutory facilities and working hours are not regulated. The employees association got its affiliation to INTUC and organised this strike for three months demanding the regulation of working hours and provision of statutory welfare facilities. Finally the management conceded the demands and implemented the same.

Strike-3

The trade unions of Sangam dairy are formed as joint action committee to achieve the twin objectives. One is that the management may take the unions into confidence for the development of the unit. The other one is immediate placement for the dependents of diceased employees. At the first stage management receives the representation of the JAC, and it has not responded properly. The joint action committee issued strike notice on 16-9-1994. As a result the management responded and 5 people were taken into employment.

Strike - 4

One of the unions in Sangam dairy namely Sangam Karmika Samaikya affiliated to CITU was established in the year 1995. This union launched the strike for one month raising the slogans against the corruption at the high level management. The management finally assured to take necessary steps for putting an end to the corruption.

JOINT COMMITTEES

No job in any company is better understood by anyone than the person who does it, whether he be a floor sweeper, factory mechanic or President of the company. The person who understands the job knows the problems as well as the feasible solution. This is the rationale for worker participation in decision-making.

Worker's participation in Management has been considered to be one of the synergetic techniques of management. The concept of participative management goes hand in hand with the idea of industrial democracy. Ours is the largest democracy in the world and, therefore, the stress on participative management by academicians and the government alike is genuine and understandable.

The logic behind worker's participation in management, is to create an atmosphere where workers and management feel close to each other and work in union to further the development and prosperity of the industry and the nation.

A concept of industrial democracy has emerged in which workers and management both are involved in decision-making process. Decision-making in modern times is not the concern of management alone, the workers are equally concerned about the matters concerning them. If workers are allowed to participate in decision-making process, they may feel that they have a better understanding of industrial processes in which they take part. Workers' participation help to maintain discipline in the industry and improve industrial relations.

Both Vijaya dairy and Sangam dairy are more concerned not only about the quality of the product but also about the industrial atmosphere in the organisation.

The management of the organisations are striving hard to maintain peace in the organisations by promoting harmonious relations between employees and the management. The joint committees constituted in the study units illustrating participative management are presented below. Canteen Committee, Safety Committee, Works Committee, Productivity Committee and Quality Control Committee.

Table 6.14: Awareness about the Bipartite Committees

Response	*Frequency*	*Per cent*	*Cumulative Per cent*
Yes	71	23.3	23.3
No	234	76.7	100.0
Total	305	100.0	

Table 6.14 shows that majority of the respondents do not have awareness about the committees and they have expressed that the management does not constitute committees with the representatives of workers and management, whereas the other respondents (23.3 per cent) have agreed that the management constitutes committees with the equal representatives of workers and management.

Canteen Committee

The canteen committee has been constituted with the equal participation of both management and workers' representatives. This committee meets once in a month. In this meeting they review the expenditure incurred during the month and prepare an estimates budget for the coming month.

The personnel officer will preside over the committee meeting every month. The purchase, preparation and sales are supervised by the workers' representatives.

As mentioned in preceding chapter both the units of Vijayawada and Guntur have provided canteen with all facilities and they are maintained well and the food items served in the canteen are offered at subsidised rates. Cleanliness and hygiene are given an important feature of these canteens. It is interesting to know to what extent these facilities are utilised by the workers. With this end in view the respondents were asked whether they are using the canteen services. Their views are presented in Table 6.15.

Table 6.15: Whether Using Canteen Services

Response	*Frequency*	*Per cent*	*Cumulative Per cent*
Yes	234	76.7	76.7
No	71	23.3	100.0
Total	305	100.0	

As one can expect it is found that more than three-fourth 76.7 per cent of the respondents make use of the canteen services. But only 23.3 per cent expressed that they seldom use the services of the canteen though they take their lunch which they carry from home in the canteen and relax during the rest period.

Table 6.16: Canteen Committee Functioning

Response	*Frequency*	*Per cent*	*Cumulative Per cent*
Good	81	26.6	26.6
Average	68	22.3	48.9
Poor	156	51.1	100.0
Total	305	100.0	

Table 6.16 inferred that more than half of the respondents have felt that the canteen committee's functioning is 'poor', followed by more than one-fourth as 'good' and the rest of them expressed its functioning as 'average'.

Safety Committee

Though the dairy industry does not involve hazardous nature of work giving rise to accidents, the management has not neglected the safety aspect of the employees. They intend to provide a work environment in which the workers take up their operations without any concern or apprehension about the possible accidents. The management has provided safety equipment to the workers, such as gum boots, gloves, goggles and protective clothing. The machinery is properly fenced and the management endeavors to create awareness about safety among the workers by organising orientation programmes, safety weeks and checking safety posters at strategic places in the industry. An officer in the production department who is qualified and trained is kept incharge of the safety programme in both the units under study.

This committee is constituted with safety officer as the president and the other members are the functional heads of production, plant, civil with equal representatives of workers.

The committee looks after the safety of the workers at the workplace. The committee meets once in 6 months. In this meeting, they assess the possible causes of accidents if any and take necessary decisions in order to prevent them.

Table 6.17: Safety Awareness

Response	*Frequency*	*Per cent*	*Cumulative Per cent*
Yes	116	38.0	38.0
No	189	62.0	100.0
Total	305	100.0	

Table 6.17 tells that majority of the respondents lack safety awareness in the organisation whereas the other respondents have awareness.

Table 6.18: Are Safety Measures Adequate

Response	*Frequency*	*Per cent*	*Cumulative Per cent*
Yes	122	40.0	40.0
No	183	60.0	100.0
Total	305	100.0	

Table 6.18 reveals that majority of the respondents have expressed that the safety precautions taken in the units are inadequate. Whereas 40 per cent of the respondents have expressed a contrary view.

Table 6.19: Functioning of Safety Committee

Response	*Frequency*	*Per cent*	*Cumulative Per cent*
Good	38	12.5	12.5
Average	62	20.3	32.8
Poor	205	67.2	100.0
Total	305	100.0	

Table 6.19 demonstrates that majority (67.2%) of the respondents have expressed that the functioning of the safety committee is poor. But more than one-fifth of the respondents have opined that the level of functioning of the safety committee is average. The remaining 12.5 per cent of the respondents have expressed that functioning of the committee is good.

Works Committee

In both the units the composition of the works committee is on the same lines. The committee is comprises of 3 Board of Directors, Deputy General Manager (Plant) and the General Manager and Senior Accounts Officer. From the union side an equal number of representatives are associated in the committee.

Table 6.20: Awareness about Works Committee

Response	*Frequency*	*Per cent*	*Cumulative Per cent*
Yes	109	35.7	35.7
No	196	64.3	100.0
Total	305	100.0	

Table 6.20 indicates that majority (64.3%) of the respondents are not aware of the existence of works committee. Whereas the remaining has awareness about this body.

Table 6.21: Works Committee Functioning

Response	*Frequency*	*Per cent*	*Cumulative Per cent*
Good	40	13.1	13.1
Average	59	19.3	32.5
Poor	206	67.5	100.0
Total	305	100.0	

Table 6.21 depicts that more than two-third of the respondents have stated that the functioning of works committee is poor. From out of the remaining, nearly one-fifth have felt average and for the rest it is good.

Production Committee

This committee was constituted in both the units recently in the year 1998. The members include DGM Production as the president, and other functional heads. There are no member representatives from the workers side.

The main objective is to assess the progress in meeting production targets periodically and also monitor on the quality aspects. If any hurdles are noticed in production matters they are sought to be removed. The committee meets periodically depending upon the need.

Quality Control Committee

In order to survive in the market, the industry has to maintain the quality of its products. In this regard the management pays utmost attention. It is aware of the growing competition in the dairy industry.

The Quality Control Committee was also constituted recently in the units with the president as Quality Control Officer and the functional heads as members.

Besides these 5 statutory and non-statutory joint committees, Sangam dairy constituted another joint committee namely Death Relief Fund Committee.

Death Relief Fund Committee

Death Relief Fund Committee consists of managing director as the chairman of the committee, welfare officer is the convener, all the functional heads as the members from management side. All the presidents of trade unions are the employee representatives on this committee. The objective of the committee is to provide financial relief to the deceased employees' family by identifying the dependents. The committee also fixes the priorities as per the stipulated procedure. The committee meets whenever the need arises.

DISCIPLINE

Bremblett observes that "discipline does not mean a strict and technical observance of rigid rules and regulations. It simply means working, cooperating and behaving in a normal and orderly way, as any responsible person would expect an employee to do."[15] In short, discipline is employee's self-control which prompts him to willingly cooperate with the organisational standards and objectives.

Absence of discipline tells upon the functioning of organisations and the society. Importance of discipline has to be realised by all concerned and maintenance of discipline should be joint responsibility of both the workers and management. Discipline is a two-way traffic and breach of discipline on the part of the either party in industry will cause unrest. The approach to managing discipline depends, to a great extent, upon managerial philosophy, culture and attitude towards the employees. A negative approach to discipline relies heavily on punitive measures and in line with the traditional managerial attitude of "hire and fire" and obedience to orders. On the other hand, a constructive approach stresses on modifying forbidden behaviour by taking positive steps like educating, counselling, etc. The concept of positive discipline promotion aims at the generation of a sense of self-discipline and disciplined behaviour in all the human beings in a dynamic organisational setting, instead of discipline imposed by force or punishment. The approach to the disciplinary action in most cases should be corrective rather than punitive. Further, the positive discipline maintenance should form an intergral part of human resource development efforts of an organisation. Some case studies are presented for portraying the various facets of discipline prevailing in the two units. The actual names are not used to safeguard the confidentiality. Instead pseudonyms are used.

Case Studies in Vijaya Dairy

Case Study-1: Dereliction of Duty

Appa Rao, assistant dairy officer, as usual attended for the duty in processing section in third shift. The second shift manager had handed over 2700 liters of buttermilk in vat no. 5 and it was given for laboratory sample at 4:30 pm during third shift and received the result of fat 0.1 per cent, SNF 7.88 per cent, Acidity 0.125 per cent and WB negative. In addition to the above quantity of buttermilk the delinquent employee has received during his shift 2,000 liters of sweet cream buttermilk kept in the same vat no. 5 and thus he has 4,700 liters of sweet buttermilk on hand during his shift. Whereas he has utilised 700 liters of butter milk only for processing and left 4000 liters of buttermilk without processing and shown it as balance available. In the beginning of the first shift on 12-1-99 at 3 AM quality control laboratory had drawn sample from the above buttermilk vat no. 5 and issued a report with the remarks that it is “not fit for processing”

Hence, as per the laboratory report 4000 liters of sweet cream buttermilk was spoiled on 12-1-99 at processing section. This has happened due to gross negligence of Appa Rao. An explanation was called for from the delinquent officer for the said lapses. The management received explanation from the officer along with the remarks of the dairy manager (processing). The dairy manager (processing) has stated in his remarks categorically that this has happened only due to the negligence of Appa Rao, the delinquent officer.

Keeping in view the remarks of the manager, the disciplinary authority appointed Subrahmanyarn as an enquiry officer to enquire into the allegations levelled against Appa Rao. In the course of enquiry Rao deposed his evidence stating that Israil stopped operation of sweet buttermilk without his knowledge and that he was not intimated about the fact of the addition of 2000 liters of buttermilk in vat no. 5 received during his shift. The CSE stated that there was no sufficient staff on that particular day and only one employee by name Israil had knowledge of processing who did not cooperate with the delinquent officer. Further he stated that in order to safeguard the whole milk received from Nellore tanker he had to attend to it immediately for its re-pasteurisation. He has also given importance to re-pasteurisation of reconstituted skimmed milk which was having high temperature.

The enquiry officer opined that the delinquent officer did not bestow his attention in processing the butter milk which is expected of him. Therefore, he came to the conclusion that the allegation of negligence of work or negligence in performing his duties and causing damage to the property of the management is proved beyond doubt and the same constitutes misconduct under clauses 9, 10 and

35 of rule 5 of conduct discipline and appeal rule of 1983. The extent of loss to the management is 1360 liters. After receiving the report from the enquiry officer the disciplinary authority has communicated this report to the delinquent officer with a direction to submit his remarks. Since the disciplinary authority did not satisfy with the remarks of the delinquent officer, issued a show-cause notice to the delinquent officer stating that why disciplinary action (i.e. stoppage of annual increment for a period of one year without cumulative effect) should not be initiated against him for the misconduct.

As the disciplinary authority was not satisfied with the explanation of the delinquent officer, he was awarded punishment of stoppage of annual increment for a period of one year without cumulative effect since the allegations are proved beyond doubt and the misconduct (dereliction of duty) is established.

Case Study-2: Misappropriation

The facts of the case in brief are that it is brought to the notice of the general manager that Venkat Rao, fodder development officer, had drawn Rs. 15,000 on 2-5-98 to meet the expenditure for conducting general body meeting to be held on 9-5-98. Out of the said amount Rs. 8,326 was spent on general body meeting and the balance amount was remitted in accounts section on 24-9-98, that is after four months, which amounts to temporary misappropriation of company's funds. Therefore, the management called for an explanation from the delinquent employee for the said lapse. The delinquent employee had submitted his explanation to the management. The explanation submitted by him was not found to be satisfactory, Anjaneyulu, retd. Sub-judge was appointed as an enquiry officer for conducting detailed enquiry into the alleged charges issued against the delinquent. The enquiry officer, duly following the enquiry procedure and also the principles of natural justice, conducted enquiry and sent his enquiry report to the management as directed in the stipulated time. The enquiry officer while arriving at the final conclusion took into consideration all the evidence adduced by both the parties and perused the documentary evidence filed before him by the both parties and confirmed that the delinquent committed misconduct and also thereby the charges levelled against him are proved. The enquiry officer had submitted his report to the management and in turn the management communicated the same to Venkat Rao with a direction to submit his explanation asking why proposed punishment (that is stoppage of one annual grade increment) should not be imposed for the misconduct. The employee had submitted his explanation which was not found to be satisfactory and convincing to the management. Therefore the management finally issued punishment orders of stoppage of annual grade increment for a period of one year without cumulative effect for the proven misconduct (temporary misappropriation of the unit funds).

Case Study-3: Unauthorised Absence

The facts of the case in brief are that Srinivas, field assistant was sanctioned leave from 18/02/97 to 16/03/97 on private affairs and after expiry of the said leave he absented himself from duty with effect from 17/03/97 to 3/9/97. Later he submitted leave application along with joining report dated 4-9-97, after a lapse of six months. Absenting consecutively for more than 8 days constitutes misconduct as per certified standing orders. As his absence caused dislocation to the routine work the management proposed to initiate disciplinary action against him. Accordingly the management issued charge memo to the said employee directing him to submit his explanation for the charges. The said employee did not submit any explanation and more over absconded from his duties with effect from 1-12-97 to 11-12-97 without permission of the management. The same also amounts to misconduct as per certified standing orders. Therefore the management again called for explanation of the said employee for his unauthorised absence and for absconding from duties within a stipulated time and also with a direction to resume duty forthwith. The following charges were framed against the employee.

Charge 1: Willful and habitual absence from duties without any leave application or prior permission.

Charge 2: Insubordination or dis-obedience to the orders of the superiors.

It is held that the charges levelled against the delinquent employee are established beyond doubt. Further the enquiry officer opined that the absence beyond eight days is an offence which constitutes misconduct. The enquiry officer submitted his enquiry report to the management. The management after communicating the enquiry report and after issuing show cause notice to the delinquent employee issued punishment of withholding annual grade increment for one year without cumulative effect.

Case Studies in Sangam Dairy

Case study 1: Theft, fraud and dishonesty

Raja Rao, sales supervisor, has collected 73 tubs on 7-3-2001. Further the said sales supervisor tampered the records by correcting the number of tubs by adding 1 before the number of tubs actually received, i.e. 73 and made it as 173 received. Thus the attitude of the employee indicates that he intended causing loss of the property of the establishment to the tune of Rs. 7,958 towards 100 tampered number of tubs.

Further due to the security alertness only 10 tubs of toned milk was prevented from going outside the dairy; otherwise the establishment might have incurred some more loss. Thus the said employee committed misconduct under standing orders item 35(d). The management called for explanation and after having received explanation from the employee framed charges since the explanation is not satisfactory. The management appointed Ramana, Manager (Training) as enquiry officer who conducted enquiry into the charges levelled against the said employee and submitted his findings to the management. The management issued a show cause notice to the delinquent employee duly enclosing the enquiry report and directed him to submit his explanation why punishment of stoppage of two annual grade increments shall not be imposed. Further the management having been dissatisfied with the explanation of the delinquent employee awarded punishment of stoppage of two annual grade increments with cumulative effect.

Case Study 2: Unauthorised Absence and Fraud

Venugopal, working in Sangam dairy, was deputed to Nagarjunasagar milk sales route along with vehicle on 31-05-1999 night. He collected sales proceeds worth of Rs. 10,740 from the commission agents and it was not remitted to the management. Moreover he absconded from duties from 1-6-1999 to 13-7-1999.

B. Rajesh, manager (fodder) was appointed as enquiry officer to conduct enquiry into the charges levelled against Venugopal. The enquiry officer conducted enquiry on 24-9-1999 and during the enquiry the employee was present and admitted all the charges levelled against him before the enquiry officer. In view of the admission of charges the enquiry officer concluded the enquiry by following the procedure and submitted enquiry report to the management. The managing director, that is disciplinary authority, immediately after receiving the report from the enquiry officer, issued a show cause notice proposing punishment of removal from service, while directing the delinquent to remit the amount of Rs. 10,740 with eighteen per cent interest. The delinquent employee submitted his explanation and expressed his willingness to re-pay the amount of Rs. 10,740 along with interest. On perusal of the explanation of the delinquent employee, the managing director taking a lenient view basing on his age, previous record, and family obligations decided to modify the impugned order and proposed stoppage of three annual grade increments due to him in the year 2000, 2001, 2002 with cumulative effect. The amount due to the management from the delinquent employee i.e., Rs. 10,740 with Rs. 967 as interest, which comes to Rs. 11,707 was ordered to be recovered from him on or before 31-11-1999.

Further, on the request of the delinquent employee the managing director issued orders to recover the said amount of Rs. 11,707 from the pay revision commission arrears payable to him and balance if any shall be recovered from his leave salary. In view of the above, the managing director passed order duly lifting suspension orders and for reinstatement of the deliquent employee and the suspension period was regularised as on duty.

Case 3: Misappropriation

Siva Ram, Junior Assistant was charged for misappropriation of sale proceeds of stores material worth rupees Rs. 19,713.32 stores at milk chilling centre, Vinukonda. Having not been satisfied with the explanation of the junior assistant, the management has appointed B. Satish (fodder) as an enquiry officer to conduct domestic enquiry against the charges levelled against the junior assistant. The enquiry officer conducted enquiry duly following the principles of natural justice and submitted his enquiry report to the enquiry officer stating that the charges are proved beyond doubt. Therefore, the management issued a final show cause notice to the delinquent employee indicating the proposed punishment of stoppage of three annual increments with cumulative effect. Besides the management also directed the delinquent employee to remit back the amount of Rs. 19,713.32.

The delinquent employee had submitted his explanation to the show cause notice issued by the management. The management was not satisfied with the explanation of the delinquent employee and taking into consideration of his previous service record decided to confirm the proposed punishment of stoppage of three annual increments and recovery of Rs. 19,713.32 and Rs. 3,358.23 towards further short remittance by the delinquent employee.

Hence the management had issued orders directing the delinquent employee to remit the amount of Rs. 23,071.55 in the cash counter on or before 27-1-2001; otherwise the amount would be recovered from his future salary bill. Then the management lifted the suspension orders and reinstated the said employee into service.

Case Study 4: Damaging the Property (Negligence)

The case in brief is that one Prakesh, assistant dairy manager, was incharge of the powder section and while he was on duty on 5/5/98 midnight failed to identify the burning of skimmed milk powder which caused loss as this powder was not found to be fit for utilisation. The management came to the conclusion that the incident has not occurred suddenly but in a continuous manner due to his negligence; therefore the management issued a charge memo to the delinquent employee for his alleged misconduct, i.e. dishonesty, damage to the property of the management, falsification of records, negligence, and absence from work spot, under rule 5(1) and 5(5), 5(10), and 5(33). Since the explanation submitted by the delinquent employee was not found to be satisfactory, it is decided to initiate disciplinary action against him and appointed an enquiry officer and directed him to conduct enquiry as early as possible and to submit his report. The enquiry officer, duly following the procedure and principles of natural justice, conducted enquiry and submitted his findings to the management stating the charges levelled against the delinquent employee are found to be proved beyond doubt. The management issued a show cause notice to the delinquent employee enclosing the enquiry report requiring him to submit his explanation/ remarks on the report. Having not been satisfied with the explanation of the delinquent employee, the management had issued a final show cause notice to the delinquent employee as to why a punishment of stoppage of three annual grade increments with cumulative effect should not be imposed. Besides recovery of Rs. 15,765 towards damage of 250 kgs skimmed milk, the management after taking into consideration the explanation of the delinquent employee, his past service etc reduced the punishment and confirmed the punishment of stoppage of two annual grade increments out of which one increment with cumulative effect and another one without cumulative effect. Further the management also ordered for recovery of Rs. 15,765 for the damage incurred by the delinquent employee.

Case Study 5: Unauthorised Absence and Tampering of Records

The case in brief is that Swamy was chargesheeted for alleged misconduct, i.e. unauthorised absence from 6-1-1999 to 14-1-1999, tampering of attendance register, theft, fraud or dishonesty, and habitual breach of standing orders, while he was working as milk dispatcher during the period, i.e 28/9/98, 30-9-98, and 6-10-98. Further for short remittance of Rs. 6,461 on 8-10-98. Swamy has submitted his explanation to the management and since the explanation is not satisfactory the management appointed Eswar (Assistant manager—procurement and input) as enquiry officer to conduct enquiry into the charges levelled into against the employee.

The enquiry officer has conducted the enquiry duly following the principles of natural justice and submitted the report to the management, stating that the charges against the delinquent employee are proved beyond doubt. The management issued show cause notice to the delinquent employee duly enclosing the enquiry report requiring an explanation. The delinquent employee has submitted his explanation to the show cause notice. Having not been satisfied with the explanation the management issued a final show cause notice as to why their proposed punishment, i.e. stoppage of three annual grade increment with cumulative effect and recovery of short remittance amount of Rs. 6,461 with 18 per cent interest should not be imposed. The delinquent employee did not submit his explanation even after receipt of this notice and reminders on 2-12-99 and 24-12-99. Further the delinquent employee did not remit the said amount of Rs. 6,461 plus 18 per cent interest till 10-4-2000. However keeping in view of his past record the management decided to impose punishment, i.e. stoppage of two annual grade increments with cumulative effect and to recover an amount of Rs. 969 only towards interest since the delinquent employee had subsequently remitted back the short remittance amount Rs. 6,461.

Case Study 6: Absconding from duties

The case in brief is that Veeraiah, the worker was chargesheeted for the alleged misconduct, i.e. absconding from his duties from 21-12-99 to 10-2-2002. However the delinquent employee applied leave intermittently from 9-4-2000 to 14-2-2000, 17-4-2000 to 14-5-2000, 23-5-2000 to 26-5-2000, 30-5-2000 to 6-6-2000, 8-6-2000 to 13-6-2000, 16-6-2000 to 17-8-2000, 28-10-2000 to 30-10-2000, 1-11-2000 to 2-11-2000, 4-11-2000 to 5-11-2000 and 19-11-2000 to 11-5-2001. He was admitted into duties pending disciplinary action on 12-5-2001. The delinquent employee before finalisation of disciplinary action again absconded from his duties from 8-7-2001 to 31-7-2001 and from 17-8-2001 till he was reinstated into duty. The management after taking into consideration the report of the enquiry officer Sarma (Fodder) issued show cause notice to the delinquent employee duly enclosing the report; the management further issued chargesheet for the misconduct, i.e. absconding duty after commencement of the disciplinary proceedings and appointed another enquiry officer to conduct enquiry against the additional charges against the delinquent employee. Both the enquiry officers have submitted their enquiry reports after conducting the enquiry duly following the procedure under the principles of natural justice stating that the charges levelled against the delinquent employee are proved beyond doubt.

The management issued a show cause notice to the delinquent employee duly enclosing the enquiry reports and also proposing the punishment of removal from service. The delinquent employee has submitted his explanation which was not found to be satisfactory and hence the management issued final show cause notice proposing the punishment of removal from service and requiring him to submit reasons as to why the proposed punishment should not be imposed against him.

The management having not been satisfied with the explanation decided to issue punishment orders duly modifying the proposed punishment of removal from service as fresh appointment, i.e keeping him in minimum pay in the time scale of Rs. 2,750 to 5,150 from the date of his joining.

Case Study 7: Habitual breach of rules and disobedience

The case in brief is that Gouse, senior assistant, who has unauthorised absence and irregular attendance. He had applied medical leave on 20-9-2001 for 20 days from 12-9-2001. Further he had applied medical leave on 26-11-2001 for sanction of leave from 8-11-2001 to 28-11-2001 and extended leave up to 4-12-2001 but he has resumed duty on 18-11-2001, further he had absconded from duties from 11-4-2002 to till the date of issue of charge memo without any leave application.

Further he was transferred to marketing section and directed him to resume duty on 3-4-2002 but he joined duty on 8-4-2002. Therefore the management has issued chargesheet against the employee for the alleged misconduct, i.e. unauthorised absence, disobedience, leaving the work spot during working hours and habitual breach of rules. The delinquent employee has submitted his explanation and it was not found to be satisfactory. Therefore, management had appointed Raghu, Manager training, as enquiry officer who conducted enquiry on the charge levelled against the delinquent employee duly following the procedure and principles of natural justice and sent his report to the management. The management after receiving the enquiry report issued a show cause notice to the delinquent employee as to why disciplinary action should not be initiated against him since the charges were proved during enquiry. The delinquent employee submitted his explanation and as it was not satisfactory the management again issued as final show cause notice indicating the punishment of stoppage of one annual grade increment with cumulative effect. Whereas the said show cause notice sent by registered post was returned by the postal authorities as undelivered.

Therefore the final show cause was pasted on the notice board on 2-9-2002. Even then he has not submitted explanation. Then the management decided to confirm the proposed punishment, i.e. stoppage of one annual grade increment, with cumulative affect and the delinquent employee was ordered accordingly.

Case Study 8: Unauthorised absence

Jacob was chargesheeted by the management for the misconduct of unauthorised absence under habitual breach of rules. Jacob had applied medical leave from 16-3-99 to 21-3-1999 and requested for permission to avail weekly holiday. Later he absconded from his duties from 23/3/99 onwards till 7-9-2000 without any leave application and he has not turned up even after his explanation to the charge in spite of charge memo on 10-7-1999. Therefore the management had decided to initiate disciplinary action against the said employee and appointed Hanumantha Rao, in-charge manager (cooperatives), as an enquiry officer. The enquiry officer, duly following the procedure and the principles of natural justice, conducted enquiry against the charges levelled against the delinquent employee.

Since the delinquent employee failed to attend the enquiry even after taking steps for serving the enquiry notice by registered post and through publication of the said notice in Enadu daily local newspaper. The enquiry officer was constrained to conduct enquiry ex-parte (in the absence of the delinquent employee). Taking into consideration the documentary evidence and other evidences, the enquiry officer completed his enquiry and sent his findings to the management duly holding that the charges were proved. The management after receiving the findings of the enquiry officer, issued a show cause notice to the delinquent employee indicating the punishment of removal from the service. The delinquent employee responded to the final show cause notice and offered his explanation which is not convincing. The management, having dissatisfied with the explanation of the delinquent employee, finally decided to impose the reduced punishment, i.e reduction of pay to the lower minimum of the pay scale instead of proposed punishment of removal from service, keeping in view of his family conditions and hoping that he will change his attitude. Thus, the management finally awarded punishment of reduction to lower pay, i.e. Rs. 2750 in the time scale of 2750-5150 with immediate effect.

Table 6.22: Awareness of Company Rules and Regulations Relating to Discipline

Response	*Frequency*	*Per cent*	*Cumulative Per cent*
Yes	155	50.8	50.8
No	150	49.2	100.0
Total	305	100.0	

Table 6.32 illustrates that more than half of the respondents have awareness of company rules and regulations relating to discipline while the other respondents lack such awareness.

Table 6.23: Show Cause or Charge Sheet Received by the Respondents

Response	*Frequency*	*Per cent*	*Cumulative Per cent*
Yes	56	18.4	18.4
No	249	81.6	100.0
Total	305	100.0	

Table 6.23 tells us that the absolute majority (81.6%) of the respondents never received show cause or

chargesheet, whereas the other (18.4%) respondents have received.

Table 6.24: Rating the Overall Employee Discipline

Employee Response	*Frequency*	*Per cent*	*Cumulative Per cent*
Highly disciplined	69	22.6	22.6
Moderately disciplined	150	49.2	71.8
Just disciplined	70	23.0	94.8
Indisciplined	16	5.2	100.0
Total	305	100.0	

Table 6.24 explains that nearly half of 'the respondents rated the overall employee discipline as 'moderately disciplined'. This is followed by twenty-three per cent of employees who rated as 'just disciplined'. Nearly the same per cent of the respondents felt that employees are 'highly disciplined'. Contrary to this a few employees stated as 'indisciplined'.

Table 6.25: Rating Overall Industrial Relations

Response	*Frequency*	*Per cent*	*Cumulative Per cent*
Good	66	21.6	21.6
Satisfactory	194	63.6	85.2
Poor	45	14.8	100.0
Total	305	100.0	

Table 6.25 shows that majority of the respondents rated overall industrial relations as 'satisfactory'. This is followed by more than one-fifth of the respondents who rated as 'good'. The other respondents rated as 'poor'.

Table 6.26 depicts that the majority of the respondents are 'satisfied' with overall union-management relations. More than one-fifth of the respondents rated as 'good'. The remaining respondents felt that the overall union-management relations are 'poor'.

Table 6.26: Rating Overall Union Management Relations

Response	*Frequency*	*Per cent*	*Cumulative Per cent*
Good	66	21.6	21.6
Satisfactory	198	64.9	86.6
Poor	41	13.4	100.0
Total	305	100.0	

GRIEVANCE REDRESSAL

Michael Jucius defines grievance as "any discontent or dissatisfaction, whether expressed or not, whether valid or not, arising out of anything connected with the company that an employee thinks, believes, or even feels is unfair, unjust or inequitable."[16] According to Flippo, "A complaint becomes a grievance when the employee feels that an injustice has been committed. If the supervisor ignores the complaint and dissatisfaction grows within the employee, it usually assumes the status of a grievance. A grievance in business organisation is always expressed, either verbally or in writing... A grievance is usually more formal in character than a complaint. It can, of course, be either valid or ridiculous, and must grow out of something connected with company operations or policy. In many instances, it must involve an interpretation or application of provisions of the labour contract."[17]

The National Commission on Labour has given a statutory backing for the formulation of an effective grievance procedure which should be simple, flexible, less cumbersome, and more or less on the lines of the present model grievance procedure.

A grievance procedure should normally provide for three steps, namely, (a) approach to the immediate superior, (b) appeal to the department head/manager, and (c) appeal to the bipartite grievance committee representing management and the recognised union. The constitution of the committee should have a provision that in case no unanimous decision is possible, the unsettled grievance may be referred to an arbitrator.

Matters Relating to Grievance in Dairy Industry

Employees may represent grievances on matters relating to wages, increments, allowances, leave, transfer, promotions, seniority, work assignment, non-extention of any benefits due under co-operative federation rules, employees working conditions and service and related matters. Any employee or a small group of employees or a union can represent grievances orally or in writing.

Grievance Machinery

Table 6.27: Grievance Machinery

Unit	*E.G.R. Officer*	*E.G.R. Review Officer*
Milk Chilling Center/Cooling Center/Dairy	Manager (or) Controlling Officer	Joint Directors/ General Manager/ Deputy Directors
Region	Asst. Engineer (C)/Regional Asst./Executive Eng. (Civil)/ Dairy Engineer/ Senior Dairy Engineer	Director (Civil Projects)/Director (Eng. Projects)
Milk Products Factories	Personnel Officers (or)/ Welfare Officers, Asst. Personnel Officer (or) Asst. Welfare Officer	General Manager
Head Office	Welfare Officer	Joint Director (Per. & Adm)

As shown in table 6.27 grievances are represented at various levels to the employee grievance redressal officers and in case of dissatisfaction the grievances are referred to review officers. For unit milk chilling centre/cooling center/ dairy redressal officer is either manager or controlling officer in case of dissatisfaction the grievance is referred to joint directors/general managers/deputy directors. Grievances in a region are referred to assistant engineer (C)/regional assistant and executive engineer/executive engineer (civil)/ dairy engineer/senior dairy engineer. In case of dissatisfaction the grievance is referred to director (civil and projects)/director (engineering and projects). Grievance in milk products factories shall be referred to personnel officers or assistant welfare officer. The general manager is the reviewing officer. In case of the grievance in the head office, welfare officer is the redressal officer and joint director (personnel and administration) will review the grievances.

In addition to the above, there is employees grievance redressal cell for which the welfare officer will be in-charge and he will work directly under joint director (personnel and administration). There are also shop level and plant level councils at all milk product factories to settle the problems relating to production and working conditions etc.

Grievance Procedure

The redressal officers will receive the grievances and register them, assign it a number and furnish acknowledgement to the aggrieved employee. The redressal officer is the link between the employees and management to collect information on the grievance and follow-up action. He will liaise with all concerned authorities whether below or above him for redressal of the grievance. There are prescribed time limits for settlement of grievances. The redressal officer must intimate action within three days of registration of grievance. The grievance should be settled by the redressal officer within one month. If he fails to settle the grievance, the aggrieved party may approach the redressal review officer. The redressal officer should inform the review officer in writing within three days why he is not able to settle yet. The redressal officer will submit a list of delayed cases to the grievance cell at head office and also to the review officer with reasons. All such delayed cases referred to the review officer should be settled by him directly within one month by his initiative and appropriate action. If he fails to settle the grievance within three days of the expiry of the prescribed time, he shall report to the grievance cell with reasons and also inform to the party with reasons in writing. The aggrieved may also approach the cell in such cases. The cell should finalise the settlement of the grievance within one month from the date of its reference to it.

The grievance handling procedure in any organisation depends on the organisational policies. While formulating the policy the management will prepare some guidelines. The unit officers will follow the guidelines while handling the grievances. Sometimes the workers instead of directly taking the grievance to the appropriate authority seek the help of the union. The union in turn takes up the matter with the grievance officer in the unit.

Table 6.28: Approaching Unions for Grievance Redressal

Response	*Frequency*	*Per cent*	*Cumulative Per cent*
Yes	108	35.4	35.4
No	197	64.6	100.0
Total	305	100.0	

Table 6.28 reveals that more than one-third of the respondents approach the unions for grievance redressal whereas nearly two-third of the respondents do not approach unions for grievance redressal.

Table 6.29: Awareness of the Grievance Procedure

Response	*Frequency*	*Per cent*	*Cumulative Per cent*
Yes	129	42.3	42.3
No	176	57.7	100.0
Total	305	100.0	

Table 6.29 narrates that more than majority of the respondents lack awareness about the grievance procedure whereas the other respondents have awareness of the existing grievance procedure.

Table 6.30: Do you have Grievance Anytime

Response	*Frequency*	*Per cent*	*Cumulative Per cent*
Yes	73	23.9	23.9
No	232	76.1	100.0
Total	305	100.0	

Table 6.30 infers that more than three-fourth of the respondents do not have any grievance at all whereas the rest of the respondents expressed that they have grievances at sometime or other.

Table 6.31: Rating the Grievance Settlement Machinery

Response	*Frequency*	*Per cent*	*Cumulative Per cent*
Good	23	7.5	7.5
Satisfactory	147	48.2	55.7
Poor	135	44.3	100.0
Total	305	100.0	

Table 6.31 indicates that nearly half of the respondents are satisfied with the grievance settlement machinery in the organisations. This is contradicted by 44.3 per cent of the respondents by expressing that the machinery of grievance settlement is 'poor' or in effective. The rest of the respondents' have expressed that the machinery is 'good'.

Voluntary Retirement Scheme

This is a scheme for reduction of excess manpower. Excess manpower with substantial cost is threatening the viability of Milk dairies. With the current trends of business, the fixed costs have become unrelated to market realities. Organisation needs to be restructured pruning the manpower strength as an immediate alternative. In case of adoption of VRS the financial position would dramatically change putting the organisation on sound financial ground.

In the study by NDDB in 1988, 1243 employees were identified as surplus. In 1995 the Vijaya dairy found 794 employees as surplus. In a phased manner the Vijaya dairy applied VRS to 427 employees. On similar lines recently the management of Sangam dairy has also extended VRS for 28 employees in the first phase.

REFERENCES

1. Heneman, Jr, Herbert G. and. Turnbull, John G (eds.), *Personnel Administration and Labour Relations,* 5.
2. *International Institute of Labour Studies,* (1972). Bulletin No. 10, 3.
3. Punekar, S.D. and Manorama G. Savur, (1969). *Management-White Collar Relations,* Bombay, Popular Prakasan, 244.
4. Arthur Kornhauser (edited), (1954). *Industrial Conflicts,* New York: McGraw Hill Book Company, 3.
5. Mathur, A.S. (1968). *Labour Policy and Industrial Relations in India.* Ram Prasad & Sons, 4.
6. This Act has been amended many times and the recent *Industrial Disputes (Amendment) Act, 1982* has relevance to industrial conflict resolution in the sense that it proposed amendments for speedier resolution of conflicts.
7. Frederick Harbison and John Coleman stated that the attitudes and policies of management towards union change because of number of factors. The possible choices of management in this regard comprise of (a) Fighting the union (b) Armed Truce (c) Working hormony (d) Union management co-operation. For details see Harbison, Frederick H., and Coleman John R., (1951) *Goals and Strategies in Collective Bargaining,* New York: Harper and Row Inc.
8. Pigors and Myers have added one more concept, i.e *'Fighting the Union'.* According to this concept the Management tries to

fight the union in subtle ways. Outright discrimination against union members and refusal to bargain collectively cannot be practiced openly as such actions would become unlawful. As far as dairy units under study is considered, the management has never tried to curb the growth of union nor showed discrimination against union members.

9. Paul, Pigors and Charles, A. Myers (1973). *Personnel Administration.* Tokyo, McGraw Hill, Hogakusha Ltd., 156.

10. Murthy, B.S. (1986). *Profile of Trade Unions* (a study in Orisa), Delhi: BR Publishing Corporation, l.

11. Johri, C.K. (1967). *Unionism in a Developing Economy,* (issued under the auspices of the Sri Ram Centre for Industrial Relations) New Delhi: Asia Publishing House, viii.

12. Sodhi, J.S. (1995). Issues, Trends and Developments in Industrial Relations in India and other South Asian Countries, in *Indian Journal of Industrial Relations,* Vol. 30 No. 4, 369.

13. Sur, Mary. (1965). *Collective Bargaining—A Comparative Study of Developments in India and other Countries.* Bombay: Asia Publishing House, 71.

14. International Labour Organisation, (1973). *Collective Bargaining: A Workers Education Manual,* Geneva.

15. Bremblett, Eari R. (1961). Maintenance of Discipline. In *Management Personnel, Quarterly,* Vol., No. 1, Autumn, 10.

16. Jucius, J.M. (1977). *Personnel Management,* 4.

17. Flippo, Edwin, B. (1976) *Principles of Personnel Management,* 430.

7

Commitment

An attempt is made from chapter 3 to chapter 6 to analyse various HRM activities such as recruitment, selection, HRD, wage and salary administration, employee welfare and industrial relations. One of the outcomes of HRM activities is employee commitment (Bear Michael, 1985).[1]

In this chapter a conceptual framework of commitment is provided and to study the levels of commitment, the researcher makes an effort to elicit the views of the respondents. Item analysis and regrouped results based on quartile values have been presented. Further to find out whether the work commitment is associated with the independent and organisational variables the chi-square test has been applied.

ASPECTS OF COMMITMENT

Commitment has both individual and institutional aspects. At the individual level, a person with a high commitment to the job puts in his or her sincere, honest, efficient and sustained hard work. In its institutional or organisational aspect, it symbolises a feeling of belongingness, a sense of pride in self and group achievements and a spirit of determination and dedication in making efforts to accomplish and further the goals of the organisation.[2]

Indeed, commitment emerges only when the employees identify with the aims and objectives of the organisation as their own. Also, when their professionalism is synchronised with the functional as well as organisational goals. Such a commitment can be consciously built up through a genuine sense of participation and self-importance among the members of the organisation. This broadly involves associating the employees in the organisational processes, like setting the organisational goals at various levels, planning for task accomplishment, decision-making as well as implementation process. In other words, it means shaping of the entire organisational culture and climate which will be conducive to commitment. At the same time, the employees must perceive that the leadership wants to follow participative style of management in a genuine sense. It may not be out of place to mention here that the 360° Leadership Assessment chart being used by the MNC, GE of USA gives a lot of importance to "Commitment". Commitment, indeed, is quite important for leaders in particular, and all employees in general.

The employee involvement can be brought about and sustained when one and all in the organisation work together and involve themselves in the organisation. No technology, no system, no amount of capital investment can guarantee success unless the organisation has a committed, dedicated and motivated workforce at all levels. Here the role of top management is very crucial since he has to evolve the right climate. Commitment to work embraces the aspect of fully integrating the individual goals with the goals of the organisation in which continuous effort is required to be made by all levels of the society including the managers.[3]

Commitment is the urge of the individual or a group of individuals to attain the objective of the organisation which aims at excellence. Work commitment is primarily seen as an attitude, as a discipline, as a philosophy of work and as an obligation to society. There should be commitment right from top to bottom by giving them a sense of ownership.[4]

Stages of Commitment

The commitment of workers to the industrial employment is a more complicated process than recruitment.

Hiring of workers may be relatively easy, but keeping them consistently at work tends to be more difficult. A committed worker is one who stays on the job, and who has severed his major connections with the native place. He is a permanent member of the industrial working force, receiving wages and being dependent for making a living on enterprise managements which offer him work and direct his activities at the workplace.[5]

In the commitment of workers to industrial employment, it is useful to distinguish four stages or points on the continuum of behavioral change which mark the transition of the worker from traditional societies into adherence to an industrial way of life, these stages are as follows: the uncommitted worker; the partially or semi-committed worker, the generally committed worker and the specifically committed worker.[6]

Uncommitted Worker

The uncommitted worker has no intention of entering industrial employment on any continuing basis. His is a temporary stay for an immediate purpose—perhaps to get a needed sum of money to liquidate tax obligations, or to buy a bride, or to tide over his family during a period of famine, price decline, or other emergency. Although the length of the initial stay may be determined by the immediate need for income from industrial employment, it does constitute a break with the rural tribal background, and it may be a first step toward further migrations to industrial work and even to more permanent commitment as time goes on. Welfare Programmes like housing, canteen, crèche, education and transportation facilities etc., will have a great bearing on further migrations to industrial work and to become the rural migrant worker to be more committed to his industrial employment. In a number of the newly industrialising countries uncommitted workers constitute a major proportion of the industrial labour force.

Semi Committed Worker

The semi-committed worker is a man at the margin of two ways of life. He works more or less regularly in industry but maintains his connections with the land, the tribe or the village. His periods of industrial employment may be no longer than those of the uncommitted workers; the primary difference is that he contemplates spending a major part of his adult life shifting between agricultural and industrial employment, while the uncommitted worker regards industrial employment as only temporary. In many cases the wife and the family remain on the tribal land or village where she supports herself and the children. The industrial "bachelor", as in Kenya, will send his small amounts of money and return home periodically. The semi-committed worker has no option except leaving his wife and children in the village due to lack of housing facilities, job security etc., in the urban or industrial centres. The semi-committed workers generally show high turnover rates. They belong neither to the tribe nor to the urban industrial life.

Generally Committed Worker

The generally committed worker is one who has completely cut off his connections with the village to become a permanent member of an urban or industrial workforce. This involves just more than just being an urban dweller, it requires an adjustment to all the institutional aspects of urban living and industrial employment. The securities of the generally committed worker is geared to the availability of industrial employment and provision of welfare programmes like housing, canteen, education and transportation facilities etc., for he no longer has strong ties to the rural or tribal society. He may be a textile worker, a steel worker, a dock worker, or a truck driver, and in some societies he may have tried his hand at different occupations in a variety of industries. He may be committed to a craft, occupation or profession through an apprenticeship or education. But whatever his occupation, he must sell his labour to maintain himself and his family. All advanced economies depend mainly on this kind of committed labour, or on the more specifically committed worker as described below.

Specifically Committed Worker

The specifically committed worker is one who is permanently attached not only to the industrial way of life, but to a particular employer and often to a particular occupation as well. He is a member not just of the industrial labour force but rather of a small and closely prescribed segment of it. He is committed to a particular enterprise by virtue of work experience, specific training, welfare programmes, seniority rules, pension rights or personal obligation. He is immobile, and inextricably rooted in the culture of a particular establishment. In Japan, for example, industrial employment commonly has involved a life commitment to a single firm. Indeed, the contemporary Japanese,[7] as worker has been as bound by custom to his employer as if he were in the closed circle of a pre-industrial tribe. He would not think of seeking alternate employment, nor would his employer ever try to dismiss him. He has had permanent membership in the enterprise.

COMMITMENT—ITEM ANALYSIS

To know the overall opinions of the respondents towards employees' commitment, an effort has been made to quantify the responses by using the method of summated ratings.

At the first stage, a set of items were selected and they were given responses on four point scale. Then each response was given scores ranging from one to four.

After constructing the tool it was pre-tested with a small sample of 60. The scores were summed up and analysed for their reliability. It was found that except one item, all the items had very high correlation coefficient with the total scores. The item which had low coefficient of correlation was dropped and the final tool was prepared.

Commitment is closely related to job satisfaction. It is generally believed that commitment of employees is the result of high satisfaction. The industrial work, the industry as a place of work, the job, the management and the desire to participate in management has been encouraged by the co-operative principles. Their career growth is linked with the flourishment of dairy industry.

To know the level of commitment of the respondents, 12 statements have been selected from various research studies. (Rao. M.S.A. (1965),[8] Vaid K.N. (1968),[9] Sheth N.R. (1968),[10] Sharma B.R. (1968),[11] Kannappan Subbaiah (1970),[12] Sheth N.R. (1971),[13] Jain Sagar C. (1971).[14] These statements have four point response pattern i.e. strongly agree, agree, disagree, strongly disagree. These responses are scored and summated. The score analysis is given in table 7.1.

Table 7.1: Commitment

Scores	*Frequency*	*Per cent*	*Cumulative Per cent*
14.00	1	.3	.3
15.00	1	.3	.7
16.00	26	8.5	9.2
17.00	7	2.3	11.5
18.00	14	4.6	16.1
19.00	5	1.6	17.7
20.00	9	3.0	20.7
21.00	10	3.3	23.9
22.00	13	4.3	28.2
23.00	6	2.0	30.2
24.00	24	7.9	38.0
25.00	14	4.6	42.6
26.00	52	17.0	59.7
27.00	56	18.4	78.0
28.00	28	9.0	87.2
29.00	11	3.6	90.8

30.00	14	4.6	95.4
31.00	3	1.0	96.4
32.00	1	.3	96.7
34.00	1	.3	97.0
36.00	6	2.0	99.0
38.00	2	.7	99.7
46.00	1	.3	100.0
Total	305	100.0	

There are 12 statements and these scores range was 46 and 14.

No. of Statements	12
Response pattern	4, 3, 2, 1
Maximum Scores	46
Minimum Scores	14

Further to find out the variables which affect the level of commitment, data have been cross tabulated. First of all the frequency table of level of commitment scores are regrouped on the basis of first and third quartile values and then results have been presented.

Table 7.2: Commitment

Quartile Values	*Frequency*	*Per cent*	*Cumulative Per cent*
High (21)	116	38.0	38.0
Middle (21-26)	180	59.0	97.0
Low (27+)	9	3.0	100.0
Total	305	100.0	

As shown in table 7.2 a majority that is fifty-nine per cent of respondents have moderate level of commitment followed by thirty-eight per cent of respondents whose level of commitment was high. Only three per cent of the respondents have low level of commitment.

It is understood from the above analysis that majority of the respondents in both the dairies have commitment to the organisation. From this it can be inferred that they are satisfied with the welfare programmes, social security measures and fair compensation and benefits. It may also be said that the employees are specifically committed to the dairy units since they are permanently attached to the employers of these units.

Is work commitment associated with the sex of the respondents? To find out the answer, data relating to the sex of the respondents and their work commitment have been cross tabulated. The results of the analysis are presented in Table 7.3.

Table 7.3: Work Commitment by Sex

Sex	*Commitment regrouped*			*Total*
	Low	*Moderate*	*High*	
Male	102	157	9	268
Female	14	23	-	37
Total	116	180	9	305

$X^2 = 1.314$ df = 2 p = .519 Conti. Coeff = .065

It is evident from table 7.3 that in the case of a majority of the respondents from both the sexes, the level of commitment was moderate. However, further analysis reveals that comparatively large proportion of female respondent commitment was moderate. But interestingly, no female respondents could get score to reach higher level of commitment whereas nine male respondents could score high. To test whether there is any significant association between the two variables, chi-square test was used. The results show that the association is statistically not significant. That is whether the employee is male or female does not tell us about their level of commitment.

There seem to be no association between work commitment and sex. Whether the employee is male or female does not make any difference in his/her commitment. The commitment of an employee may not be based on sex because the welfare measures, social security and job satisfaction largely contribute to the employee's commitment irrespective of the sex differences.

Is work commitment associated with the educational background of the respondents? To find out the answer, data relating to the educational background of the respondents and their work commitment have been cross tabulated. The results of the analysis are presented in Table 7.4.

Table 7.4: Work Commitment by Educational Background

Education	*Commitment regrouped*			*Total*
	Low	*Moderate*	*High*	
Elementary level	4	11	-	15
High school level	52	61	-	113
Intermediate	16	40	6	62
Graduation	23	47	3	73
Post-graduation/professional	21	20		41
Technical		1		1
Total	116	180	9	305

$X^2 = 25.461$ df = 10 p = .005 Conti. Coefff =.278

It is evident from table 7.4 that a majority of the respondents' level of commitment was moderate. However, further analysis reveals that most of the respondents have high school education (113), intermediate (62), graduation (73), post-graduation/professional (41). To test whether there is any significant association between the two variables, chi-square test was used. The results show that the association is statistically significant. Hence, the employees' educational background tells us about their level of commitment. Most of the respondents (180) are moderately committed whereas more than one-third (116) of total respondents' level of commitment is 'low'. But nine respondents having

Intermediate and degree qualifications are 'highly' committed.

As revealed from the above analysis the commitment of the employees increases with higher educational background. The respondents having intermediate and degree qualifications are highly committed. This may be due to the fact that the employees with higher qualifications will have higher aspirations for career development and personal growth in the organisation. It is also observed that majority of the respondents with educational background are committed to the organisation.

Is work commitment associated with the indebtedness of the respondents? To find out the answer, data relating to the indebtedness of the respondents and their work commitment were cross tabulated. The results of the analysis are presented in Table 7.5.

Table 7.5: Work Commitment by Indebtedness

Elementary level	*Commitment regrouped*			*Total*
	Low	*Moderate*	*High*	
Yes	65	95	6	166
No	51	85	3	139
Total	116	180	9	305

$X^2 = .862$ df = 2 p = .650 Conti. Coeff =.053

It is indicated from table 7.5 that more than half of the respondents were indebted and their level of commitment was moderate. This is followed by low level of commitment. Six respondents were highly committed even though they were indebted. To test whether there is any significant association between the two variables, chi-square test was used. The results show that the association is statistically not significant. That is whether the respondents are indebted or not does not tell us about their level of commitment.

There seem to be no relationship between indebtedness and commitment of the employee. The indebtedness of the employee may not have any bearing on the commitment of the employee if welfare and social security measures are properly implemented by the organisation.

Is work commitment associated with the number of dependents of the respondents? To find out the answer, data relating to the number of dependents of the respondents and their work commitment were cross tabulated. The results of the analysis are presented in Table 7.6.

Table 7.6: Work commitment by number of dependents

Number of Dependents	*Commitment regrouped*			*Total*
	Low	*Moderate*	*High*	
.00	2	2		4
1.00	9	8	1	18
2.00	24	39		63
3.00	38	38	4	80
4.00	25	62	4	91
5.00	17	25		42
6.00	1	6		7
Total	116	180	9	305

X^2 = 16.823 df = 12 P =.156 . Conti. Coeff = .229

It is understood from table 7.6 that the level of commitment among large number of the respondents (91) who have four dependents, was moderate. However further analysis shows that the commitment among most of the respondents having two to five dependents, it was moderate. Whereas one-third of the respondents have dependents between two to five and their commitment is 'low'. Interestingly, the respondents having three to four dependents are found to have high commitment. To test whether there is any significant association between the two variables, chi-square test was used. The results show that the association is statistically not significant. Hence the employees' commitment is not based on number of dependents.

The number of dependents of the employee may not affect the employees commitment if the well being and the opportunities for career development are taken care of by the organisation.

Is work commitment associated with the rural/urban background of the respondents? To find out the answer, data relating to the rural/urban background of the respondents and their work commitment have been cross tabulated. The results of the analysis are presented in Table 7.7.

Table 7.7 Work Commitment by Rural/Urban Background

Rural/Urban Background	*Commitment regrouped*			*Total*
	Low	*Moderate*	*High*	
Rural	99	154	9	262
Urban	17	26		43
Total	116	180	9	305

$X^2 = 1.525$ df = 2 p = .467 Conti. Coeff =.071

It is evident from table 7.7 that a majority of the respondents from both the Rural/Urban background, have moderate commitment. However, further analysis reveals that more than one-third (116) of the total respondents' (99 rural, 17 urban respondents) have low commitment. Interestingly, few (9) rural respondents were highly committed. To test whether there is any significant association between the two variables, Chi-square test was used. The results show that the association is statistically not significant. Hence the employee's background either rural or urban does not tell us about their level of commitment.

The commitment of the employees is not influenced by the rural or urban background when once he becomes a committed worker. The generally committed worker is one who has completely cut off his connections with village or native place to become a permanent member of an urban or industrial workforce. He will not have any strong ties with the rural or urban society.

Is work commitment associated with the organisation of the respondents? To find out the answer, data relating to the organisation of the respondents and their work commitment were cross tabulated. The results of the analysis are presented in Table 7.8.

Table 7.8: Work Commitment by the Organisation

Organisation	*Commitment regrouped*			*Total*
	Low	*Moderate*	*High*	
Vijaya dairy	76	99	5	180
Sangam dairy	40	81	4	125
Total	116	180	9	305

$X^2 = 3.272$ df = 2 p = .195 Conti. Coeff =.103

It is evident from table 7.8 that among majority of the respondents from both the organisations, the level of commitment was moderate. However further analysis reveals that comparatively large proportion of Sangam Dairy respondents had moderate commitment. More than one-third (116) in both the organisations the respondents' commitment is 'low'. Whereas five respondents from the Vijaya dairy and four respondents from Sangam dairy were highly committed. To test whether there is any significant association between the two variables, chi-square test was used. The results show that the association is statistically not significant. That is whether the employees belong to Sangam dairy or Vijaya dairy does not tell us about their level of commitment.

Whether the employees belong to Vijaya or Sangam dairy, it has not made any difference between the commitment of the employees. That is to say there may not be much difference between the two organisations under study so far as the welfare and social security measures are concerned. The employees have work commitment in both the organisations.

Is work commitment associated with the category of the respondents? To find out the answer, data relating to the category of the respondents and their work commitment, were cross tabulated. The results of the analysis are presented in Table 7.9.

Table 7.9: Work Commitment by Category

Category	*Commitment regrouped*			*Total*
	Low	*Moderate*	*High*	
Managerial	25	29	1	55
Non-managerial	91	151	8	250
Total	116	180	9	305

$X^2 = 1.713$ df = 2 p = .425 Conti. Coeff = .075

It is evident from table 7.9 that a majority of the respondents from managerial category in both the units have moderate commitment. However, further analysis reveals that comparatively large proportion of non-managerial respondents' commitment was also moderate. This is followed by non-managerial (91) and managerial (25) respondents whose commitment is low. But comparatively more non-managerial respondents (8) than managerial category (1) were highly committed. To test whether there is any significant association between the two variables, chi-square test was used. The results show that the association is statistically not significant. That is whether the employee is managerial or non-managerial category does not tell us about their level of commitment.

The level of commitment does not depend on the category of employees (managerial or non-managerial) as it is evident in the above statistical analysis. It is found from the study that in both the cadres the amenities, perks and other benefits are satisfactorily provided by the management. Both the cadres are found to have commitment. Hence there is not much difference between commitment levels of the said cadres of employees.

Is work commitment associated with the caste of the respondents? To find out the answer, data relating to the caste of the respondents and their work commitment have been cross tabulated. The results of the analysis are presented in Table 7.10.

Table 7.10: Work Commitment by Caste

Caste	*Commitment regrouped*			*Total*
	Low	*Moderate*	*High*	
Open category	81	135	7	223
Backward classes	31	31		62
Scheduled caste	4	14	2	20
Total	116	180	9	305

$X^2 = 10.791$ df = 4 p = .029 Conti. Coeff = .185

It is evident from table 7.10 that a majority of the respondents from all the categories have moderate level of commitment. But interestingly, no BC respondents could get score to reach higher level of commitment. Whereas OC (7) and SC (2) respondents could score high. To test whether there is any significant association between the two variables, chi-square test was used. The results show that the association is statistically significant.

The association between caste and commitment is statistically significant. Among the OCs majority of the employees have moderate to high commitment since they have higher aspiration level. They work hard for fulfilling their aspirations. Their socio-economic background also contributes for improving their qualifications and also for achieving higher positions in the organisations. Among BCs normally the aspiration level may be low as evidenced by 50 per cent of them having low commitment. Among SCs majority of them have moderate commitment. Since they have low aspiration level, they are satisfied with whatever facilities that are provided by the management. In some way or other, caste may also influence the commitment level of the employees.

Is work commitment associated with the age of the respondents? To find out the answer, data relating to the age of the respondents and their work commitment have been cross tabulated. The results of the analysis are presented in Table 7.11.

Table 7.11: Age

Age	*Commitment regrouped*			*Total*
	Low	*Moderate*	*High*	
27-43 years	22	49	6	77
44-51 years	55	88	3	146
52-57 years	39	43		82
Total	116	180	9	305

X^2 = 13.627 df = 4 p = .009 Conti. Coeff =.207

It is evident from table 7.11 that a large number of respondents of middle age have moderate level of commitment. However, further analysis reveals that comparatively larger proportion of respondents of middle age group had moderate commitment than respondents from younger age group. But interestingly, no older respondents could get score to reach higher level of commitment whereas six younger respondents and three middle age respondents could score high. To test whether there is any significant association between the two variables, chi-square test was used. The results show that the association is statistically significant. That is the employees who are young and middle aged are highly committed than the respondents from the older age.

It is observed from the above analysis that the association between the age and commitment is statistically significant. The lower age respondents are more committed than the older since they strive for advancement in their career; they work hard for improving their qualifications and skills for achieving higher positions in the organisation. Accordingly they have more commitment to the organisation upto the age of 50 years. The employees above the age of 50 have low commitment since they do not visualize the career advancement at the fag-end of their service before their retirement. They may not be able to maintain health status also. Physically, they may not be able to withstand hard work with the deterioration of health. Their commitment may also be diluted.

Is work commitment associated with the gross salary of the respondents? To find out the answer, data relating to the gross salary of the respondents and their work commitment have been cross tabulated. The results of the analysis are presented in Table 7.12.

Table 7.12: Work Commitment by Gross Salary

Gross Salary (in Rs.)	*Commitment regrouped*			*Total*
	Low	*Moderate*	*High*	
3900-7400	22	57	-	79
7401-11000	60	73	8	141
11001-70000	34	50	1	85
Total	116	180	9	305

X^2 = 13.343 df = 4 p =.010 Conti. Coeff =.205

It is evident from table 7.12 that more than half of the respondents from the 'middle range of gross salary have moderate level of commitment. But interestingly, no respondent from low salary could get score to reach higher level of commitment while as many as eight respondents whose gross salary was medium, could score high. To test whether there is any significant association between the two variables, chi-square test was used. The results show that the association is statistically significant. That is the employees with higher gross salary have higher level of commitment.

As revealed from the above analysis, the association between gross salary and commitment is statistically significant. The employees with higher gross salary have higher level of commitment because, higher salary will enhance their economic status and they can fulfill their life requirements. They can get life satisfaction and also job satisfaction; with this sense of satisfaction and fulfillment in life their commitment will also increase.

Is work commitment associated with the net salary of the respondents? To find out the answer, data relating to the net salary of the respondents and their work commitment have been cross tabulated. The results of the analysis are presented in Table 7.13.

Table 7.13: Work Commitment by Net Salary

Net Salary (in Rs.)	*Commitment regrouped*			*Total*
	Low	*Moderate*	*High*	
1800-3800	19	52	2	73
3801-6700	66	86	6	158
6701-16000	31	42	1	74
Total	116	180	9	305

$X^2 = 7.147$ df = 4 p = .128 Conti. Coeff = .151

It is evident from table 7.13 that a majority of the respondents from the medium net salary have moderate level of commitment. To test whether there is any significant association between the two variables, chi-square test was used. The results show that the association is statistically not significant. That is employee's net salary does not tell us about their level of commitment.

The above analysis shows that the association between net salary and commitment is statistically not significant. Net salary denotes take home pay. It is found from the study that the net pay has no impact on commitment of the employee since most of the employees are satisfied with the gross salary and their economic status also is determined by the gross salary. Though the net salary is less than the gross salary by way of deductions, the present employees get satisfaction because they are contributing to future savings and for acquiring assets such as housing, land, and other permanent assets for future security of life.

It is found that the higher the educational background that higher the level of commitment. This could be probably because of the job they perform. People with higher qualifications are generally given white collar jobs and they are made responsible for the duties assigned with enough autonomy to plan and perform their work.

With regard to caste background the study has found that the upper caste respondents are more committed than the others. This might be because of their higher level of aspirations which can be fulfilled by performing the activities with commitment.

It is observed in the study that the higher the age the lower the level of commitment. The rationale behind this could be that people in older age group might fulfill their aspirations are put off them. However, the younger people who are energetic with higher level of ambitions might be performing the job with commitment to meet their career ambitions.

With respect to the association between gross salary and commitment it is found that higher the salary higher the commitment. This might be because salary is one of the major outcomes of the job. When the job provides good income people are likely to work with more commitment.

Based on the above analysis presented in this chapter it can be concluded that the commitment has association with educational background, caste, age and gross salary.

REFERENCES

1. Michael, Beer et al. (1985). New York: The Free Press.

2. Sujith, Sen and Shallendra, Saxeena (1997). "Sincerity and commitment for corporate success", in *Personnel Today*. Calcutta: National Institute of Personnel Management, Vol. XVIII. No. 3, 16.

3. Parida, S. (1999). "Employee Involvement for Organisational Excellence" in *Personnel Today*. Calcutta: National Institute of Personnel Management, Vol. XIX. No. 4, 23.

4. Myers, Charles A. (1958). *Labour Problems in the Industrialisation in India,* Cambridge: Harvard University Press.

5. Clark Kerr, Harbison et al. (1962). *Industrialism and Industrial Man,* London and Edinburgh: Heineman Educational Books Ltd.

6. *Ibid.*

7. Abegglien, James C. (1958). *The Japanese Factory,* Glencoe Illinois: The Free Press.

8. Rao, M.S.A. (1965). "Labour Commitment—its Implications for Labour Policy." *Indian Journal of Industrial Relations,* Vol. No. 1.

9. Vaid, K.N. (1968) *The New Worker—A Study at Kata.* Bombay: Asia Publishing House.

10. Sheth, N.R. (1968). *The Social Frame Work of an Indian Factory*. Bombay: Oxford University Press.

11. Sarma, B.R. (1968, July). Commitment to Industrial Work: A Case of Indian Automobile Worker. *Indian Journal of Industrial Relations,* Vol. 4, No. 1.

12. Kannappan, Subbaiah (1970). Labour Force Commitment in Early Stages of Industrialisation. *Industrial Journal of Industrial Relations,* Vol. 5, No. 3.

13. Seth, N.R. (1971, Feb). The Problems of Labour Commitment. *Economic and Political Weekly,* Vol. 9.

14. Jain, Sagar C. (1971). *Indian Manager: His Social Origin and Career.* New Delhi: Somaiah Publications Pvt. Ltd.

Job Satisfaction

This chapter deals with the determinants of job satisfaction. To know the overall view of the respondents towards employees' job satisfaction, item analysis and regrouped results were presented. Further, whether job satisfaction is associated with the independent and organisational variables or not, was tested by applying the chi-square test. The results were discussed.

The term "job satisfaction" refers to an employee's general attitude toward his job. Locke[1] defines job satisfaction as a "pleasurable or positive emotional state resulting from the appraisal of one's job or job experiences. "To the extent that a person's job fulfils his dominant need and is consistent with his expectations and values, the job will be satisfying.[2]

The importance of job satisfaction is fairly evident from a description of the importance of maintaining morale in any industry. If an employee is not satisfied with his work, then both the quantity and quality of his output will suffer.

Determinants of Job Satisfaction

According to Abraham Korman, there are two types of variables which determine the job satisfaction of an individual. These are: (1) Organisational variables, and (2) Personal variables.

Organisational Variables

Occupational Level

The higher the level of the job, the greater the

satisfaction of the individual. This is because higher level jobs carry greater prestige and self-control. This relationship between occupational level and job satisfaction stems from social reference group theory in that our society values some jobs more than others. Hence, people in the valued jobs will like them more than those who are in non-valued jobs. The relationship may also stem from the need-fulfillment theory. People in higher level jobs find most of their needs satisfied than when they are in lower level ones.

Job Content

The greater the variation in job content and the less the repetitiveness with which the tasks must be performed, the greater the satisfaction of the individuals involved. Since job content in terms of variety and nature of tasks called for is a function of occupational level, the theoretical arguments given above apply here also.

Considerate Leadership

People like to be treated with consideration. Hence considerate leadership results in higher job satisfaction than inconsiderate leadership.

Pay and Promotional Opportunities

All other things being equal these two variables are positively related to job satisfaction

Interaction in the Work Group

Here the question is when is interaction in the work group a source of job satisfaction and when it is not? Interaction is most satisfying when

(i) it results in the cognition that other person's attitudes are similar to one's own, since this permits the ready calculability of the other's behaviour and constitutes a validation of one's self;

(ii) it results in being accepted by others; and

(iii) it facilitates the achievement of goals.

Personal Variables

For some people, it appears most jobs will be dissatisfying irrespective of the organisational conditions involved, whereas for others, most jobs will be satisfying. Personal variables like age, educational level, sex, etc., are responsible for this difference.

Age

Most of the evidence on the relation between age and job satisfaction, holding such factors as occupational level constant, seems to indicate that there is generally a positive relationship between the two variables upto the pre-retirement years and then there is a sharp decrease in satisfaction. An individual aspires for better and more prestigious jobs in later years of his life. Finding his channels for advancement blocked his satisfaction declines.

Educational Level

With occupational level held constant there is a negative relationship between the educational level and job satisfaction. The higher the education, the higher the reference group which the individual looks for guidance to evaluate his job rewards.

Role Perception

Different individuals hold different perceptions about their role, i.e. the kind of activities and behaviours they should engage in to perform their job successfully. Job satisfaction is determined by this factor also. The more accurate the role perception of an individual the greater his satisfaction.

Sex

There is as yet no consistent evidence as to whether women are more satisfied with their jobs than men, holding such factors as job and occupational level constant. One might predict this to be the case, considering the generally lower occupational aspiration of women.

Determinants of job satisfaction listed by some other authors:

Table 8.1: Determinants of Job Satisfaction

Author	*Nature of the study*	*Determinants of job satisfaction*
Stagner, Flebbe And Wood (1952)	Working on the rail-road; a study of job satisfaction (*Personnel Psychology,* 1952, 5,293-306). This is a study of 715 male unionised rail-road workers.	1. General working conditions. 2. Union-management relations 3. General quality of supervision 4. Grievance handling procedures
Gadel (1953)	Productivity and satisfaction of full and part-time female employees (*Personnel Psychology,* 1953, 6, 327-342). This is a study of 301 women doing typing and routine clerical work. Sixty per cent of this number were at least 40 years old and more were married.	1. Type of work 2. Working conditions 3. Pay 4. Co-workers 5. Ease of commuting to 6. Advancement opportunities *For older Group:* 1. Security 2. Supervision 3. Company prestige 4. Working hours
Ross and Zander (1957)	Need satisfaction and employee turnover (*Personnel Psychology,* 1957, 10, 327-338). This is a study of skilled women in a large company.	1. Recognition 2. Autonomy 3. Doing important work 4. Fair evaluation of work done
Durganand Sinha (1958)	Job satisfaction in office and manual workers (*Indian Journal of Social work,* 1958, 19, 39-46).	1. Job status 2. Type of work 3. Supervisory behaviour 4. Work group.

Job Satisfaction—Item Analysis

To know the overall view of the respondents towards employees Job Satisfaction an effort has been made to quantify responses by using the method of summated ratings.

At the first stage, a set of items were selected and they were given responses on five point scale. There each response was given scores ranging from five to one.

After constructing the tool it was pre-tested with a small sample of 60. These scores were summed and analysed for reliability. It was found that except one items, all the item had very high correlation coefficient with the total scores. The item which had low coefficient of correlation was dropped and the final tool was prepared

Job satisfaction refers to an employee's general attitude towards job. To the extent that a person's job fulfils his dominant needs and is consistent with his expectations and values, the job will be satisfying. Number of characteristics such as pay and benefits, supervision, working conditions, the nature of work itself and dairy industry policies, influence job satisfaction. The respondents' level of job satisfaction on the whole is moderate.

To know the level of satisfaction of the respondents, 15 statements have been selected from various research studies. (Pestonjee, D.M. (1967),[3] Sinha, D. and Aggarawal, U.N. (1971),[4] Dwivedi, N. (1973),[5] Gyanendra, P.S. (1973)[6] and Dafturarcn (1982).[7] These statements have five point response pattern i.e. very high, high, average, low, very low. These responses are scored and summated. The score analysis is given in Table 8.2.

Table 8.2: Job Satisfaction

Scores	*Frequency*	*Per cent*	*Cumulative Per cent*
21.00	1	.3	.3
27.00	1	.3	.7
29.00	1	.3	1.0
30.00	2	.7	1.6
31.00	3	1.0	2.6

Scores	*Frequency*	*Per cent*	*Cumulative Per cent*
32.00	2	.7	3.3
34.00	5	1.6	4.9
35.00	3	1.0	5.9
36.00	7	2.3	8.2
38.00	2	.7	8.9
39.00	14	4.6	13.4
40.00	3	1.0	14.4
41.00	16	5.2	19.7
42.00	15	4.9	24.6
43.00	17	5.6	30.2
44.00	9	3.0	33.0
45.00	43	14.1	47.2
46.00	18	5.9	53.1
47.00	38	12.5	65.6
48.00	21	6.9	72.5
49.00	24	7.9	80.3
50.00	22	7.2	87.5
51.00	12	3.9	91.5
52.00	6	2.0	93.4
53.00	3	1.0	94.4
54.00	5	1.6	96.1
55.00	3	1.0	97.0
56.00	5	1.6	98.7
57.00	1	.3	99.0
58.00	1	.3	99.3
59.00	1	.3	99.7
63.00	1	.3	100.0
Total	305	100.0	

There are 15 statements and the scores range was 63 and 21

No. of statements	15
Response pattern	5, 4, 3, 2, 1 (scores)
Maximum Score	63
Minimum Score	21

Further to find out the variables that **affect the level** of job satisfaction data were cross tabulated. **First of all** the frequency table of level of job satisfaction was regrouped on the basis of first and third quartile values and then results have been presented.

Table 8.3: Job Satisfaction

Quartile Values	*Frequency*	*Per cent*	*Cumulative Per cent*
High (42)	15	4.9	4.9
Medium (42-48)	206	67.5	72.5
Low (49+)	84	27.5	100.0
Total	305	100.0	

As shown in Table 8.3 that a majority of respondents have moderate level of job satisfaction followed by 27.5 per cent of respondents' low level of job satisfaction. Nearly 5 per cent of the respondents have high level of job satisfaction.

Is job satisfaction associated with sex of the respondents? To find out the answer, data relating to sex of the respondents and their job satisfaction have been cross tabulated. The results of the analysis are presented in Table 8.4.

Table 8.4: Job Satisfaction by Sex

Sex	*Job satisfaction regrouped*			*Total*
	Low	*Moderate*	*High*	
Male	15	174	79	268
Female		32	5	37
Total	15	206	84	305

$X^2 = 7.317$ df = 2 p = .026 Conti. Coeff = .153

It is evident from Table 8.4 that a majority of the respondents from both the sexes have moderate level of satisfaction. However, further analysis reveals that comparatively large proportion of female respondents' satisfaction was moderate. But interestingly, female respondents (5) could get score to reach higher level of satisfaction whereas (79) male respondents could score high. To test whether there is any significant association between the two variables, chi-square test was used. The results show that the association is statistically significant. That is male respondents are moderately (174) and highly satisfied (79).

As evident from the above analysis, majority of the male respondents have moderate and high job satisfaction. Among the female respondents majority of them have moderate satisfaction. The proportion of males having high satisfaction is less than that of females. By this one can understand that though the number of females who are working in the organisations is less than males, majority of the females have job satisfaction since they get economic independence and security on account of their earning capacity

Is job satisfaction associated with the educational background of the respondents? To find out the answer, data relating to the educational background of the respondents and their job satisfaction have been cross tabulated. The results of the analysis are presented in Table 8.5.

Table 8.5: Job Satisfaction by Educational Background

Education	*Job satisfaction regrouped*			*Total*
	Low	*Moderate*	*High*	
Elementary level		12	3	15
High school level	5	84	24	113
Intermediate	7	34	21	62
Graduation	2	50	21	73
Post-graduation/ professional	1	25	15	41
Technical		1		1
Total	15	206	84	305

X^2 = 14.579 df = 10 p = .148 Conti. Coeff = .214

It is evident from Table 8.5 that a majority of the respondents' educational background, and their level of job satisfaction is moderate. However, further analysis reveals that most of the respondents have high school (84), intermediate (34), graduation (50) and post-graduation/ professional (25) educational background. It is observed from the above analysis that only one employee with technical qualification has moderate satisfaction. To test whether there is any significant association between the two variables, chi-square test was used. The results show that the association is statistically not significant. Hence, the employees' educational background does not tell us about their level of job satisfaction.

As it is found from the above analysis, the association between the educational background and job satisfaction is not significant because employees with higher educational qualifications have higher aspirations for career advancement. Sometimes it may not possible for them to achieve the positions commensurate with their qualifications. In private enterprises career development may not depend on educational qualification. As a result employees with high academic qualifications may not have job satisfaction as per their expectations. Moreover the academic qualifications have no impact on the career development of the employees in the organisations under study.

Is job satisfaction associated with indebtedness of the respondents? To find out the answer, data relating to indebtedness of the respondents and their job satisfaction have been cross tabulated. The results of the analysis are presented in Table 8.6.

Table 8.6: Job Satisfaction by Indebtedness

Male	*Job satisfaction regrouped*			*Total*
	Low	*Moderate*	*High*	
Yes	11	107	48	166
No	4	99	36	139
Total	15	206	84	305

$X^2 = 2.924$ df = 2 p = .232 Conti. Coeff = .097

It is indicated from table 8.6 that more than half of the respondents' with indebtedness have moderate job satisfaction and nearly one-third have high level of job satisfaction. 11 respondents with indebtedness showed low job satisfaction. To test whether there is any significant association between the two variables, chi-square test was used. The results show that the association is statistically is not significant. That is the respondents' indebtedness does not tell us about their level of job satisfaction.

As revealed from the above analysis the association between indebtedness and job satisfaction is not significant, and so indebtedness may not be having any impact on job satisfaction of employees when they are happy with the amenities and facilities provided by the management. If the organisation is providing adequate emoluments, welfare and social security measures, the indebtedness may not effect job satisfaction of the employee.

Is job satisfaction associated with the number of dependents of the respondents? To find the answer, data relating to the number of dependents of the respondents and their job satisfaction have been cross tabulated. The results of the analysis are presented in Table 8.7.

Table 8.7: Job Satisfaction by Number of Dependents

Number of Dependents	*Job satisfaction regrouped*			*Total*
	Low	*Moderate*	*High*	
.00		3	1	4
1.00		14	4	18
2.00	2	44	17	63
3.00	4	56	20	80
4.00	7	62	22	91
5.00	2	21	19	42
6.00		6	1	7
Total	15	206	84	305

$X^2 = 11.922$ df = 12 p = .452 Conti. Coeff = .194

It is understood from table 8.7 that among majority of the respondents number of dependents and level of job satisfaction is moderate. However, further analysis shows that among most of the respondents having two to five dependents, their job satisfaction is moderate. Whereas with 15 respondents having dependents between two to five, the level of job satisfaction is 'low'. But more than one-fourth of the total respondents have high job satisfaction though majority of them have three to five number of dependents. To test whether there is any significant association between the two variables, chi-square test was used. The results show that the association is statistically not significant. Hence, the employees' job satisfaction is not based on number of dependents.

As revealed from the above analysis the employees job satisfaction is not based on number of dependents. There is no association between the number of dependents and job satisfaction because as observed from table 8.7 majority of respondents have only 1-4 dependents. A very few dependents have 5 or 6 dependents. Since most of the respondents have 1-4 dependents, it may not effect their job satisfaction. Moreover, when the employees are satisfied with the amenities and benefits, the number of dependents may not have any bearing on the job satisfaction.

Is job satisfaction associated with the rural/urban background of the respondents? To find the answer, data relating to the rural/urban background of the respondents and their job satisfaction have been cross tabulated. The results of the analysis are presented in Table 8.8.

It is evident from table 8.8 that a majority of the respondents are from both the rural/urban background and their level of job satisfaction is moderate. However, further analysis reveals that more than one-fourth of the total respondents' (72 rural + 12 urban = 84) job satisfaction level is high. Interestingly, very few (14 rural + 1 urban =

15) respondents' level of job satisfaction is low. To test whether there is any significant association between the two variables, chi-square test was used. The results show that the association is statistically not significant. Hence the employees' background either rural or urban does not tell us about their level of job satisfaction.

Table 8.8: Job Satisfaction by Rural/Urban Background

Rural/Urban Background	*Job satisfaction regrouped*			*Total*
	Low	*Moderate*	*High*	
Rural	14	176	72	262
Urban	1	30	12	43
Total	15	206	84	305

X^2 = .723 df = 2 p = .697 Conti. Coeff = .049

It is observed from the above analysis that there is no association between rural, urban background and job satisfaction. It makes no difference whether the employee is from rural or urban background when the working conditions and benefits satisfy the employees. When the employees of both the backgrounds equally share the benefits the differential background may not effect their job satisfaction.

Is job satisfaction associated with the organisation of the respondents? To find the answer, data relating to the organisation-wise respondents and their job satisfaction have been cross tabulated. The results of the analysis are presented in Table 8.9.

Table 8.9: Job Satisfaction by the Organisation

Organisation	*Job satisfaction regrouped*			*Total*
	Low	*Moderate*	*High*	
Vijaya Dairy	15	128	37	180
Sangam Dairy		78	47	125
Total	15	206	84	305

X^2 = 19.027 df = 2 p = .000 Conti. Coeff = .242

It is evident from table 8.9 that a majority of the respondents from both the organisations have moderate level of job satisfaction. However, further analysis reveals that comparatively large proportion of Vijaya dairy respondents' job satisfaction is moderate. But interestingly no Sangam dairy respondent could get score to lower level of job satisfaction. The Sangam dairy respondents (47) could get score to reach high level of job satisfaction. To test whether there is any significant association between these two variables, chi-square test was used. The results show that. the association is statistically significant. That is in both the organisations, majority of the respondents have moderate level of job satisfaction. Especially Sangam dairy respondents' job satisfaction is comparatively high. 15 Vijaya dairy respondents expressed their low level of job satisfaction.

As noticed from table 8.9 all the respondents of Sangam dairy have moderate and high level of job satisfaction when compared to those of Vijaya dairy respondents. It may be noted that some of the respondents of Vijaya dairy have low level of job satisfaction while none of the respondents of Sangam dairy is represented in low level of job satisfaction. The researcher himself observed during the study that the Sangam dairy seems to have an edge over Vijaya dairy in some aspects of HRM practices leading to better job satisfaction of the employees of Sangam dairy.

Table 8.10: Job Satisfaction by Category

Category	*Job satisfaction regrouped*			*Total*
	Low	*Moderate*	*High*	
Managerial	5	39	11	55
Non-managerial	10	167	73	250
Total	15	206	84	305

$X^2 = 3.874$ df = 2 p = .144 Conti. Coeff = .112

Is job satisfaction associated with the category of the respondents? To find out the answer, data relating to the category wise respondents and their job satisfaction have been cross tabulated. The results of the analysis are presented in Table 8.10.

It is evident from table 8.10 that a majority of the respondents from both the categories have moderate level of job satisfaction. Both the managerial (11) and non-managerial (73) respondents could get score to reach high level of job satisfaction. But the proportion of non-managerial respondents having high job satisfaction is higher when compared to the managerial respondents. To test whether there is any significant association between these two variables, chi-square test was used. The results show that the association is statistically not significant. That is, in both the categories, majority of the respondents have moderate level of job satisfaction. Non-managerial respondents (10) and managerial respondents (5) expressed their low level of job satisfaction.

It is observed from the above analysis that there is no significant difference between the two categories as regards job satisfaction. It may be presumed that the employees of both the categories are equally satisfied with the amenities, facilities and emoluments which are made available in the organisation according to their cadres.

Table 8.11: Job Satisfaction by Caste

Caste	*Job satisfaction regrouped*			*Total*
	Low	*Moderate*	*High*	
Open category	12	151	60	223
Backward classes	2	41	19	62
Scheduled caste	1	14	5	20
Total	15	206	84	305

$X^2 = .792$ df = 4 p = .939 Conti. Coeff = .051

Is job satisfaction associated with the caste of the respondents? To find out the answer, data relating to the caste of the respondents and their job satisfaction have been cross tabulated. The results of the analysis are presented in Table 8.11.

It is evident from table 8.11 that a majority of the respondents from all the castes have moderate level of job satisfaction. However, further analysis reveals that comparatively large proportion of OC and BC respondents' job satisfaction is moderate. The respondents from OC (60), BC (19) and SC (5) could score high. To test whether there is any significant association between the two variables, chi-square test was used. The results show that the association is statistically not significant. Hence, the employee's caste OC, BC and SC does not tell us about their level of job satisfaction.

From the above analysis it is understood that there is no association between job satisfaction and caste. From this it may be stated that in organised industries the perks, amenities and emoluments are extended to their employees according to their nature of work and cadre but not according to caste.

Is job satisfaction associated with the age of the respondents? To find out the answer, data relating to the age of the respondents and their job satisfaction have been cross tabulated. The results of the analysis are presented in Table 8.12.

Table 8.12: Job Satisfaction by Age

Age	*Job satisfaction regrouped*			*Total*
	Low	*Moderate*	*High*	
27-43 years	4	37	36	77
44-51 years	5	103	38	146
52-57 years	6	66	10	82
Total	15	206	84	305

X^2 = 25.647 df = 4 p = .000 Conti. Coeff = .279

It is evident from table 8.12 that a majority of the respondents from all the ages have moderate level of job satisfaction. However, further analysis reveals that comparatively large proportion of respondents' job satisfaction is moderate in the age group between 44 to 51 years. But interestingly, from all the age groups 84 respondents are having high job satisfaction. To test whether there is any significant association between the two variables, chi-square test was used. The results show that the association is statistically significant. That is the employees in the age group between 27 to 43 (36 respondents) and 44 to 51 years (38 respondents) are having high job satisfaction. In the age group 52 to 57 years (10 respondents) also scored high level of job satisfaction.

As evident from the above analysis the association between age and job satisfaction is statistically significant. From 27-51 years the job satisfaction of the respondents is on the increase because during the said period of life they work hard for their career development. With their commitment to the organisation they achieve not only their career development, correspondingly they get their benefits and emoluments commensurate with their experience and skills. So the job satisfaction also increases with their job and experience upto 51 years. Beyond this age also considerably a good number of the respondents have moderate job satisfaction due to hike in salary and superannuation benefits.

Table 8.13: Job Satisfaction by Gross Salary

Gross Salary (in Rs.)	*Job satisfaction regrouped*			*Total*
	Low	*Moderate*	*High*	
3900-7400	4	48	27	79
7401-11000	6	88	47	141
11001-70000	5	70	10	85
Total	15	206	84	305

$X^2 = 14.801$ df = 4 p = .005 Conti. Coeff = .215

Is job satisfaction associated with the gross salary of the respondents? To find the answer, data relating to the gross salary of the respondents and their job satisfaction have been cross tabulated. The results of the analysis are presented in Table 8.13.

It is evident from table 8.13 that in terms of gross salary, among majority of the respondents' the level of job satisfaction is moderate. This is followed by 84 respondents having high level of job satisfaction. To test whether there is any significant association between the two variables, chi-square test was used. The results show that the association is statistically significant. Most of the respondents have moderate (206) to high (84) job satisfaction.

The above analysis shows that the association between the gross salary and job satisfaction is statistically significant. That is to say that majority of respondents is moderately and highly satisfied with their gross salary. It appears that the emoluments in terms of gross salary are adequate to fulfill the needs and aspirations of the employees. The gross salary is commensurate with their qualifications and experience. When the emoluments are satisfactory, it tends to lead to job satisfaction. Moreover, the gross salary enhances the social and economic status of the employee.

Table 8.14: Job Satisfaction by Net Salary

Net Salary (in Rs.)	*Job satisfaction regrouped*			*Total*
	Low	*Moderate*	*High*	
1800-3800		42	31	73
3801-6700	12	100	46	158
6701-16000	3	64	7	74
Total	15	206	84	305

$X^2 = 26.273$ df = 4 p = .000 Conti. Coeff =.282

Is job satisfaction associated with the net salary of the respondents? To find out the answer, data relating to the net salary of the respondents and their job satisfaction have been cross tabulated. The results of the analysis are presented in Table 8.14.

It is. evident from table 8.14 that in terms of net salary, among majority of the respondents, the level of job satisfaction is moderate. However, further analysis reveals that comparatively large proportion of respondents having net salary of Rs. 1800 to Rs. 3800 and Rs. 3801 to Rs. 6700 show high job satisfaction. To test whether there is any significant association between the two variables, chi-square test was used. The results show that the association is statistically significant. So, the employees' net salary tells us about their level of job satisfaction.

The above analysis shows that as in the case of gross salary, majority of the employees show moderate to high job satisfaction in respect of their net salary. That is to say the respondents take home salary is also quite adequate to fulfil their needs and requirements for their maintenance.

With respect to the gender it is found that the level of job satisfaction among the men is higher than the women. This might be because of the work they perform almost all the woman employees in both dairies are given clerical assignments which they might have felt, over a period of time, routine without any autonomy and opportunities for upgradation etc.

Organisation-wise it is found that Sangam dairy respondents are more satisfied than its counterpart. This might be because of autonomy given, acceptable supervision and leadership and benefits such as death relief fund, effective co-operative credit societies etc. The level of satisfaction among respondents in the age group of 27-51 years was higher than the older age group (52-57). This could be because that the people in older age group might be moving towards retirement after performing their duties after a long period.

Based on the above analysis presented in this chapter it can be concluded that the job satisfaction has association with sex, organisation, age, gross salary and net salary.

REFERENCES

1. Locke, E.A. (1976). The Nature and Cause of Job Satisfaction. In M.E. Dunnette (ed.) *Handbook of Industrial and Organisational Psychology.* Chicago: Rand McNally College.

2. Tripati, P.C. (1996). *Personnel Management and Industrial Relations.* New Delhi: Sultan Chand & Sons, 105.

3. Pestonjee, D.M. (1967). *A Study of Employee's Morale and Job Satisfaction as Related to Organisational Structures.* Aligarh: Aligarh Muslim University (un-published thesis).

4. Sinha, D. and Agarwal, U.N. (1971). Job Satisfaction and General Adjustment of Indian White-collar Workers. *Indian Journal of Industrial Relations,* 6. 357-367.

5. Dwived, N. (1973). *A Study of the Effect of the Financial Incentives on Job Satisfaction of Blue Color Workers.* Varanasi: Unpublished Doctorate Thesis.

6. Gyanendra, P.S. (1973). A Study of Some Determinations of Job Satisfaction among Underground and Ground Colliery Workers. *Indian Journal of Industrial Relations,* 8. 375-381.

7. Daftuar, C.N. (1982). *Job Attitudes in Indian Management—A Study in Need Deficiencies and Need Importance.* Delhi: Concept Publishing Co.

9

Causal Analysis

In this research study there are four major variables namely employee welfare, job satisfaction, commitment and level of satisfaction on recruitment and selection practices. In earlier chapter how the independent variables such as Age, Education, Caste etc., effect these major variables has been discussed.

In this chapter an effort is made to examine how these major variables are inter-correlated and if inter-correlated then to investigate if other variables do effect these correlations.

It can be observed from the above correlation matrix that there exists relationship between

(i) Employee Welfare and Commitment.

(ii) Job Satisfaction and Commitment.

(iii) Job Satisfaction and Level of Satisfaction on Recruitment and Selection.

(iv) Commitment and Level of Satisfaction on Recruitment and Selection.

These three inter-correlated variables were further examined by using partial correlation to know that there are other variables which are also effecting other major variables.

Tabel 9.2 shows the correlation between commitment and job satisfaction when the effects of gross salary are

Table 9.1: Correlations Matrix

Major Variables	*Employee Welfare*	*Job Satisfaction*	*Commitment*	*Level of Satisfaction /Acceptance*
Employee Welfare				
Pearson Correlation	1.000	.089	.337**	.025
Sig (1-tailed)		.060	.000	.330
N	305	305	305	305
Job Satisfaction				
Pearson Correlation	0.89	1.000	.253**	.341**
Sig (1-tailed)	.060		.000	.000
N	305	305	305	305
Commitment				
Pearson Correlation	.337**	.253**	1.000	.094*
Sig (1-tailed)	.000	.000		.050
N	305	305	305	305
Level of Satisfaction Acceptance				
Pearson Correlation	.025	.341**	.094*	1.000
Sig (1-tailed)	.330	.000	.050	
N	305	305	305	305

**. Correlation is significant at the 0.01 level (1-tailed).

*. Correlation is significant at the 0.05 level (1-tailed).

controlled by using partial correlation and the conclusions are as follows:

Table 9.2: Partial Correlation Co-efficient

Correlation Co-efficient between	*Controlling for*	*Partial Correlation Co-efficient*
Commitment and job satisfaction	Gross salary	.2464
Commitment and job satisfaction	Age and gross salary	.2183
Commitment and Employee Welfare	Gross salary, caste, education	.3511
Job satisfaction and level of satisfaction on Recruitment and Selection	Gross salary, Organisation, Net Salary	.2860

It is evident that the original co-efficient of correlation between the variables commitment and job satisfaction was 0.253 after controlling the effects of gross salary the co-efficient of correlation has come down to .246 which shows that the original correlation between the variables (Commitment and Job Satisfaction) has been effected by the other one (Gross salary) but the effect is very marginal. Thus it can be concluded that the two variables, i.e. commitment and job satisfaction are correlated. In other words it can be inferred that if the employees are satisfied with the jobs they are likely to have high work commitment.

In the sample units most of the employees are satisfied with their nature of work, in other words the place of work and working conditions are congenial. Their wages, salaries, fringe and other benefits are on par with state government employees. General working environment is conducive. The two way communication process enhances their working relations more meaningfully. Incentives for better performance, and the authority structure in the organisation satisfied the employees, hence job satisfaction of employees leads to high work commitment.

It is evident that the original co-efficient of correlation between the variables commitment and job satisfaction was 0.253. After controlling the effects of age and gross salary the co-efficient of correlation has come down to 0.218 which shows that the original correlation between the variables (Commitment and job satisfaction) has been effected a little by the other two (age and gross salary) but the effect is very marginal. Thus, it can be inferred that the two variables, i.e. commitment and job satisfaction are correlated. In other words it can be inferred that if the employees are satisfied with the jobs they are likely to have high work commitment.

Most of the respondents are in the age group of 27-50 years. Their gross salary is below Rs. 11,000 which is on par with state government salaries (as per fifth pay commission revised scales). Besides salary, the employees believe that work is necessary for self-development.

It is depicted that the original co-efficient of correlation between the commitment and employee welfare was .337 after controlling the effects of the gross salary, caste and education the co-efficient of correlation has come up to .351 which shows that the original correlation between the variables (commitment and employee welfare has been effected by the other three (gross salary, caste and education) but the effect is marginal.

Thus, it can be concluded that the two variables, i.e., commitment and employee welfare are correlated.

Employee welfare programmes like housing, canteen facilities, social security measures etc play a vital role in the commitment of workers. In dairy industry there is wide coverage of welfare programmes, i.e. washing allowances recreational facilities, leave travel concession, co-operative credit society, canteen which provides working lunch at the cost of Rs. 3.00, housing facilities, various loan facilities, consumer cooperative stores, allowances and a unique

Table 9.3: Job Commitment and its Predicting Variables

Model	*Unstandardised Coefficients*		*Standardised Coefficients*	*t*	*Sig.*
	B	*Std. Error*	*Beta*		
1. (constant)	18.060	3.408		5.300	.000
Age	–.150	.044	–.198	–3.403	.001
Education background	–.174	.224	–.043	–.776	.439
Employee welfare	5.269E-02	.008	.330	6.225	.000
Job satisfaction	.162	.048	.189	3.358	.001
Level of satisfaction on recruitment and selection	3.110E-04	.043	.000	.007	.994
Your present gross salary	–2.282E-05	.000	–.023	–.379	.705
Your take home pay	5.239E-05	.000	.035	.603	.547

(a) Dependent Variable: Commitment

scheme for the deceased members of the family and other employee welfare programmes have great impact on employees that will obviously lead to commitment of the job.

It is depicted that the original co-efficient of correlation between the variables, job satisfaction and level of satisfaction on recruitment and selection practices was 0.341. After controlling the effects of the gross salary, organisation and net salary it has come down to 0.286. Which shows that the original correlation between the variables (job satisfaction and level of satisfaction on recruitment and selection practices) has been effected by the other three (gross salary, organisation and net salary). However, their effect is negligible. Thus, it can be concluded that the two variables, i.e. job satisfaction and level of satisfaction on recruitment and selection practices are correlated.

Job satisfaction refers to an employees' general feeling of satisfaction on the job which acts as a motivation to work or serve better. It represents a constellation of a person's attitudes towards or about the job. It is a function of satisfaction with different aspects of the job security, good salary as good as state government jobs. The place of work is very nearer to their native places; even migrated people are accommodated in quarters. Actually they seek to enter into these units through the employment exchange. Their mode of selection is written test for managerial personnel followed by interview. Their placement, probation period and other terms and conditions are good. Thus the employees are satisfied with recruitment and selection practices of dairy units.

Job Commitment and Its Predicting or Continuing Variables

In the preceding sections it has been found that job commitment is one of the most significant variables in the context of human resource management practices.

In other words the job commitment has emerged as critical variables so far as HRM practices are concerned,

Model Summary

Model	*R*	*R Square*	*Adjusted R Square*	*Std. Error of the Estimate*
1.	.448[a]	.201	.182	4.3286

Model Summary

Model	*Change Statistics*				
	R Square Change	*F Change*	*df1*	*df2*	*Sig F Change*
1.	.201	10.648	7	297	.000

a. Predictors: (Constant), Your take home pay, employee welfare, level of satisfaction/acceptance, education background, job satisfaction, age, your present gross salary.

which means to examine and enhance the quality of HRM practices. From this study it is revealed that a manager has to give his major concern to job commitment. With this in mind, an effort has been made to identify some of the variables, which contribute to the job commitment. For this purpose regression analysis was applied on job commitment as a dependent variable and a set of 7 independent variables i.e. age, education, employee welfare, job satisfaction, level of satisfaction on recruitment and selection practices, present gross salary and take home pay.

The analysis shows that employee welfare (Beta equals to .330) is the most significant contributor to job commitment.

That means if management is planning to enhance level of job commitment it has to take up employee welfare seriously.

Young people in the sample units are committed. Basically their profile is different from the older employees. Younger employees believe that work is necessary for self development. They strongly agree that the productive work is an important source of life satisfaction. They feel that work gives them an independent status in their life and also brings recognition and status in the society. It depends upon whether one is productively employed or not. They further have expressed that they are proud of working for this organisation. Their personal and professional values and organisational values are rather identical. New employees are willing to put in greater efforts for the betterment of the organisation because they get their satisfaction from it. Hence organisations are advised to design the employee development programmes which would promote the commitment of younger employees.

Next to employee welfare it is the age of the employee which contributes to job commitment. The results show negative contribution which means that lower the age higher the commitment. It may be inferred that management has to focus job commitment activities more on young people than old.

In fact, both the managements have concentrated to extend employee welfare facilities in accordance with their financial viability. There is a greater need to introduce new employee welfare measures based on needs of individuals because present employees' aspirations are high in all aspects of their life. Studies suggest that new schemes in the new economic environment might enable the employees of today to perform their jobs meaningfully. Besides the existing benefits, new measures like access of internet, opportunity for multi-skills learning, interaction with other executives are essential for the managerial personnel. Whereas in the case of the non-managerial personnel up-gradation of skills, performance-linked incentives, autonomy of work, and empower to take decisions will go a long way to make the young employees more committed.

Job satisfaction appears as third important contributor to the job commitment. The analysis further shows that the other variables' contribution is non-significant.

10

Conclusions and Suggestions

The present study is undertaken in the dairy industry of Andhra Pradesh. Two major dairy units viz., Krishna District Milk Producers Co-operative Union Ltd (Vijaya Dairy) and Guntur District Milk Producers Mutually Aided Co-operative Union Limited (Sangam Dairy), situated in Krishna district and Guntur district respectively, have been selected. Their contribution to the 'white revolution' in the state is substantial. Both the units have registered incremental growth year after year. They are in the process of taking a big leap and have embarked upon ambitious expansion programme. The co-operatives which have roots in the villages engage nearly two thousand employees. If these units have to cope up with the competitive environment and make rapid strides, they have to manage their human resources effectively besides taking care of capital and other physical resources. Needless to mention that the growth and viability of the organisation depend upon the quality of its human resources. In this context the policies and practices of HRM play a vital role. The present study is an attempt to examine closely the policies and practices adopted in this regard in the two units. Recruitment and selection is the first vital function of HRM. If the management adopts the modern and scientific techniques, it can induct competent, capable human resources. One of the concerns of the study is to examine this aspect. Besides, the management has to adopt appropriate methods and strategies to develop the potential of human beings so inducted in organisations. The study seeks to examine the developmental strategies and approaches of human potential.

Objective of the Study

Objectives of the present study include assessing the human resources management practices in the dairy units under study, and towards this end to study the employment policies, assessing the HRD practices, examining the employee compensation system, to study the industrial relations climate, examining the employee welfare and social security, to study the extent of commitment and job satisfaction among the employees.

Hypotheses

Hypotheses have been formulated relating to recruitment and selection, employee welfare, job satisfaction and commitment, and to study the relationship between these variables and personnel and organisational variables. The objectives and the hypotheses provide the necessary framework for present enquiry.

Research Design

The study is descriptive in that socio-economic profile of the respondents, welfare measures, industrial relations and HRM practices obtaining in the two units under study are described in detail. It is also analytical in the sense that the statistical analysis of the association between variables, i.e. employee welfare, job satisfaction and their association with personal and organisational variables etc. are brought out. In addition, the case study method is also adopted for in depth understanding of HRM practices. The method of comparative study is also used for bringing out the similarities and dissimilarities of HRM practices in the two units under study.

A sample of 305 respondents is drawn from both the units covering both managerial and non-managerial categories on the basis of stratified random sampling. Two comprehensive schedules are designed for collecting information from management and employees. Interview and observation methods are also used in this regard. Statistical techniques are employed for qualitative analysis of data.

SOCIO-ECONOMIC PROFILE

As regards the socio-economic profile, majority of the employees belong to the age group of 44 to 51 years. The average age of the respondents is 46 years; 87.9 per cent of them are male employees, nearly three-fourth (73.1%) of the respondents belong to the open category; and the remaining belong to B.C. (20.3%) and S.C. (6.6%) categories. An overwhelming majority of them are Hindus (92.5%) and the educational level of the employees is S.S.C. (37%), and 20.3 per cent of employees completed Intermediate, 23.9 per cent of employees possess degree and 13.4 per cent have either post-graduate or professional degree.

93.6 per cent of the respondents are married, 11.8 per cent are migrated from other districts due to the paucity of employment in their home districts. 85.9 per cent have rural background; their mother tongue is Telugu (94.8%) and that of other respondents is Hindi (3%) and Urdu (2.3%). The number of dependents among 29.8 per cent of the families of respondents is 4 and 3 members in about 26 per cent of the families.

As per the residential status of the respondents, 45.9 per cent have own houses; 42.3 per cent reside in rented house; 10.8 per cent of the employees live in company quarters. The average number of living rooms is three. Distance from residence to workplace is about 5 km as stated by 68.2 per cent of the respondents. Most of the employees' mode of conveyance is city bus service. 54.4 per cent of the respondents are indebted. The average of present gross salary is Rs. 9,240 but their average take home pay is Rs. 5,725 only.

RECRUITMENT AND SELECTION

The study reveals that the majority of respondents (57 per cent) are moderately satisfied on recruitment and selection practices whereas nearly 40 per cent of respondents have low level of satisfaction. The remaining respondents (11 per cent) are highly satisfied with the recruitment and selection process.

The study shows that sex has no bearing on the level of satisfaction of employees on recruitment and selection process. The association between sex and level of satisfaction of employees on recruitment and selection process is statistically not significant.

The study reveals that the employees level of satisfaction does not depend on the number of their dependents. The association is statistically insignificant.

The results show that the employees background either rural or urban does not tell us about their level of satisfaction on recruitment and selection practices. The association is statistically not significant.

Analysis of data shows that in both Vijaya and Sangam dairies, majority of the respondents have moderate level of satisfaction, particularly respondents from Sangam Dairy are found to be highly satisfied with their recruitment and selection policies and practices. The association is statistically significant.

In both dairies younger respondents have expressed their satisfaction regarding recruitment and selection policies.

It is found that there is a significant association between the employees' gross salary and their level of satisfaction. Most of the dairy employees are satisfied the obvious reason being revised salaries. The amount of gross salary is on par with that of state government employees. Hence, the respondents seem to be satisfied with their recruitment and selection practices in the sample units.

Human Resource Development

Vijaya dairy and Sangam dairy have intended to follow HRD philosophy. But professional approach to HRD activities is lacking. Training centre which forms an integral part of HR department has clear-cut objectives such as imparting training to executives and supervisors as well as conducting on-the-job training to the operatives. It is also responsible to prepare a comprehensive and integrated plan for training and development programmes consistent with the needs of industry. Both dairies are organising training programmes for farmers, members of village level co-operative society. In addition to the operatives in their perspective plan, full-fledged training centre is to be established.

Employee training and development form an important part of the effort in building an effective teamwork that can lead to a high level of productive efficiency. Nearly two-third of the respondents have not received any induction training. 29.8 per cent of the respondents only have received training organized by the company. 8.5 per cent of the employees' wards have received vocational training. Majority of the respondents have expressed that opportunities for employee training and development are inadequate and those who have undergone training have not endeavoured to utilize their skills and knowledge.

Performance appraisal techniques have been evolved to identify the relative strengths and weaknesses of the employees in the performance of their work. 58 per cent of the respondents have felt that the criteria of performance appraisal is poor and is not very much related to work performance traits. 59 per cent of the respondents have expressed that the appraisal system lacks transparency and objectivity. The reason for this seems to be that the appraisal results are not discussed with appraisees through post-appraisal interview on properly given feedback system. 63 per cent of the respondents have expressed their view that the organisation hardly uses the appraisal results either for identifying training needs of the employees or for their development.

WAGES AND EMPLOYEE WELFARE

Majority (58.7%) of the respondents' have felt that their

salary is commensurate with qualifications and their efforts put in the organisation.

Majority (78.4%) of the respondents have perceived their salary vis-a-vis the salary in other industries as either 'high' or 'same'.

Majority (57.4%) of the respondents expressed that their salary is adequate to meet their basic needs. 29.5 per cent of respondents are eligible for incentives/perks. 78.7 per cent of the respondents have expressed dissatisfaction with the bonus payment. Vijaya dairy does not offer any bonus at all because of its continuous losses and Sangam dairy pays bonus at minimum rate (8.33 per cent) in view of this their dissatisfaction can be understood. In about 86 per cent of the respondents the satisfaction range is between high to moderate. This leads to the inference that overwhelming majority of the employees are satisfied with the welfare facilities.

The study reveals that personal factors such as sex, educational background, size of dependants in the family, caste and gross salary tend to influence the satisfaction level of the employees with regard to employee welfare. The study has found that the relationship between these factors and employee welfare is statistically significant.

Industrial Relations

Industrial relations in dairy industry have never remained static. The quality and tenor of these relations have been changing over time.

Majority (62 per cent) of the respondents are members of some union or other. The reasons for their joining the trade union include urge to be a member of the group (31.5 per cent); for protection from management (11.8 per cent), employees solidarity (9.2 per cent); monetary benefits (5.9 per cent). Of the total respondents, 83.9 per cent are ordinary members of unions and 16.1 per cent occupy some official position (office bearers) in the union. Nearly 60 per cent of the respondents have never participated in any strike and demonstration conducted by the unions, since the inception of the dairy units. More than half of the respondents (59 per cent) have not exercised the vote in union elections. This may be due to the fact that none challenged the elections to the union in Vijaya dairy. 41 per cent of them have taken part in the elections and used their voting right. These respondents appear to belong to Sangam dairy, where union elections were held in 2001. 62.3 per cent of the respondents are paying their subscriptions regularly; 33.1 per cent of the respondents are helping the union in its fund raising campaign. Half of the respondents have expressed that the union meets the expectations of its members; interestingly 86 per cent of the respondents prefer inside leadership.

Collective bargaining has come to stay in both the dairy units, particularly a trend is visible that both management and union show a preference to settle their issues amicably through this democratic method. Even among unions, they make a common cause and form a joint action committee to promote their solidarity and represent their problems in more concerted fashions before the management. When the respondents are asked about the unions influence on the management in the present scenario nearly half of them have felt that the unions' influence on management is on the increase. However, about one-fourth (25.9 per cent) of respondents have felt that the influence has declined. About 16 per cent have expressed that there is no change in the union influence.

Viewed against the above background, the parties show maturity, trust and understanding in addressing their problems and settle the same in an amicable way. In both the units a healthy tradition has come to be established that the parties try to settle their problems among themselves. In the first instance in cases where the negotiations are deadlocked, they seek the help of conciliation officer; it is also to be noted here that even when the bipartite agreement is reached by the mutual efforts of management and unions, they approach the conciliation officer for signing the agreement. When he signs the agreement the complexion changes into one of settlement which has certain additional advantages in terms of the binding effect not only on the parties to the dispute but also other workers. It is very rare that the disputes of the units are referred for adjudication. In Sangam dairy there was one dispute related to the promotion of an LDC clerk which was referred to adjudication.

Strikes form an important feature of industrial relations in the dairy units as in the case in other organisations. But the strikes here are not bitter and prolonged. Often the strikes are of sporadic nature when the joint action committee, which is formed by the unions is issue based and when workers' problems arise they are placed before the management for consideration. In general the management after perusal of the workers' demands gives a promise to settle the issue. But the management because of its lack of seriousness on its part tend to ignore the issue. This provokes the joint action committee to give either strike notice or conducting a strike in reality to get fulfillment of the management promises. But these strikes are of short duration and do not disturb the production schedules seriously.

As regards discipline, the dairy units are marked by cases of indiscipline, though their number is limited and occurrence infrequent. In cases of misconduct the dairy units are governed by the provisions of the standing orders which are in vogue. The standing orders defined clearly all the major and minor misconducts. Managements do not take the minor misconducts seriously and the concerned workers are let off either with a written warning or a reprimand. But the major misconducts are dealt with in accordance with the principles of natural justice and following the disciplinary procedure. The researcher presented nearly a dozen case studies of misconducts which vividly portray the nature of offences committed by the workmen and the rules and procedures followed by the units to dispose of the cases. The case studies reveal that major misconducts like insubordination, fraud, misappropriation of funds, dereliction of duty, unauthorized absence etc. the accused workers are clearly informed about the charges and if the explanation submitted by them is unsatisfactory then an impartial domestic enquiry is conducted by an officer of the company. Depending upon facts contained in the enquiry report, appropriate punishment is awarded when the charges are proved beyond doubt. A general tendency of the managements in the units in awarding punishment is noticed. In most of the cases of major misconducts the maximum punishments inflicted to any employee is stoppage of an annual increment with or without cumulative effect. In comparison Sangam dairy appears to deal with the cases more sternly than the Vijaya dairy. It can be noted that disposal of disciplinary cases involved inordinate delay and the managements would do well to follow the 'hot stove rule' of Mc Gregor in dealing with these matters.

Majority of the respondents (76.7 per cent) are not aware about the joint committees. They have expressed their ignorance about the existence of these committees. Only 23.3 per cent respondents have expressed that they are aware of the bipartite committees. As regards utilising canteen services 76.7 per cent respondents have said that they are using its services. They appear to be satisfied with the quality price and range of food items and beverages. Interestingly, 51.1 per cent respondents have felt that the canteen committees are not functioning satisfactorily.

Only 38 per cent of the respondents have expressed that they have safety awareness (38 per cent) and more than 60 per cent of them do not have awareness in this respect. 60 per cent of the respondents opined that safety measures undertaken by the dairy units are inadequate whereas 40 per cent of them have felt that they are adequate. As regards the functioning of the safety committee about 68 per cent of the respondents have felt that it is poor. Neither the members meet regularly nor important matters of safety discussed in the committee.

About 65 per cent of the respondents do not seem to be aware about the existence of works committee in the dairy units. About 68 per cent of the respondents have a poor opinion about the functioning of the works committee. They have felt that the committees are not convened regularly and if decisions are taken in the committee the management seldom implement them. Besides the above committees, the dairy units have also constituted production committee and quality control committee to look after the production and quality control respectively. In the course of discussion held with the management and the committee members the researcher gets the impression that both the committees discharge their functions assigned to them, more particularly the quality control committee pays utmost attention to the aspects of hygiene, cleanliness, packing and quality maintenance. Death relief committee has been constituted in Sangam dairy besides the above bipartite committees. The committee is meant to provide relief to the family of the deceased employee in case of his pre-mature death. A healthy and helpful practice is developed in this unit that in case of a pre-mature death of employee all the employees of the organisation contribute one day salary to death relief fund and the same will be handed over to the legal heirs of the deceased employee. This activity is appreciated by everyone and provides substantial relief to the distressed families.

The Grievance handling procedure in any organisation depends on the organisation policies. While formulating the policy, the management provides some guidelines to the unit officers while handling the grievances of the employees. The grievance settlement method is found to be satisfactory as stated by 48.2 per cent. 35.4 per cent of the respondents approach unions for grievance redressal. This may be attributed to their lack of awareness about the grievance machinery and credibility and helping nature of the unions.

42.3 per cent have awareness of grievance procedure; 23.9 per cent only have grievances at any time of their career in the unit. This indicates in a way the health of the organisation. The employees are encouraged to express their grievances and redress them expeditiously.

Commitment

Commitment has implication both for the individual as well as the organisation. At the individual level a person with high level of commitment tends to put in sincere, honest and sustained hard work. From the organisational angle it develops a feeling of belongingness, a sense of pride and determination to further the goals of the organisation. In view of its importance the researcher tries to identify personal variables such as sex, educational background, indebtedness, dependents, rural/urban background, caste, age, gross salary and net salary. Similarly he has also tried to identify the organisational variables like nature of management and official position of the employee in terms of managerial or non-managerial category. In the first instance item analysis and regrouped results based on quartile values scored by the respondents on the 12 statements selected for commitment, were presented. Further correlation co-efficient was applied. To find out the relationship between the different variables and commitment and to measure the significance level of the relationship, chi-square test was used. The study reveals that there is a relationship between workers' commitment and his personal aspects like educational background, caste, age and gross salary and these personal factors tend to influence significantly the level of commitment of the worker. The study could not find any evidence to establish relationship between other personal and organisational variables mentioned above.

Job Satisfaction

Job satisfaction also formed an important aspect of the study. If the worker is satisfied with the job, he tends to work productively and willingly besides he develops a positive emotional attitude towards the job, which increases his morale. It is believed that if an employee is satisfied with his job it is likely to increase his efficiency level and lead to improvement in quality and quantity of output. Similar approach and same statistical measure were used to find out the relationship between organisational and personal variables on one hand and the other worker's job satisfaction. The study found evidence that there is a relationship between sex, age, gross salary, net salary and the nature of the organisation and job satisfaction of the employee. It is found that the relationship between the personal and organisational variables and job satisfaction is statistically significant. It implies that these factors have a tendency to significantly influence the level of job satisfaction of employee.

Causal Analysis

In this research study there are four major variables namely Employee Welfare, Job Satisfaction, Commitment and Level of Satisfaction on Recruitment and Selection Practices.

An effort has been made to examine how these major variables are inter-correlated and if inter-correlated then to investigate; if other variables do effect these correlations

It is found that the original co-efficient of correlation between the variables commitment and job satisfaction was 0.253 and after controlling the effects of 'gross salary' the co-efficient of correlation has come down to 0.246 which shows that the original correlation between the variables (commitment and job satisfaction) has been effected by the other one (gross salary) but the effect is very marginal. Thus it can be concluded that the two variables, i.e. commitment and job satisfaction are correlated. In other words it can be inferred that if the employees are satisfied with the jobs they are likely to have high work commitment.

It is also found that the original co-efficient of correlation between the variables commitment and job satisfaction was 0.253. After controlling the effects of age and gross salary the co-efficient of correlation has come down to .218 which shows that the original correlation between the variables (commitment and job satisfaction) has been effected a little by the other two (age and gross salary) but the effect is very marginal. Thus, it can be inferred that the two variables, i.e. commitment and job satisfaction are correlated. In other words it can be inferred that if the employees are satisfied with the jobs they are likely to have high work commitment.

It is depicted that the original co-efficient of correlation between the commitment and employee welfare is 0.337 after controlling the effects of the gross salary, caste and education the co-efficient of correlation has come up to .351 which shows that the original correlation between the variables (commitment and employee welfare) has been effected by the other three (gross salary, caste and education) but the effect is marginal.

Thus, it can be concluded that the two variables, i.e., commitment and employee welfare are correlated.

Further it is found that the original co-efficient of correlation between the variables job satisfaction and level of satisfaction on recruitment and selection practices was .341. After controlling the effects of the variables, namely, 'gross salary', 'organisation', and 'net salary' have come down to .286, which shows that the original correlation between the variables (job satisfaction and level of satisfaction on recruitment and selection practices) has been effected by the other three variables (gross salary, organisation and net salary) but the effect is negligible. Thus, it can be concluded that the two variables, i.e. job satisfaction and level of satisfaction on recruitment and selection practices are correlated.

In other words the job commitment has emerged as critical variables so far as HRM practices are concerned, which means to examine and enhance the quality of HRM practices. From this study it is revealed that a manager has to give his major concern to job commitment. With this in mind, an effort has been made to identify some of the variables, which contribute to the job commitment. For this purpose regression analysis has been applied on job commitment as a dependent variable and a set of 7 independent variables i.e. age, education, employee welfare, job satisfaction, level of satisfaction on recruitment and selection practices, present gross salary and take home pay.

The analysis shows that employee welfare is the most significant contributor to job commitment.

That means if a management is planning to enhance level of job commitment it has to take up employee welfare seriously.

After employee welfare it is the age of the employee which is important in connection with job commitment. Results show that there is negative contribution which means that the lower the age the higher the commitment. It may be inferred that management has to focus job commitment activities more on young people than old.

Suggestions

In the light of the findings of the study and the conclusions drawn above the following suggestions may be made for improving HRM practices in the dairy units under study.

1. Dairy industry in Andhra Pradesh is at the cross roads. Its potential for contribution to economic development and employment generation emerge since it is a vital food industry for catering to the daily needs of the population. The government and the co-operative federations at the state level may take necessary steps for expanding its processing capacity from the present 2.50 lakh liters per day to 3.0 lakh liters per day being an agro-based industry both the aspects of generating

more employment in rural areas as well as using new technology must be given equal importance.

2. As revealed in the study the dairy units still follow the traditional human resource practices and in some areas the adoption of HR practices is found to be marginal. Sea-saw changes took place in the HR profession and its practices. The dairy units have to develop more professionalism by adopting the modern management principles in general and HRM practices in particular. The dairy units can follow the example of Anand dairy at Ahmadabad.

3. No method of scientific planning is found in the organisations under study. As a result the units often suffer from surplus manpower with low level of skills and competencies. Manpower planning aspects must be paid adequate attention to see that right people are placed at the right time and at the right place with right skills and background and the units do not suffer from either surplus or shortage of human resource at any point of time (Gujarat).

4. Another HR aspect which is found wanting is training and development. This aspect most broadly has four areas. Training programmes for workers at lower level, management development programmes for the executives, career development for the employees and organisational development. Induction programmes must be made, an integral aspect of the socialisation process of the new employees. The training programmes must be identified on the basis of the need and must be organized in a continual basis. Evaluation of training programmes at all levels must be scrupulously observed to see that the knowledge and skills are transferred to the job and result in increased efficiency and productivity. Career planning including promotions received a raw deal by the management. The study revealed that in case of dairy attendants they are without promotions and developmental opportunities and they retire in the same position in

which they are recruited when they join the company. The management should explore promotional avenues or incremental growth in the time scale for every three or four years to keep their morale high and work enthusiastically. Management development programmes must be need-oriented and the managers must be sent to out side the institute to receive more qualitative training. There is a need for adopting HRD philosophy and total support must be extended by the top and middle level management, also a budgetary support must be given for the HRD activities.

Superior subordinate relations inter-departmental/unit co-ordination and promotion of teams approach are essential for organisational development. The units must adapt themselves to the changes in the environment and must try to become dynamic and growth oriented.

5. The study revealed that some systems of performance appraisal are followed in the organisations. But the systems need to be qualitatively improved and transparency and objectivity must be the hallmarks of the system. The employees must be informed of the criteria of appraisal, and the results of the appraisal including the strengths and weaknesses of performance. It must be viewed as an HR device and a means of enabling their employees to improve their performance and competences. The appraisal systems must be properly integrated with promotions, reward system and growth and opportunities of the employees.

6. The study revealed that some joint committees have been constituted to promote consultation between management and workers. The working of these committees is found to be unsatisfactory. Workers participation constitute a cornerstone of the industrial relations policy in India. A thorough review of the working of these committees has to be made and steps have to be taken to strengthen participatory management

practices in the organisations. Both management and trade unions must place their trust and credibility of the committees and work honestly for their success.

7. The dairy units have grievance redressal mechanisms but the awareness of the employees about the system is low. Sometimes they approach the trade unions for grievance redressal instead of submitting their job related complaints to the appropriate authorities of the grievance redressal mechanism. The workers must be encouraged to express their grievances freely and necessary awareness be created among them, about various authorities at different levels who are concerned in the redressal of their grievances.

8. The study revealed that cases of misconduct are not infrequent in the dairy units major misconducts like absconding from duty without authorized leave, misappropriation of funds, dereliction of duty, willful insubordination, fraud, damage to the property are reported in these units. The case studies made by the researcher bring out the fact that inordinate delay is involved in disposing of these matters. The managements appear to be lenient in dealing with the cases of discipline. When charges are proved in the enquiry the punishment must be serious and commensurate with the gravity of offence.

9. A comparative study of both the Vijaya and Sangam dairies reveals that both the units have same type of technology. Sangam dairy is some what comfortably placed with regard to its financial performance. But in marketing strategies Vijaya dairy is ahead of its sister concern. In utilisation of human resource practices Sangam dairy shows more initiative and has an edge over Vijaya dairy. But it must be observed that in a competitive environment in which they are placed and when the competition is likely to be more intense in the years to come, the strategy of both the units in terms of HR practices, finance, marketing and technology are

not adequate. The units need to be more professionalized and the organisational members must be geared to meet the future challenges. They can do so if their competencies are developed to the optimum and they become result-oriented. Needless to point out that HR policies of the units must be integrated with the overall business strategic policies of the organisations.

Suggestion for Future Research

1. Since there are few studies on HRM practices particularly in dairy industry, similar studies may be undertaken in the dairy industry in other regions and also the private sector.

2. Studies focusing on job satisfaction and commitment of the employees in the various dairy units in co-operative and private sectors will throw light on the differential organisational climate and their impact on commitment of the employees.

3. Studies may also be undertaken on recruitment and selection policies and procedures followed in different dairy units in Andhra Pradesh and other states.

4. Managers are nominated by the units to undergo the management training at places like Mumbai, Ahmadabad, Anand and other places. There is a need to evaluate the training programmes offered at these centres. They not only help us to know the content but also their relevance to the units. Dairy industry is fast developing in Andhra Pradesh. Dr.Marri Chenna Reddy HRD Centre and Administrative Staff College of India serve as 'harbingers' for critical training programmes at Hyderabad. The co-operative milk federation at state level in collaboration with the above centres of learning must start a training centre at Hyderabad to cater to the special and unique needs of the dairy industry. The training and development programmes form an important and critical area of study for future researchers.

Bibliography

Agarwal, R.D. (1977). *Dynamics of Personnel Management in India.* New Delhi: Tata McGraw Hill Publishing Company.

Aswathappa, K. (1995). *Essentials of Business Environment.* Bombay: Himalaya Publishing House.

Bartholomew, D.J. (1976). *Manpower Planning.* Rupa: Penguin Modern Management Readings Distributors.

Basu, K.S. (1979). *New Dimensions in Personnel Management.* New Delhi: Macmillan & Co.

Belcher, D.W. (1962). *Wage and Salary Administration.* New Jersy: Prentice Hall.

Biswas, R.K. (1982 March). Concept of Wages under Different Labour Laws. *Labour Gazette,* 761-772.

Bremlett, Eari R. (1961-Autumn). "Maintenance of Discipline", in *Management Personnel,* Quarterly Vol, No. l.

Chandra (1968). *Grievance Procedure: A Survey of Practices in Industries in India.* Hyderabad: Administrative Staff College of India.

Gupta, V.P. (1996). *Industrial Relations.* Nagpur: Central Board for Workers Education Publications.

I.I.P.M. (1973). *Personnel Management in India.* Udaipur: S.J.C. Publications.

Johri, C.K. (1967). *Unionism in a Developing Economy.* Udaipur: S.J.C. Publications.

Laldas, D.K. (1991). *Personnel Management, Industrial Relations and Labour Welfare.* Agra: Y.K. Publishers.

Parida, S. (1999). "Employee Involvement for Organisation Excellence" in *Personnel Today.* Calcutta: National Institute of Personnel Management, Vol. xix. No. 4.

Ravisankar, S. & R.K. Mishra. (1985). *Management of Human Resources in Public Enterprises*. New Delhi: Vision Books Pvt. Ltd.

Sashibala, (1984). *Management of Small Scale Industries*. New Delhi: Deep and Deep Publishers.

Subba Rao, P. (2002). *Essential of Human Resource Management and Industrial Relations*. Mumbai: Himalaya Publishing House.

Suman, Swarup, (2001 September). *Employees Guide*. New Delhi: Employees' State Insurance Corporation, Director General.

Tripati, P.C. (1996). *Personnel Management and Industrial Relations*. New Delhi: Sultan Chand & Sons.

INDEX

D

E

F

G

H

I

L

M

N

O

P

Y